ALL GONG
AND NO DINNER

1,001 HOMELY PHRASES AND CURIOUS DOMESTIC SAYINGS

NIGEL REES

Collins

Collins
An imprint of HarperCollins*Publishers*
77–85 Fulham Palace Road
London
W6 8JB

www.collins.co.uk

First published in 2007

12 11 10 09 08 07

10 9 8 7 6 5 4 3 2 1

A catalogue record for this book is
available from the British Library.

ISBN-10 0-00-724935-7
ISBN-13 978-0-00-724935-0

Collins uses papers that are natural, renewable and recyclable products
made from wood grown in sustainable forests. The manufacturing processes
conform to the environmental regulations of the country of origin.

Edited by Caroline Taggart
Index by Lisa Footitt

Set by Rowland Phototypesetting Ltd, Bury St Edmunds, Suffolk
Printed and bound in Great Britain by Clays Ltd, St Ives plc

Contents

'Campion was relieved. If the Palinode "family language" consisted of references to the classics, a good memory and a comprehensive dictionary of quotations should go quite a long way. Miss Evadne disillusioned him. "'That's all very well,' she said to her brother. "Have you performed a Cousin Cawnthorpe?'" 'Mr Campion's heart sank. He recognized in that remark the one unbreakable code known to man, the family allusion' – Margery Allingham, More Work for the Undertaker, *Chap. 5 (1949).*

'Your family, like every other family, has a language of its own, consisting of unintelligible catchphrases, favourite but not generally known, quotations, obscure allusions, but not intrinsically funny family jokes' – A.A. Milne, 'Christmas Party' in* A Table Near the Band and Other Stories *(1950).*

'What is human life? The first third a good time; the rest remembering about it' – Mark Twain, attributed in More Maxims of Mark *(1927).*

INTRODUCTION

All Gong and No Dinner is a celebration, a recording, a remembering, a search for the origins of homely words, phrases and sayings. These may take the form of domestic catchphrases, family sayings (often unique to a particular family), household words, rhymes, old wives' sayings and proverbial wisdom.

I came across this rich seam of language almost by accident. When I devised the BBC Radio show *Quote . . . Unquote* in the mid-1970s, I thought that it would simply be a quiz about the 'big' quotations – from the Bible, Shakespeare, Oscar Wilde, Rudyard Kipling and so on.

But right from the very first week, listeners came to share with me not only quotations that they enjoyed or wanted to know more about, but also more informal sayings from everyday life. In time we tended to categorize these as 'Eavesdroppings' (overheard remarks), 'Babes and Sucklings' (children's remarks), 'Foot in Mouth' (verbal clangers) and eventually 'Family Sayings'. Wherever they came from, however, what they all had in common was that somebody felt moved to quote them to me.

Consequently, over the past 30 years of the programme's life, I have been the happy recipient of hundreds of thousands of these 'conversation clippings'. Often they were accompanied by an inquiry as to whether – if they were not obviously unique to the sender – anybody else knew of them.

I have tried to keep pace with these queries and with all this material ever since. Apart from giving air space to a small fraction of them on *Quote . . . Unquote* itself, I have explored the subject in two earlier works

– *As We Say In Our House: a book of family sayings* (1994) and *Oops, Pardon Mrs Arden!: an embarrassment of domestic catchphrases* (2001). I am grateful to Robson Books for permission to quote material from both of them. In addition, I have sought evidence of origins and usage through a quarterly publication, *The 'Quote ... Unquote' Newsletter* and through the *Quote ... Unquote* website (www.btwebworld.com/quote-unquote).

I am, of course, hugely grateful to all the correspondents mentioned in what follows who have shared with me their own domestic phrases and sayings. Quite simply, the book could not have existed without their willingness to reveal what has been said and what still may be said in their homes and families. The names of these helpful people, whether they be readers or listeners, are mentioned in the individual entries alongside the information with which they have supplied me.

I emphasize the fact that *All Gong and No Dinner* is devoted to the domestic side of this part of the English language. Words and phrases may catch on from all kinds of sources – broadcasting, show business, films, the office or workplace, the services – but here I concentrate on those that are most common in the home environment, wherever they originated and to wherever they may get passed on. One of the recurring themes of the book is that an informant's parent or grandparent used to say the phrase, to which is added the comment, 'And I find myself saying it too.' In this way, colourful phrases are handed down through the generations – and long may they continue to be so.

This book is a reference dictionary but, given the subject matter, I have tried to make it as friendly and easy to read as I can.

I need to point out one or two things, however. It is not written in 'dictionary-ese'. In fact, where the entries become rather chatty, this is because they are based on my replies to people approaching the *Quote ... Unquote* radio show, newsletter or website with queries about their own family sayings. Sometimes it has simply not been possible to point to an origin, in which case I say so.

I have sometimes used the term 'nannyism' to describe the bossy injunctions from actual nannies or from other grown-ups who have this tendency. As for 'Wellerism', this is the term for a form of comparison in which a saying or proverbial expression is attributed to an amusingly inapposite source. Mieder & Kingsbury in their *Dictionary of Wellerisms* (1994) note that a Wellerism usually consists of three parts: a statement, a speaker who makes the remark and a phrase or clause that places the utterance in a new light or an incompatible setting. The type was known long before Dickens gave a fondness for uttering these jocular remarks to Sam Weller. For example, from *Pickwick Papers*, Chap. 23 (1837): 'It's over, and can't be helped, and that's one consolation, as they always say in Turkey, ven they cut the wrong man's head off.'

It should be apparent from the entries when a saying is unique to one family and when it is to be found quite widely. Where possible, I have indicated where my informants lived at the time they got in touch with me, because this might just have some bearing on the phrase's origin. I have also put in an informant's age (where I know it), if only to help make clear when a saying might have arisen or become popular. On the whole, I have tended not to include dialect expressions – as these are really something else. Where a date is given after an informant's name, this refers to the year in which I received the information, not to when the phrase may have come into use.

But I would be the first to concede that all this dating and placing is very approximate. The chapter divisions are at times arbitrary and so to find a particular expression, it is always best to look first in the keyword index at the back of the book.

I make no great claims for the importance of all the hundreds of phrases and sayings in this book. Like most catchphrases, they are silly but fun and, at their best, can produce a warmly nostalgic glow. Apart from which, as Frank Muir once said to me about some other trifling activity (in his case, writing letters to *The Times*), '**They're just a way of getting you through the day.**'

Well, we could all do with a little help in that department . . .

Nigel Rees
London 2007

ABBREVIATIONS & ACKNOWLEDGEMENTS

A number of sources are mentioned with great regularity. Accordingly, I refer to them by a short title, namely:

Apperson: G.L. Apperson, *English Proverbs and Proverbial Phrases* (1929)

Casson/Grenfell: Sir Hugh Casson & Joyce Grenfell, *Nanny Says*, ed. Diana, Lady Avebury (1972)

ODP: *The Oxford Dictionary of Proverbs* (2003 edn)

OED2: *The Oxford English Dictionary*, 2nd edn (1989), CD-ROM version 3.0 (2002)

Partridge/Catch Phrases: Eric Partridge, *A Dictionary of Catch Phrases*, 2nd edn, edited by Paul Beale (1985)

Partridge/Slang: Eric Partridge, *A Dictionary of Slang and Unconventional English*, 8th edn, edited by Paul Beale (1984)

Wickenden: The sayings of Florence May Wickenden (1910–73) were communicated to me by her daughter, Rosaline Gibson, of Sevenoaks, Kent

Widdowson: Professor J.D.A. Widdowson – whose name I use when quoting from the Survey of English Language and Folklore, which he initiated in 1964 for what is now the National Centre for English Cultural Tradition at the University of Sheffield. I have also quoted several observations from his chapter entitled 'The Language of the Child Culture …' in *They Don't Speak Our Language*, ed. Sinclair Rogers (1976).

I would also like to thank several organisations for permission to reproduce the following extracts:

Extract from 'Let's Stop Somebody from Doing Something' by A. P. Herbert reprinted with permission of A P Watt Ltd on behalf of the Executors of the Estate of Jocelyn Herbert, M T Perkins and Polly M V R Perkins. Copyright © A P Herbert 1930.

Extract from 'The Cough Drop Shop' by Leslie Sarony reprinted with permission of EMI Music Publishing Ltd. Copyright © Leslie Sarony 1932.

Extract from 'Don't Tell My Mother I'm Living in Sin; Or, See What It Done to Me' by A P Herbert from *Laughing Ann* (1925) reprinted with permission of A P Watt Ltd on behalf of the Executors of the Estate of Jocelyn Herbert, M T Perkins and Polly M V R Perkins. Copyright © A P Herbert 1925.

Extract from *The Wonder of Words* by Isaac Goldberg reprinted with permission of Peter Owen Publishers Ltd. Copyright © Isaac Goldberg 1938.

Extract from *Who's Afraid of Virginia Woolf?* by Edward Albee reprinted with permission of WMA, LLC on behalf of Edward Albee. Copyright © Edward Albee 1962.

Chapter 1

AS THE SAYING GOES …

Boniface, the landlord in George Farquhar's play The Beaux' Stratagem *(1707), has a curious verbal mannerism. After almost every phrase he adds,* '**As the saying is …**', *but this was in itself a well-established phrase even then. In 1548, Hugh Latimer in* The Sermon on the Ploughers *had:* 'And I fear me this land is not yet ripe to be ploughed. For as the saying is: it lacketh weathering.' *Similarly, the addition of* '**as they say**' *to heighten or qualify a remark is a long-established practice. It is a verbal tic of the Nurse in Shakespeare,* Romeo and Juliet, *II.iv.162 (1594):* 'But first let me tell ye, if ye should lead her in a fool's paradise, as they say, it were a very gross kind of behaviour, as they say.' *Nowadays,* '**as the saying goes**' *seems to be the preferred usage. To begin with, here is a general selection of the things people say with almost audible quotation marks round them.*

that accounts for the coke in the milkanut 'What you say after something has been explained' – Rosie Cullen on a saying of her grandmother's (2001). But did people ever say **that accounts for the milk in the coconut**? Yes, they did. *Partridge/Catch Phrases* has 'accounts for/explains the milk in coconut' as an American catchphrase meaning 'that explains the puzzle or elucidates the mystery', dating from 1853 and only a little later in the UK.

after done and said all Meaning presumably 'when all is said and done', this was an expression used by the grandmother of Peter Kirkby, Rudgeway, Gloucestershire (2000).

all sorts *Street Talk: The Language of Coronation Street* (1986) defines this as 'all sorts of people, things or activities. Often said pejoratively of people, as in, "You get all sorts in a neighbourhood like that."' The proverb 'It takes all sorts to make a world' was known by 1620. There may also be a modern allusion to Bassett's Liquorice Allsorts, a brand of confectionery that comes in many different colours and shapes.

as black as the Earl of Hell's riding boots Could this phrase be the answer to a query: 'Can you shed any light on an expression that my mother used to use, back in the unlit days of World War II: "It's as black as itchell outside"' – James Sumner (2002)? *Partridge/Slang* has the phrase meaning 'pitch-dark' in naval use from the turn of the 18th/19th century.

Adam Severs came across the expression 'the night's **as black as the inside of a cow**' in Somerville & Ross, *Some Experiences of an Irish RM*, Chap. 10 (1899), and wondered if this was its origin. Not quite. Joe Kralich found this in Mark Twain's *Roughing It*, Chap. 4 (1891): 'Made the place as "dark as the inside of a cow," as the conductor phrased it in his picturesque way.'

between you (and) me and the gatepost (or **bedpost** or **doorpost**) Confidentially – a phrase suggesting (lightly and not very seriously) that a secret is about to be imparted and that it should be kept. Known by 1832. Charles Dickens, *Nicholas Nickleby*, Chap. 10 (1839) has: 'Between you and me and the post, sir, it will be a very nice portrait.' The previous year, Dickens had written in a letter, 'Between you and me and the general post.'

I wasn't born on Pancake Day I'm not fooled that easily. 'My grandmother in the Midlands would say this when I was a child. For some time I assumed it was a common expression so could not understand why everyone looked at me as if I were from another planet whenever I used it myself' – Keith St John, Cheshire (2003). What the connection is between Pancake Day and being foolish, I can't say.

butter fingers! What you cry when a person has dropped something. Date of origin unknown, but first found in connection with a cricketer who lets the ball slip through his fingers. 'At every bad attempt to catch, and every failure to stop the ball, he launched his personal displeasure at the head of the devoted individual in such denunciations as ...

butter-fingers, muff, humbug, and so forth' – Charles Dickens, *The Pickwick Papers*, Chap. 7 (1837); 'Swinging the hammer with a will, [he] discharged a smashing blow on his own knuckles … He crushed down an oath and substituted the harmless comment, "butter fingers!"' – R.L. Stevenson & Lloyd Osbourne, *The Wrong Box*, Chap. 5 (1889).

look what the cat's brought in/dragged in An expression of disdain for someone of bedraggled or weary appearance , or simply for someone who is unwelcome. The earliest 'brought' version was spotted by the *OED2* in 1928. 'Dragged' occurs in the film *Bus Stop* (US 1956).

Charlie Farnsbarns A foolish person whose name one cannot remember or does not care to. Although this moderately well-known expression escaped Eric Partridge and his reviser, Paul Beale, in *Partridge/Slang*, Beale wrote to me (1985), 'Charlie Farnsbarns was a very popular equivalent of e.g. "Mrs Thing" or "Old Ooja", i.e. "Old whatsisname". Much play was made with the name in the BBC radio show *Much Binding In the Marsh*, but whether Richard Murdoch and Kenneth Horne actually invented it, or whether they borrowed it "out of the air", I'm afraid I don't know. They would mention especially, I remember, a magnificent motorcar called a "Farnsbarns Special" or something like, say, a "Farnsbarns Straight Eight". This was in the period, roughly 1945–50, while I was at school – I recall a very jolly aunt of mine who was vastly amused by the name and used it a lot.'

Of course, a 'Charlie' (as in 'chase me, Charlie', 'proper Charlie' and 'right Charlie') has long been a slightly derogative name to apply to an ordinary bloke. In Australia, it may also be a shortening of 'Charlie Wheeler', rhyming slang for 'Sheila', a girl – as recorded in Sydney Baker, *The Australian Language* (1945). 'Farnsbarns' has the numbing assonance needed to describe a bit of a nonentity. The phrase probably came out of the services (possibly RAF) in the Second World War.

'Small boys brought up in the city of Lincoln, as I was, will testify that if one left a door open, someone would be sure to say, "**Do you come from Bardney?**" Bardney is nine miles south-east of Lincoln and there was formerly an Abbey there, presumably with an "ever-open door".' So Steve Race, the musician and broadcaster, wrote to me (1993). *Apperson* finds this expression being discussed in *Notes & Queries* by 1905.

Compare: 'Anyone who leaves a door open in Gloucestershire is liable to be asked, "Do you come from Winchcombe?" This is said to be a survival of the pilgrimage to Hayles, when the Abbot requested the good people of Winchcombe to throw open their doors to house the many pilgrims' – Eric R. Delderfield, *The Visitors' Brief Guide to the Cotswold Country* (1959).

'If someone came into the room and left the door open, my Father-in-Law would shout, "Topsham – they always leave the doors open in Topsham." This is a saying heard in many parts of Devon, according to local people' – Mrs B. Penberthy, Cullompton, Devon (2002).

'"Born in Sussex!" (if I hadn't shut the door)' – Alison Adcock, Oxford (2004).

do you think I fell off the Christmas tree? Do you take me for an innocent? *Partridge/Catch Phrases* dates 'I didn't fall off a Christmas tree' to the mid-1940s and claims it was found more in the services than among civilians. Partridge glosses it as, 'I know my way about – I'm not to be fooled.' In BBC TV, *Hancock's Half Hour*, 'Sid in Love' (1 April 1960), a female bus conductor says it to Hancock who is trying to convince her that Sid James is a film casting director.

Colin Price asked (2004) about the saying **don't look at me in that tone of voice** and this released numerous recollections from the 1950s/60s. Marian Griffith thought that it could be extended to include '… you smell a funny colour.' Steve Hill concurred: 'At junior school in Yorkshire, early fifties, we used this quote and completed it as follows: "Don't look at me in that tone of voice – it smells a funny colour!"'

Several respondents were pretty certain that the saying came up in the BBC radio *Goon Show,* also in the 1950s. So far I have only found this (but obviously an allusion): in 'Drums along the Mersey' (11 October 1956), Neddie Seagoon (Harry Secombe) said, 'I seem to recognize that tone of face.'

Colin Price himself then googled his way to an attribution to Senator Thaddeus Caraway (Democrat–Arkansas) in the 1929 *Congressional Record.*

Finally, Peter Young courteously pointed out that, as ever, it is a *Punch* joke dating from 1884. Indeed, it was included in the *Oxford Dictionary of Quotations* until the 1992 edition, since when it has been dropped: 'Don't look at me, Sir, with – ah – in that tone of voice.'

the donkey's been on the strawberries In 2005, Ruth Appleby from Newcastle asked about an odd line in Shelagh Delaney's play, *A Taste of Honey,* Act 1, Sc. 1 (1958). Peter, the mother's 'friend', announces, 'Well, I won't be round tomorrow; the cat's been on the strawberries.' Ruth added, 'I don't really have any idea of what this could mean and I was wondering if anyone knows.'

Curiously enough, they do. Ian Forsyth remembered, 'There are certainly sayings in this vein. As a schoolboy in the North East, I worked part time in a butcher's shop and then in a Co-Op warehouse. In both places, roundsmen would jocularly call out, "Won't be round tomorrow; the donkey got away again!"' Kenneth Neate agreed with this sort of provenance: 'It is meant to be attributed to a coster-monger selling fruit from his barrow. The more often used version is "Shan't be round tomorrow, the donkey's peed on the strawberries". Anthony Newley uses the line as a postscript to his rendition of "As I Was Going to Strawberry Fair", but slurs the rude word, as I remember.'

Not quite. Newley pauses before using the p-word in the line 'The donkey's *pinched* all the strawberries.' This was in the novelty version of the traditional folksong with which he had a hit in 1960.

'My father had a small coal business. We used to go with a borrowed horse and cart to the railway sidings to unload the coal to take home. As a child I used to "help" push the truck around the houses. People were often reluctant or unable to pay and would hide behind the door. One of dad's sayings was, "The wheel's come off the donkey's barrow. We shan't be round tomorrow"' – Jean Rowe, Gimingham, Norfolk (2006).

See also YOU DON'T GIVE DONKEYS STRAWBERRIES (page 341).

easy, tiger! To calm passions. Tim Cornford, Bradford, Yorkshire (2005), wanted to know where it came from. Still looking.

Mike Elvy wrote (2004), 'A friend of mine was recently fingered by a pickpocket on the Underground. I wanted to quote her a poem that I read many years ago about "Fellow Feeling", but I am unable to find it.' Well, Muriel Smith recalled this from a tear-off calendar 'many years ago':

> **A fellow feeling makes one wond'rous kind –**
> And yet methinks the poet would have changed his mind
> If, in a crowd, he chanced to find
> A fellow feeling in his coat behind.

Indeed, this turns out to be one of those verses that people used to put in autograph books etc. On the internet I came across a facsimile of Alice

Hackwood's autograph book which includes more or less the same verse contributed by someone from Wenvoe, near Cardiff, on 26 April 1916. So it is by Anon. But who was the poet who wrote the opening quotation? Not exactly a poet – it is from the actor David Garrick's 'An Occasional Prologue on Quitting the Theatre' (1776).

David Hyman asked (2003) about the saying **to fill one's boots**, meaning 'to take as much as one likes of a good thing'. I had not encountered the phrase, but then stumbled upon this use of it: 'Graham Norton is like a man making up for lost time. An actor until his late twenties, he spent most of his time "resting" … Who can really blame him if he's now filling his boots, and hyperactively running around a studio in spangly jackets for five nights of the week?' – *The Independent* (14 March 2003). Could the phrase, like Graham Norton, be Irish, I wonder? Is the idea that one fills one's boots with food or beer?

Chris Anderson commented, 'I am surprised that you have not come across the expression "fill your boots" before. I served on the lower deck of the Royal Navy from early 1945 to late 1947, where it was very common indeed. For instance, it was the (forbidden) practice for a birthday boy to tour the mess decks begging a sip of everyone's tot of rum. It was called "offering sippers", and a generous invitation was to "gulpers". Rum was a currency – men would do a week's laundry in exchange for a tot (one eighth of a pint, I seem to remember). "Fill your boots" was said to anyone who begged a favour, which might be anything from a drink to the loan of a pen. It meant "Have as much as you wish", but was also used sarcastically post facto.'

Mat Coward added, 'I'm not sure when I first became aware of this phrase, but certainly knew it well in the late 70s, early 80s, in Hampstead, where I used to play darts. Its usage in that context was as follows. Say my opponent threw a very low score, or missed an out shot, then as I stepped up to the oche supporters would call, "Go on, son – fill your boots." They meant that I now had a chance to take advantage of my opponent's misses by (depending on the state of the game) scoring heavily or finishing. I always assumed the substance that one filled one's boots with was beer. Quite possibly Irish, as you suggest, given the geographical, sporting and cultural milieu.'

David Kennard (ex-Croydon, now Mill Valley, California) was also intrigued: 'My late father often used to say "fill your boots!" to me, meaning "take plenty". When I asked him where the idea came from, he said it referred to sea-boots (most of the first half of his life was in the merchant marine). He speculated that, when packing up to go to sea, a mariner would have a kit bag (a long, roly-poly canvas bag in the mid-20th century) and the boots would go in there, and you'd literally "fill your boots" with socks, clothes and (more importantly) several of the little treats that make life at sea bearable: tobacco, chocolate, pictures of loved ones etc. The more of these treats you could pack in, the better.'

'A battalion, sometimes thought to be from The Seaforth Highlanders, was being entertained by a group from ENSA. Being close to Christmas, the show took the form of a pantomime. Inevitably, the Fairy Queen had to make her appearance but in this case *she* was a *he*, and his opening lines went as follows:

> Oh, I am the Fairy Queen
> Of whom you are so fond,
> Please tell me, tell me, tell me
> Where shall I put my wand?

'Foreseeing a predictable answer from 700 thoroughly bored jocks, the Regimental Sergeant Major leapt to his feet and uttered the immortal words, "**First man who speaks – seven days confined to barracks.**"

'Subsequently, in my family, any request for information, such as "Where shall I put this plate?" was met by my father with "First man who speaks ..." Since my father became Chief of the General Staff, one wonders what became of the gallant originator' – James Cassels, Errol, Perthshire (2002).

from great guns and women's tongues, good Lord deliver us ...
Obviously, the last four words are from the Litany in the Book of Common Prayer, but what of the rest? Moshe Brody of Kfar Sava, Israel, wrote (2004), 'This fragment is a corruption of an anonymous sailor's "prayer" dating back to the early mid-1800s, and was occasionally inscribed on articles of pottery that would be used in establishments catering to seafarers and the like. Presumably it might also have been written on other items, but I have seen it only on pottery, such as bowls and pitchers. It's a humorous short verse and like many a good limerick, the complete saying appears in various similar forms, and goes like this:

> From rocks and sands and barren lands
> Kind fortune keep me free,
> And from great guns and women's tongues
> Good God deliver me.

Also:

> From rocks and sands and barren lands
> Good fortune set me free.
> And from great guns and women's tongues
> O, Lord, deliver me.'

'Said of someone's childish humour, "That's what I like about you – **funny but never vulgar**"' – Tony Malin, Blandford Forum (2003). I wonder if this was inspired by the remark attributed to W.S. Gilbert?

A Quaker singer, David Bispham, noted in his *Recollections* (1920) that he had heard Gilbert say something like it to Sir Herbert Beerbohm Tree about his Hamlet. On the stage of the Haymarket Theatre, London, after the first performance in 1892, Gilbert said, 'My dear fellow, I never saw anything so funny in my life, and yet it was not in the least vulgar.'

At the time, the line quickly went round in its abbreviated form, and apparently Tree put up a brave show of not being offended. He wrote to Gilbert on 25 March 1893, 'By the bye, my wife told me that you were under the impression that I might have been offended at some witticism of yours about my Hamlet. Let me assure you it was not so. On the contrary, it was I believe *I* who circulated the story. There could be no harm, as I knew you had not seen me act the part, and moreover, while I am a great admirer of your wit, I have also too high an opinion of my work to be hurt by it.'

Hesketh Pearson in his 1956 biography of Tree seems to think this letter shows the actor claiming not only to have circulated the story against himself but to have *invented* it. On the other hand, in his earlier biography of Gilbert and Sullivan (1935) Pearson had reported Bernard Shaw as telling him that Gilbert complained shortly before his death (1911) of the way ill-natured witticisms had been fathered on him and instanced the description of Tree. There seems little doubt, though, that he did say it.

Shaw himself had used the phrase in a review of pantomime in *London Music* on 23 January 1897: 'Pray understand that I do not want the pantomime artists to be "funny without being vulgar". That is the mere snobbery of criticism. Every comedian should have vulgarity at his fingers' ends.'

J.B. Booth in *Old Pink 'Un Days* (1924) recalled an exchange in a London theatre after Pavlova's successes, when a large lady from Oldham or Wigan was attempting to pass herself off as a Russian dancer. 'What do you think of her?' asked one. Came the reply: 'Funny without being Volga.'

give the man a putty medal An ironical suggestion that someone should be given recognition for something done or said. In other words, no medal at all. Recorded in the 19th century by J. Redding Ware in *Passing English of the Victorian Era* (1909).

to go down hill like a greased pig 'To deteriorate perhaps through drink or just laziness' – Tim Thomson (2001).

God bless the Duke of Argyll! What Scots Highlanders were supposed to exclaim when scratching themselves. Why? Because a Duke of Argyll is said to have erected scratching posts on his estates for cattle and sheep. His herdsmen would use the posts for the same purpose and give this shout by way of thanks for the relief they afforded. Nobody knows which duke this was or when the saying became established. *Brewer's Dictionary of Phrase & Fable* (1894 edn), while relating the foregoing, spells it 'Argyle'.

'My grandmother (1875–1969) had many strange sayings. If anything, like a piece of furniture or equipment of any sort, was falling to bits, broken, or ceased functioning, Granny would say it had "**gone to kickeriboo**" (if that's the spelling). She pronounced "gone" as "gorn"' – Malcolm G. Sturgess, Salisbury, Wiltshire (2004). *Partridge/Slang* has 'kickeraboo' or ' – poo', meaning 'dead' and derives it from 'kick over the bucket'. He considers it to be West Indies 'pidgin' from the late 18th century.

'When annoyed with someone, my mother would often say that she'd **"have his guts for garters"**. Can you throw any light on this?' – Angela Browne (2006). For such a well-known expression, this has been little discussed and researched by reference books. The *OED2* produces only two citations from the 1930s for what it calls 'a hyperbolic threat'.

Mark English noted (2006), 'P.W. Joyce's *English As We Speak It In Ireland* (1910), p. 128, cites this from the *Irish Penny Magazine* (date not given): "A poor woman who is about to be robbed shrieks out for help; when the villain says to her: 'Not another word or I'll stick you like a pig and give you your guts for garters.' "'

Partridge/Catch Phrases does, however, do well on it. In fact, as might be suspected, the expression is a venerable one. In Robert Greene's *The Scottish History of James the Fourth*, Act 3, Sc. 2 (1598), we find: 'I'll make garters of thy guts, thou villain, if thou enter this office.' In Ben Jonson's *Cynthia's Revels: or, The Fountain of Self-Love* (1616), there is: 'I will garter my hose with your guts.' Partridge suggests it became a mainstream expression in the 18th century.

oh, '[H]arry ain't it "orrid when yer 'ot an' in an 'urry an' you 'ave to 'old yer 'at on wi' yer 'and! 'Something that my late father used to say' – Stephen Watkins, Rochford, Essex (2001). A sort of cross between a tongue-twister and a test of aitch-dropping. Compare DON'T BLOW ON IT (page 69) and HARRY'S HAT, next.

Harry's hat was hanging on the hatstand in the hall A *Quote ... Unquote* listener asked about the following verse in 2001:

> Harry went to Hampstead.
> Harry lost his hat.
> Harry's mother said to Harry,

'Harry, where's your hat?'
Harry said he'd lost it.
It wasn't true at all.
Harry's hat was hanging on the hatstand in the hall.

I do not know whether the original text had all the Hs in, as here, or whether they had all been removed, as when it is spoken.

Nevertheless, I am assuming that this verse gave rise to the title for an amateur revue I took part in at the Cockpit Theatre, London, in 1970 – it was called *'Arry's 'At Was 'Anging on the 'Atstand in the 'All*. Beyond that, I have found nothing.

An anonymous listener did, however, tell me of a similar saying: 'My grandmother, whose name was Anne, had a saying, delivered in a music-hall Cockney accent, whenever she accidentally mispronounced a word or dropped an 'aitch, which she frequently did. It was: "Hannie 'ang your 'at on the 'ook in the 'all!"'

have you got a match?/I haven't got one to match you – *Wickenden*. Compare BUT I'VE A PHOTO OF GENERAL BULLER ... (page 330).

how's your telephone, Bill? My maternal Grandma – Amy Catherine Gleave (1886–1976) – wore a hearing aid, somewhere about the size of Jodrell Bank or Goonhilly Down, which was pinned to the front of her capacious bosom. To relocate this instrument she would turn her bosom in the direction from which she supposed sound was coming. She would then turn up the volume so that all sorts of howls and whines were emitted. After a while, Grandma would invariably give up the attempt, turn off the machine and lapse into brooding silence. Then she would plot how to disrupt our activities.

Her finest moment came once when we were sitting round the tea-table, debating the great issues of the day and, as usual, excluding the poor old thing from our conversation. Suddenly, she erupted with the startling inquiry. It took us only a moment or two to realize that not one of us round the tea-table was called 'Bill'. More slowly, it dawned that Grandma had embarked on one of her many pet theories, that she was being overcharged for her telephone calls. From that day on, in our family, the phrase 'How's your telephone, Bill?' has been ritually employed whenever anybody has wanted to change the subject. Or to bring a conversation to a juddering halt.

Someone not from our family once told me that their deaf granny had come up with the equally efficacious, 'But wasn't he a Smith-Bosanquet?' – which had a similarly emasculating effect on conversation. Compare: 'My father's family used to say, "**Butter's up**" whenever someone suddenly changed the subject of a conversation. The story is that there was a dinner party with some fairly important guests, and a deep political discussion was going on. During a lull in the conversation, an elderly (and slightly deaf) relation turned to a neighbour and said, "Did you know, butter's up ..."' – Sally Lambert, Oxford (2002). 'When somebody is going on a bit, we interrupt with, "**But a wet bird never flies at night**"' – Gordon Salkilld, Sutton, Surrey (2001).

I am warming the whole of creation One of Linda Irene's 14 children recalled (2000) that their mother would warm her rear by the fire with these words. It was only much later that a pun was perceived.

I don't know what the world's coming to Traditional moan. 'As their grandparents said' – quoted in Richard Hoggart, *The Uses of Literacy* (1957).

Margaret Martin of New Malden, Surrey, wrote (1993), 'My mother communicated in epigrams: "No, you can't go to the seaside – **I have a bone in my leg**."' This all-purpose humorous excuse for non-activity – sometimes '... in my throat/arm/etc.' – dates back to the 16th century, as *Apperson* makes clear.

Anthony Fisher recalled (1997), 'As a child in the early forties I would frequently summon my father to come upstairs to read me a story. He obviously found this a rather tiresome chore and to relieve him of this duty my mother would reply, "He can't come now, he has a bone in his leg." Even at my early age, I thought this a pretty, er, lame excuse, as mobility would have been even more difficult without a bone in his leg – but what on earth could have been the origin of this curious expression?'

It is fairly pointless seeking a reason for this feeble prevarication. The obviousness of the statement – like 'He's got two ears on his head' – is an indication that it is not to be taken in any way seriously.

'When my grandmother had been told something surprising, she would often say, in a broad Belfast accent, "God bless us and save us, said 'oul Mrs Davis, **I never knew herrings was fish**' – Michael Collins, Belfast (2003).

I once had a donkey. I'd just got it learned to live without eating when it went and died on me 'My paternal grandfather said this' – Denis Sharp, Arundel (2002).
'My mother's mother came from Stockport and my mother would often say, "As my mother used to say, '**I won't boil my cabbages twice**'" – meaning she did not want to repeat herself' – Sheila Sharman, East Yorkshire (2002).

I'm as calm as a cucumber 'Said by my mother when she was het up'
– Margaret Philip, Diss (2000). 'As *cool* as a cucumber' dates back
to 1615 …

'My mother-in-law heard this on a bus in Huddersfield. It was spoken
by a portly woman to her equally portly husband. They were squashed
together on the one seat and she said to him, "Move over, Daddy.
I've only got one cheek on!"' – Enid Grattan-Guinness, Barnet,
Hertfordshire (1978).

if me no ifs and but me no buts So far, the earliest appearance found of
'If me no ifs' is in Mrs Gaskell's *Wives and Daughters* (1864–6) and 'but
me no buts' is in Susannah Centlivre's play *The Busie Body* (1708) – but
no early citation has yet been found for the two phrases joined together.
Nevertheless, injunctions against the weasely use of the words 'if' and
'but' are of long standing. In Rabelais, *Pantagruel*, Bk 3, Chap. 10 (1532),
in French, is this: '"In your propositions," said Pantagruel, "there are so
many ifs and buts that I know not how to make anything of them."' The
future Richard III in Shakespeare's play, III.iv.75 (1592) says, 'Talk'st
thou to me of ifs! Thou art a traitor:/Off with his head.' A probably
modern American proverb is '"Ifs" and "buts" butter no bread' (no date).

'My grandfather, who was a veteran of the Battle of the Somme, used to
say, "**If things don't change, they'll stop as they are.**" As a child, this
struck me as rather astute' – John Blick (2005).

'Whenever my mother went on a bus, at the first jolt she would say, "**If we have an accident, get me out of this vest**"' – Owen Wainwright, Vazon, Guernsey (no date).

to be/stand in someone else's shoes To be in someone else's place; to know what it feels like to be someone else. Originally, 'to be in someone else's coat'. *Brewer's Dictionary of Phrase & Fable* (1894) adds: 'Among the ancient Northmen, when a man adopted a son, the person adopted put on the shoes of the adopter' – quoting an 1834 source.

'My father was born in 1895. If he was using string or a lead and it became tangled, he would say it had a half-crown in it. I have never heard anyone else use such an expression. Now I am in my 70s and the vacuum cleaner lead was knotted when I was using it recently and I found myself saying, "Wait a minute, **it has a half-crown in it**." I hadn't thought of the saying for years' – Ruby White, Epping, Essex (2004).

'Whenever a door opened by itself or one thought that a person had come into the room when they had not, my mother would say, "**It must be Billy Winkle.**" It could be an entirely unique family saying, but I'm sure it must come from somewhere else' – Jo Marshall, Twickenham, Middlesex (2000).

'A saying from my maternal grandfather who died in the early 1960s: **"It remains to be seen, the monkey said, as he swept the muck under the carpet"'** – Ann Bamford, Cumbria (2006). A Wellerism – compare from the US in 1942: '"That remains to be seen," said the elephant, as he walked in the fresh cement.'

'cos me did 'This is a thing my family says and is based on an interchange between my grandfather and my aunt Jessie, who was then aged only three. There were seven children in the family, so they all helped with the washing up. My grandfather was busy writing notes for a speech when Jessie dropped a cup which smashed noisily on to the stone floor of the scullery. Grandad rushed out and said angrily to her, "What did you do that for?" Her answer: "Because me did. I couldn't help it, Dad." Since then, shortened to "'Cos-me-did", we've used it to explain any inexplicable behaviour, thus: **"It's a case of 'cos-me-did"'** – Estelle Boxell-Hutson, Maylandsea, Essex (2000).

Johnson's at the door 'Indicating that someone has a drip on the end of their nose' – Gillian Fuller, Bromley, Kent (2006). I am sure there must be a story behind this delightful expression, but we have not turned it up yet.

joke over Either said by the teller of a joke that has misfired or by the person to whom it has been told. By the 1920s. 'If no one laughed at his or other passing jokes, my uncle would slip this in with quick resignation' – Robert Priddy, Nesoddtangen, Norway (1998).

According to Roger Wilmut, *Kindly Leave the Stage!* (1985), the Yorkshire comedian Dick Henderson had a sort of catchphrase, in his act, when he would say, 'Ha! Ha! – joke over' at the conclusion of an obvious joke.

to keep the memory green Actively not to forget about something or someone treasured. 'Green' here presumably means 'alive, fresh or young', as in a plant. Date of origin unknown. In *Our Old Home* (1863), Nathaniel Hawthorne describes encountering a gravestone in Bebington churchyard, Cheshire, that was 'beautifully embossed letters of living green, a bas-relief of velvet moss on the marble slab! ... [Nature had taken] such wonderful pains "to keep his memory green." Perhaps the proverbial phrase, just quoted, may have had its origin in the natural phenomenon here described.'

'As a Midlander married to a Northern man, I often find he has odd little sayings that I had no idea existed – nor, indeed, know what they mean. My favourite is "**laughing teacakes**" and it is used of someone who benefits from something at someone else's expense. It's rather like "laughing all the way to the bank", only more gleeful and patronizing' – Wendy-Ann Street, Ipswich (2002).

like kissing your sister I first encountered this simile from the Canadian-born singer and actress Isabelle Lucas (1927–97) on *Quote ... Unquote* (19 January 1982). She quoted an overheard remark concerning cottage cheese and I took it to mean that, as opposed to kissing someone in a sexual sense, it was 'not the real thing'. That was where it rested until I came across these other two remarks – both significantly North American and describing other unsatisfactory experiences: '[A tied ball game is] like kissing your sister' – Eddie Erdelatz, US football coach, quoted in *The Washington Post* (9 November 1953); 'Listening to a radio service is like kissing your sister, it fails to give the proper stimulation' – *Lime Springs* (Iowa) *Sun Herald* (15 October 1931).

(it was) like pulling the wings off a butterfly 'Said of a particularly easy task or boasting about how easy it was to get one's own back on someone' – Tony Malin, Blandford Forum (2003). This is certainly a turn of phrase, but it is surprisingly little recorded.

like the barber's cat – full of wind and water 'When trying to reinforce an argument with "so and so said", this was the reply (if a male was quoted), ("water" to rhyme with "hatter")' – Margaret Martin, Surrey (1993).

Partridge/Slang has 'like the barber's cat – all wind and piss', and dates it from the late 19th century. John Beaumont, Hertfordshire (2000), added that his grandfather used to say after a good Sunday dinner, 'I'm full of wind and water like a barber's cat.' This was around the time of the Second World War.

'My father would say, "I'm farting like a barber's cat" – often as a result of too much home-brewed beer. He never explained if the cat was used as a scapegoat or whether the presence of various potions in a barber's shop caused cats this problem' – Matthew Hind, Buckinghamshire (2002).

a little bird told me What you say when you tell someone you have learned something about them from somebody you are coyly not going to name – though they can probably guess. It has been a proverbial phrase since the 18th century. Just possibly inspired by this passage from

Ecclesiastes 10:20: 'Curse not the king, no not in thy thought; and curse not the rich in thy bedchamber: for a bird of the air shall carry the voice, and that which hath wings shall tell the matter.'

'My mother used to say **"a loud laugh denotes the vacant mind"'**
– Mrs Jean Wigget, Kent (1995). She had been anticipated in this informal proverb. Lord Byron, in a letter to Augusta Leigh (19 December 1816), wrote, 'I remember a methodist preacher who on perceiving a profane grin on the faces of part of his congregation – exclaimed "no *hopes* for *them* as *laughs*".' In a note to *Hints from Horace*, Byron gave the name of the preacher as John Stickles.

A.A. Wright wrote (2001), 'When things go right, I find myself muttering, **"Lovely – tell your mother!"** I think I have heard my brother use the phrase and I know that my father used to use it. Is it a catchphrase of a music-hall performer of (say) 1900–14?'

Well, no sign of it in *Partridge/Catch Phrases*, though he does have 'Go home and tell your mother she wants you' as perhaps originating in Australia of the 1930s.

Ian Forsyth comments, 'This was used by my mother in County Durham and also my wife's father in West Middlesex when things turned out just right. Incidentally, the phrase as cited implies a breath after the first word. As we remember hearing it, it would be 'Lovelytellyourmother' with no pause. The snappiness and inverted word order were the appeal (rather like Jewish "Now he tells me").'

Cliff Blake adds, 'This was used in S.E. London in the form "It's lovely – tell your Mum!" It was often said to a child delivering something on behalf of its parent, or – jokingly – when someone was passing a minor object to a friend.'

major fall of soot 'What you say after a good sneeze. I once said this, without thinking, to a person who'd sneezed violently. He was black. Oops!' – Ann Bamford, Cumbria (2006).

Meredith we're in! This shout of triumph originated in a music-hall sketch called 'The Bailiff' (or 'Moses and Son'), performed by Fred Kitchen (his dates sometimes given as 1872–1950), the leading comedian with Fred Karno's company. The sketch was first seen in 1907 and the phrase was uttered each time a bailiff and his assistant looked like gaining entrance to the house.

Kitchen has the phrase on his gravestone in West Norwood cemetery, South London, and I have seen it:

> Fred Kitchen . . .
> Passed away
> 1 April 1951
> aged 77 years
> Beloved by all who knew him
> MEREDITH, WE'RE IN.

Alison Richards recalled (2006) a Wellerism that her mother used to employ: '**"Merely a trifle" – said the monkey, as he spat on the sponge cake.**' Alas, this particular one does not appear in Mieder & Kingsbury's *Dictionary of Wellerisms* (1994).

In 2006, Paul Wilkinson wanted to know about a comment of his father's, in 1930s Australia, about 'the deep perdition into which society was then sinking': '**A nation rots in the lap of ease/And spreads the canker worm of a foul disease.**' Paul says his father was a 'Victorian through every vital part of his being' and, although I could not put my finger on an exact source, this couplet certainly uses a clutch of phrases popular in the 19th century.

David Challener found these uses in Vol. 32 of the Revd C.H. Spurgeon's sermons (1886): 'He never expected when he became a deep-sea fisherman that he was going to sleep in the lap of ease' and 'In truth a foul disease had cankered his brow'.

I turned up this similar couplet from Patrick Brontë's 'Winter-Night Meditations' (but I have been unable to confirm what this is, except that it is 19th century and presumably was written by the father of the Brontë sisters): 'Oft fostered on the lap of ease,/Grow racking pain, and foul disease.'

'Foul disease' became a euphemism for syphilis.

neat but not gaudy A quirky comment coupled with some outlandish image, e.g. 'Neat but not gaudy – like a bull's arse tied up with a bicycle chain' – told me by a (sensibly) anonymous correspondent from the Cotswolds in 1994.

Partridge/Catch Phrases suggests that the initial phrase was established by about 1800, though in 1631 there had been the similar 'Comely, not gaudy'. Shakespeare in *Hamlet*, I.iii.71 (1600) has:

> Rich, not gaudy;
> For the apparel oft proclaims the man ...

The Revd Samuel Wesley wrote in 'An Epistle to a Friend concerning Poetry' (1700), 'Style is the dress of thought; a modest dress,/Neat, but not gaudy, will true critics please.'

Charles Lamb wrote to William Wordsworth (June 1806), 'A little thin flowery border round, neat not gaudy.' Then variations were introduced – as by John Ruskin, writing in the *Architectural Magazine* (November 1838): 'That admiration of the "neat but gaudy [*sic*]" which is commonly reported to have influenced the devil when he painted his tail pea green.'

Indeed, *Partridge* cites, 'Neat, but not gaudy, as the monkey said, when he painted his tail sky-blue' and '... painted his bottom pink and tied up his tail with pea-green'.

'A saying from my maternal grandfather who died in the early 1960s: "Neat but not gaudy, the monkey said as he painted the cat's bottom green"' – Ann Bamford, Cumbria (2006). See also AS THE MONKEY (page 275); SKY-BLUE PINK ... (page 333).

'My mother (1896–1968) used to say, "**'No answer' was the stern reply**", especially if her children didn't answer her questions. Now I, my husband and my son often use the phrase – especially if there's no reply when we phone each other! I have tried to trace its origins with no success, though I have a feeling it may come from a monologue' – Mrs M. White, Surrey (1994).

Indeed, this ironic comment on the fact that no one has replied or said a word was known by the 1930s but in various forms, including '"**No answer, no answer" came the loud reply**' and '"**Shrieks of silence" was the stern reply**'. If these are quotations, the original source has not been identified. Compare, however:

> But answer came there none –
> And this was scarcely odd, because
> They'd eaten every one.

– Lewis Carroll, *Through the Looking Glass* (1872) – 'The Walrus and the Carpenter' episode.

'But answer came there none' also appears in Sir Walter Scott, *The Bridal of Triermain* (1813) and almost in Shakespeare: 'But answer made it none' – *Hamlet* (I.ii.215). It has also been suggested that the phrase might have been a joke response to the opening question in Walter De La Mare's poem 'The Listeners' (1912), '"Is there anybody there?" said the Traveller,/Knocking on the moonlit door.' The actual answer in the poem is '"Tell them I came, and no one answered,/That I kept my word," he said.'

Among variations: 'No answer, no answer came the loud reply' – an Edinburgh grandmother of the Revd Lorna Rattray (1994), in the 1960s; 'Silence was the stern reply' – Paul Beale (1994); '"No answer was the stern reply,/The old fishmonger has gone by" – this was current in my 1920s childhood in North Lancashire, said lugubriously. Either a monologue (Billy Bennett?) or an earlier hammy melodrama as source' – N.P. Griffin, Lancashire (1997); 'My father used to complete this as a non-rhyming couplet: "No answer came the stern reply/As he got on his bike and walked away!"' – Dick Frazer, Norfolk (1997). 'My husband used to say, "No answer was the stern reply" with the following ending "... the fog grew thicker"' – Heather Bosence, Minster in Thanet, Kent (2006).

'My father's comrade in the army was a child psychologist in the real world and had written in his diary after one of his leaves, "Took Ellen (3) to the zoo. Had her walk backwards to the elephant enclosure, then swung her round. **No reaction to the elephant**." We use it when one of us is unimpressed by some amazing achievement by the other. For example, I rushed in to where they were all eating breakfast crying, "Guess what, I passed *all* my A-levels!" They all just looked at me like grazing cattle might look at a passing motor car. "No reaction to the elephant, then?" I complained' – Estelle Boxell-Hutson, Maylandsea, Essex (2000).

**not a word about the pig and how it died, and whose small potatoes
it ate** 'My grandmother (92) has this saying – I'd love to know where it
comes from' – Kate Pool, London SW10 (1995).

The only clue I have found is a headline in *Punch* (20 August 1864) –
'Not a Word about the Pig' – though there are several other references
to this short phrase in 19th-century literature. *Partridge/Slang* has 'Not a
word of the pudding' = 'say nothing about the matter', dating from the
late 17th century.

Perhaps the following is somehow related? 'Some years ago when my
children were small and I would attempt to encourage them to eat up
the meal put before them, my mother-in-law, in her wisdom, would say,
"Don't force them, dear, an old woman forced a pig once and it died"'
– Wendy Graham, Finchampstead, Berkshire (2004).

A Mr Howells introduced Mark Twain at a seventieth birthday dinner
at Delmonico's restaurant, New York City (5 December 1905), with
these words: 'I will try not to be greedy on your behalf in wishing the
health of our honored and, in view of his great age, our revered guest.
I will not say, "**Oh King, live forever!**" but "Oh King, live as long as
you like!"'

It has been a traditional toast or wish that kings live forever or, at the
very least, a long time. The Japanese cry '*Banzai*', directed at the
Emperor, literally means no more than 'ten thousand years', but what it
more usually signifies is 'for a long time'. In full, '*Tenno heika banzai*' –
'Long live the Emperor', a phrase which goes back into Japanese
history, despite its appropriation by the nationalist movements of the
1930s.

The phrase is still in use. If literally translated, it is really no different
from 'Zadok the priest, and Nathan the prophet, anointed Solomon
king. And all the people rejoiced and said, God save the king. Long live
the king, *may the king live for ever*. Amen. Alleluia' – which has been
spoken or sung at the coronation of almost every English sovereign since

William of Normandy was crowned in Westminster Abbey on Christmas Day 1066.

Jonathan Swift includes 'may you live a thousand years' among the conversational chestnuts in *Polite Conversation* (1738). The Sergeant in Charles Dickens, *Great Expectations*, Chap. 5 (1860–1) incorporates it in a toast. See also TRUE, O KING! (page 49).

(it's) on the puppy's shelf It's on the floor. Described as 'a wonderful old Surrey saying, collected in the early 1960s from nonagenarians various' – Cherry Norman, Tadworth, Surrey (2001). I have not found this recorded elsewhere.

put it in a glass case and throw sugar at it 'What on earth does this mean? My Irish grandpa used to say it' – Pat Stimpson, Keston, Kent (2001). The Irish-born broadcaster Terry Wogan has also been known to use it. Other versions heard include: 'Hang it on the wall ...', 'Put it in a box ...' and 'Put it in a big pot ...' I think the general idea is that this is a way to celebrate something that you like or which takes your fancy.

to put one's puddings out for treacle To put oneself forward for a reward (as though to receive sauce on a dessert), though a double meaning is not far away. In May 1994, Teresa Gorman MP accused Michael Heseltine of disloyalty to Prime Minister John Major by saying that he was 'putting his puddings out for treacle'. Mrs Gorman subsequently explained her expression to Alan Watkins in the *Independent on Sunday* (12 June 1994): '[It] was used in our neighbourhood about any woman considered to be putting herself forward for attention – or suspected of paying the tradesmen's bills in "kind"!'

'I recall hearing this on a 1935–45 wartime radio comedy programme.
A character in a "soppy" voice said, "They told us to put our puddings
out for treacle. I put mine out, and somebody pinched me pudding!'
– John Smart, Essex (2000). Indeed, 'Somebody pinched me puddin'!'
was used at about that time by the variety act Collinson and Breen.
Their explanation was that 'Somebody said, "All put your puddin's out
for treacle", and I put mine out and somebody pinched it!'

   Partridge/Catch Phrases has, rather, 'Put your pudden up for treacle!' as
'encouragement to be forthcoming' and quotes Edgar T. Brown (1977):
'I met the phrase in the Army in 1914 and my informant told me that it
relates to prison. If you were unwise enough to "hold your pudden out
for treacle" it would have been swiped by another inmate, who "knew
the ropes" better than you did.'

sailors don't care 'I am moved to ask if you are familiar with this
saying. I assume it means that mariners are not dismayed by storms
and tempests or by the appearance of mermaids' – Stephen W. Davies
(2001). Yes, it is an encouragement not to be over-cautious.
Partridge/Catch Phrases suggests that it was current by the late 19th
century.

to give a/the Scarborough warning To give no warning at all. This
is sometimes wrongly said to derive from the occasion when Thomas
Stafford entered and took possession of Scarborough Castle before the
townsmen were aware of his approach. But that took place in 1557 and
the phrase had been recorded by 1546.

   My attention was drawn to this expression by a correspondent who,
however, put a different gloss upon it: '"He gave him the Scarborough
warning" was used by my father and his contemporaries as an obliquely
framed reference to something nasty in the future. So, "When the

manager looked him in the eye and said he was thinking of closing his department, I reckon it was the Scarborough Warning."

'Now, I am sure that this refers to the hit and run attacks on East Coast towns by German battle cruisers in the Great War – I think in 1915 – taking advantage of the fact that the Royal Navy's fleet was based in Scapa Flow and couldn't react quickly enough. There were casualties, some of them fatal – certainly people were killed in Scarborough. What I'd like to know is whether there is direct evidence of those attacks being called "The Scarborough Warning" at the time, either by the Germans or others' – Gerald Haigh (2001).

Subsequently, I received yet another, more modern, re-interpretation and re-use of the old phrase: 'In Barnsley, if someone complains at work that they feel unwell then they might be accused of issuing a "Scarborough warning", meaning that the person intends to "pull a sickie" the following day – with the implication that they will actually be taking a day trip to Scarborough!' – Liz Saunders (2002).

see you on the Christmas tree! A valedictory remark of British origin, in the 20th century, but why – what is the implication?

And what is the connection, if any, with Joan Leslie saying to Gary Cooper in the film *Sergeant York* (US 1941), 'I wouldn't have you on a Christmas tree, Alvin York'?

since Hector was a pup A very long time ago, way back when. Of American origin and mostly in American usage. Known by 1912.

Partridge/Catch Phrases gives it as the 'US equivalent' of the various 'since ...' expressions he lists, such as 'since Pontius was a pilot', and dates it '*circa* 1920'. The *Morris Dictionary of Word and Phrase Origins* (1977) suggests that W.C. Fields spoke it in a film (unidentified) and that it was popularized by a 1920s comic strip called *Polly and Her Pals*.

It seems to be the case that, in the US, large dogs were often named 'Hector' at the turn of the 19th/20th century. But it could also be an allusion to Hector in Homer's *Iliad* (in the days when all schoolchildren knew who he was) and 'pup', as the once popular colloquialism for 'kid'. Partridge in mentioning an alleged Canadian version 'since Caesar was a pup' might seem to support this.

Earlier, in James Fenimore Cooper's novel *The Prairie* (1828), there occurs the phrase, 'The dam of Hector was then a pup', but the relevance of this is not clear.

to sit about like Joe Egg From Peter Nichols, *A Day in the Death of Joe Egg*, Act 2 (1967): 'My grandma used to say, "Sitting about like Joe Egg" when she meant she had nothing to do.' Hence, the title of the play. I am not sure that this was a very widespread usage.

to sit like Piff(e)y As when a person is left in an isolated, useless position for some time and asks, 'Why am I sat here like Piffy?' British North Country usage. A longer version is, 'Sitting **like Piffy on a rock-bun**', remembered from the 1930s.

And never ask who the original Piffy was. 'When I was a lad in Macclesfield, sixty years ago, my mother often said to me, "Shape yourself, don't stand there like Piffey"' – John Heys, letter in *The Guardian* (17 August 1989). 'Waiting here like Piffey' – Graham Whitehead (2000).

Compare also: 'In the days before theme parks and garden centres, when it was quite usual to go for a Sunday picnic which included a visit to the family grave, a child in the party fell over and was comforted in these words: "Sit on your grand-dad's grave and have a rock-bun." This phrase has been used ever since in our family as slightly mocking comfort, particularly if someone has been making an inordinate fuss about some minor mishap' – Glenys Hopkins, Warrington, Cheshire (1994).

It has been suggested that 'piffy' was a type of icing dolloped on a rock bun, but only in small amounts. See also I WISH I (page 279).

On a Belfast edition of *Quote ... Unquote* (4 October 2004), the publisher Anne Tannahill said, 'Our family has a phrase when you want to pass the buck. My brother, the youngest of the family, suddenly burst out in exasperation one evening, "You might as well call me Some-of-yous!" He explained, "When the fire's low, Daddy always says, "Some of yous get a shovel of coal." Then when nobody makes a move, he says, "I said, some of yous get a shovel of coal." Then he always gets mad and shouts, "Robert, I thought I told you to get a shovel of coal!" Ever since, we always say of an unwelcome task, "Ach, sure **Some-of-yous will do it!**" (By the way, this illustrates a useful quirk of the Ulster dialect: in common with Scots, when using the second person we keep the distinction between the singular "you" and plural "yous").'

(there is) someone walking on my grave What you say when you shiver or shudder or feel goose pimples. It is an old superstition that when you shiver, someone is walking over the place of your future grave. Jonathan Swift has it in his list of conversational clichés, *Polite Conversation* (1738).

spring in the air, Mrs Jones! A seasonal greeting customarily given by the father of the writer Andrew Davies, as related on *Quote ... Unquote* (7 November 1989). Compare WINTER DRAWERS ON (page 372).

take it from here What is the particular resonance of this phrase? Connoisseurs of British radio comedy will need no reminding of *Take It From Here*, starring Jimmy Edwards, Dick Bentley, Joy Nichols *et al*, which ran on the BBC from 1948–59. But having another look through Denis Gifford's *The Golden Age of Radio*, I was rather intrigued to learn that the phrase had been used before this for another BBC show, something starring Richard Haydn (and later Arthur Marshall as Nurse Dugdale) in 1943–4.

This made me think that it must have been a catchphrase of sorts before both programmes took a hold of it. Eric Partridge is no good on this point, seemingly thinking that the second, more famous, series caused it to catch on. He does, however, come up with a meaning: 'Let's begin at this point and ignore what's been said or done or is past.'

In best BBC fashion, I decided to refer the matter upwards – to Denis Norden, who wrote *Take It From Here* with Frank Muir. Denis replied (2005), 'Back in the Forties, you'd occasionally see the instruction "Take It From Here" beside the dispensing aperture of one of the over-sized vending machines of that era. Hence the sung introduction –

> Take it from here
> Don't go away when you can
> Take it from here
> Why don't you stay and maybe
> Join in the fun
> Now the show has begun
> Half an hour of laughter beckons
> Every minute packed with seconds.

'I still wince at that last rhyme but, as you can see, the sense in which we employed the phrase "Take it from here" differed considerably from the usage assigned to it these days, which is something more along the lines of "Carry on from where I've just left off". Moreover, if there is anything to Partridge's claim that the four words achieved catchphrase status, any credit for that should go to Johnny Johnson – who set them to a tune that accorded exactly with what was then the latest and most desirable thing in four-note motor horns ...'

take my arm and call me Charlie 'My mother (who was born in 1899) used to say this when I was a child. Much more recently, I said it to an 80-year-old friend when helping her down steps. She was amazed to hear it, as she had not heard it said since *her* childhood' – Leonie Hamilton, Heswall, Wirral (2000).

Partridge/Catch Phrases has this as 'hold my hand and call me Charlie', 'mostly derisive, addressed by youth to girl', current by 1930 and obsolete by 1960.

'A quote regularly used in our family. It was passed on from my wife's mother (and her mother before that, she was Irish). When faced by an exceptional situation or circumstance, she would say, **"That's Africa for you"'** – Lance Holyoake (2002).

that's my name – don't wear it out An example of supposedly smart talk that may date from the 1950s and probably originated in the US. A good example occurs in the film of the musical *Grease* (US 1978), in which Sandy (Olivia Newton-John) is finding it difficult to get through to Danny (John Travolta) when they meet up again. She says 'Danny?' in a questioning way and he replies tartly, 'That's my name, don't wear it out.'

'My father, Alec Hepplewhite (1919–99), used to have a lot of sayings, some from his time abroad during World War II. These included **"There are not many people your size much bigger"** and **'It's only five minutes' walk, if you run!'** – Ian Hepplewhite (2003).

'My late mother used to say the washday rhyme' – Michael Grosvenor Myer, Haddenham, Cambridgeshire (2000). Also recalled by Sydney Treadgold, Wokingham, Berkshire (2000):

> They that wash on Monday
> Have all the week to dry;
> They that wash on Tuesday
> Are not so much awry;
> They that wash on Wednesday
> Are not so much to blame;
> They that wash on Thursday
> Wash for shame;
> They that wash on Friday
> Wash in need;
> **And they that wash on Saturday,**
> **Oh! they're sluts indeed.**

This is ascribed to Anon in the *Oxford Dictionary of Quotations* (1953 edn) and seems to have been recorded first in Robert Hunt, *Popular Romances of the West of England* (1865).

this won't bathe the baby Meaning 'we must stop idly doing what we are engaged in now when there are more important tasks to be done'. From BBC TV, *Hancock's Half Hour* (The Reunion Party, 25 March

1960) – *Tony Hancock:* 'Well, this isn't going to get the baby washed, is it?'

'My mother, a *very* busy lady, would sometimes sit down for a few minutes. Feeling guilty, she would arise to "This won't bathe the baby" (even though our baby days were long past). I still use it when there are things to be done' – Mrs Elizabeth Durham, Cheshire (1995).

Compare: 'From my mother about time-wasting, "This won't get the children boots, or the baby a new bonnet"' – Deborah Chesshire, Somerset (1998); 'Well, this won't buy the baby new boots' – *Wickenden. Casson/Grenfell* has: 'Now I must get on, this will never get the baby a new coat.'

'When my Ma (born 1921) had been sitting down or resting for a while, to get herself going again, she'd say, "Well, this won't pay the old woman her ninepence or knit the baby a coat"' – Jane Russ (2001); 'One of my late mother's sayings when having to find motivation after a "well-earned" rest: "Well, this won't make the baby a new frock, nor mend its old one!"' – Ann Peterson, Thornaby (2001).

'I use an expression myself when I am lazing around with a multitude of jobs around me to do, whose origin I do not know. Indeed, my friends and family don't seem to have heard of it at all. The phrase is, **"This won't catch a cat a canary"**' – Celia Burns, Sutton Coldfield (2002).

too much is not enough/never enough In 2006, I received a letter from Michael Plant who had been at school with me in another century: 'The quotation I would like you to check is one I devised for myself many years ago as a kind of family motto: TOO MUCH IS NEVER ENOUGH or (in Latin) NIMIS NUNQUAM SATIS. It's one for collectors and fanatics of all descriptions (I think I'm more of a collector than a fanatic), but is this an original thought or have I picked it up from somewhere? My intention was to offer a counterblast to "Nothing in excess", a well-worn classical adage by Anon which has come down to us as "All things in moderation" (a remarkably tedious maxim, if you ask me). The Latin version is certainly my own invention.'

By way of reply, I told Michael that I could not find anything like his Latin in such motto books as I have, but that the notion was certainly a popular one by the 1990s. On *Quote ... Unquote* in 1992, the journalist Nina Myskow recounted how her friend Renate Blauel (briefly married to Elton John) was a world-class shopper (this may have been the first time I heard the slogan 'Shop till you drop') and, on one occasion, had bought twelve pairs of shoes from Beverly Feldman of Hollywood. According to Nina, hand-tooled in the leather of the sole was the motto 'Too much is not enough'. In 1997, the Spice Girls apparently made a TV movie with the title *Too Much Is Never Enough.*

Joe Kralich subsequently came up with the convincing suggestion that something like the first outfall of this saying might have been what we find in Beaumarchais, *Le Mariage de Figaro*, Act 4, Sc. 2 (1784): '*En fait d'amour, vois-tu, trop n'est pas même assez* [With love, you see, too much is not even enough].'

Compare what Mae West wrote in her autobiography, *Goodness Had Nothing To Do With It*, Chap. 21 (1959): 'Too much of a good thing can be wonderful.'

A little after I got married, I noticed that if I made a plonking statement or a slightly pompous one (this was very rare, obviously), my wife would respond by saying, **'True, O King!'** Where did she get this from? She did not know.

I looked in Shakespeare but the closest he gets is the ironical '"True"? O God!' in *Much Ado About Nothing*, IV.i.68 (1598), though he has any number of near misses like 'True, my liege', 'Too true, my lord' and 'True, noble prince'.

In the end, I stumbled upon the answer when watching a film of Charles Laughton doing a Bible reading. He came to the bit about Nebuchadnezzar and the gentlemen who were cast into the burning fiery furnace (Daniel 3:24). Nebuchadnezzar asks, 'Did not we cast three men bound into the midst of fire?' 'They answered and said unto the king, True, O king ...'

Mrs H. Joan Langdale of Tunbridge Wells wrote to me (1988) to say, 'My father, a Classical Scholar and an Anglican priest, used to use the quotation "True, O King!" and always added, "Live for ever"' – the last phrase of which comes from Daniel 6:21. See also OH KING, LIVE FOREVER! (page 39).

Dorothy Newburn, Warrington, Cheshire asked (1999) about a variation: 'Can you please tell me the origin of the saying, "True, true, O Queen"?' This version appears in Dorothy L. Sayers, *Have His Carcase*, Chap. 9 (1932): '"True, O Queen. Live for ever" [said Lord Peter Wimsey].' In the same novel, Harriet Vane manages a 'True, O king' in Chap. 25. That phrase also occurs in some of the Billy Bunter stories by Frank Richards (1875–1961) and in the published *Diaries* of Kenneth Williams. In the entry for 5 January 1971, the comedian recounts being told by an Irishman that he was a bore on TV: 'I smiled acquiescence and said, "How true, O King!"'

up in Annie's room behind the clock A suggested location for something that has gone missing and can't be found. My wife recalled her mother using this phrase in the 1950s. Colleen Spittles, Deal, Kent, preferred (1993), 'up in Annie's room behind the wallpaper' for when 'something had disappeared, who knows where'.

Partridge/Slang has 'up in Annie's room' as a services' catchphrase from before the First World War, in reply to a query concerning someone's whereabouts. *Partridge/Catch Phrases* has 'up in Annie's room behind the clock' as the civilian version of this.

'When something was lost, my mother would say, "It's in Alice's room"' – Eugene Burden, Ascot, Berkshire (2002) – this would seem to be a conflation of 'up in Annie's room' with 'up Alice's', an evasive answer to a question like 'Where are you going?' that was in services' use by the mid-20th century.

'Whenever a television programme was not to her liking, my stepmother would describe it to my father as "**a waste of good eyesight**"' – Alan Avery, Worcester (2005).

'My late mother was a child in the Edwardian era, one hundred years ago. During her long life, there was a family-wide expression that she would come out with at times of domestic crisis: "**Oh, what a palaver – a honeymoon in the sky** ..." I suspect that this was a catchphrase from a song of the early 1900s at the time aviation by powered aircraft was happening' – A.M.B. Bell, Helston, Cornwall (2006).

Indeed, there was a song 'In My Aeroplane for Two', subtitled 'A Honeymoon in the Sky', written by Alf. J. Lawrence, Tom Mellor and Harry Gifford and published in London in 1907. Unfortunately, the phrase 'what a palaver' does not occur in the original, rather what it says here in the chorus:

> (In my) aeroplane for two,
> I will sail away with you;
> Don't waste any more time below,
> Let's get married and up we'll go
> In my aeroplane for two,
> For miles and miles we'll fly,
> Oh, what a sensation,
> A honeymoon in the sky!

'When asked once what the three worst words in the language were, my father replied, "**While you're up . . .**"'– George Ellingham (2004).

who's the daddy? Not a question of paternity but the boast of a man who is in charge.

The actor Ray Winstone popularized the phrase when he appeared in the 1977 film *Scum*. In that, it referred to the character's position as the boss among inmates of a young offenders' institution. Winstone also used it in TV ads for Holsten Pils.

However, *Who's The Daddy?* was the title of a play by Toby Young and Lloyd Evans, staged in 2005, that portrayed some of the sexual goings-on at *The Spectator* which involved the then Home Secretary David Blunkett and obviously dealt with his fathering of a child by an executive on that magazine.

he's got the wind up his tail 'My darling grandma would say this when the cat was leaping around the garden' – Pat Stimpson, Keston, Kent (2001).

from womb to tomb For the whole of a person's life. An early non-rhyming version of this idea is to be found in the 1611 King James Bible translation of Job 10:19: 'I should have been as though I had not been; I should have been carried from the womb to the grave.'

In 1662, Michael Wigglesworth's 'The Day of Doom' almost has it:

> Then to the Bar, all they drew near
> who dy'd in Infancy . . .

> But from the womb unto the tomb
> were straightway carried.

The phrase itself was quoted in 1897 from the American poet Charles Alva Lane's 'Amrita' (published some time in the previous decade):

> Nay, Soul, thy span is not from womb to tomb:
> Thine every when and where of space and years ...

Compare: **from the cradle to the grave.** This phrase appears to have been coined by Sir Richard Steele in an essay in the *Tatler*, No. 52 (1709): 'A modest Fellow never has a doubt from his Cradle to his Grave.'

'A little rule, a little sway,/A sunbeam in a winter's day,/Is all the proud and mighty have/Between the cradle and the grave' – John Dyer, *Grongar Hill* (1726).

'*DELLA CUNA ALLA TOMBA/UN BREVE PASSO* [from the cradle to the grave – a short step] 'is inscribed on a monument in Giuseppe Bonito's 'Portrait of a Gentleman' (now at Compton Verney, Warwickshire), painted in about 1750.

'That betwixt the cradle and the grave/It only once smil'd can be;/And when it once is smil'd;/There's an end to all misery' – William Blake, 'The Smile' (*circa* 1801).

Von der Wiege bis zum Grabe [From the Cradle to the Grave] – title of a symphonic poem by Franz Liszt (1881–2).

Winston Churchill said in a radio broadcast (21 March 1943), 'National compulsory insurance for all classes for all purposes from the cradle to the grave'; 'There's your National Health, friend. Look after you from the cradle to the grave' – Peter Nichols, *The National Health*, Act 2, Sc. 1 (1969).

'The move represents a tacit admission that the National Health Service has in parts of Britain lost sight of its commitment to offer care from the cradle to the grave' – *The Guardian* (28 February 1996).

In 2005, Dr Neil Tristram was watching again the episode with the hotel inspectors in *Fawlty Towers* (BBC TV, Series 1, 1975) when his ears pricked up at this exchange:

> *Guest:* This was supposed to be my table, I did ask the waiter.
> *Basil Fawlty:* Well, he's hopeless, isn't he, **you might as well ask the cat.**

He remembered that the same phrase for describing a pointless move occurs in Chap. 3 of Jerome K. Jerome's *Three Men In a Boat* (1889): 'I've found it myself now. Might just as well ask the cat to find anything as expect you people to find it.'

David Challener noted that 'ask the cat' was the most common version in a survey of works of literature online, but he also turned up 'Do not ask him to admire anything, you might as well ask the wind' in *The North British Review* for 1870 and, 'Do the Slaves desire Freedom? You might as well ask the herds of wild buffalo' in Horace Cowles Atwater, *Incidents of a Southern Tour . . .* (1857).

'If we told my mother we had been praised at school, she would say, "Oh, you are so marvellous, **you should have been born with red hair.**" I thought that this was because her mother was a red-head, but none of her six children were. When my second child *was* born with red hair, I was over the moon. Of course, she may have thought Jesus had red hair, or the Virgin Mary!' – Joan Twist, South Lincolnshire (2001).

you're only young once Quoted in Richard Hoggart, *The Uses of Literacy* (1957). This saying, as used when a young person is being urged not to let slip some opportunity or to do something that would be regretted later if it was not done, is hardly noted in proverb books.

Mieder & Co.'s *A Dictionary of American Proverbs* does however find it
in use by 1941. As **we're only young once**, the earliest citation to hand is
from D.A.G. Pearson, *Golden* (1929).

you've got to take the rough with the smooth Meaning 'you must
be prepared for the unpleasant alongside the pleasant in any human
activity', this is not much noticed in dictionaries. The *OED2* does not
have it as an expression, although it does incidentally include a 1963
example. I should have thought this might well go back to the 19th
century. The question arose when Henry Hardy sought the origins of
an Isaiah Berlin remark: 'I must learn to take the smooth with the
rough, as someone once said ...'

This is quite a popular inversion, occurring as it does in more than one
song lyric and also, as I discovered, as a slogan for Land-Rover (undated,
but perhaps 1960s/70s): 'Land-Rover takes the smooth with the rough.'

Really, this is one of those jokes that lies there waiting to be made. The
nearest I've found in my archives is what Susan Hill quoted on *Quote ...
Unquote* (29 August 1980) about a certain Conservative MP: 'With him,
one just has to learn to take the smooth with the smooth ...'

Chapter 2

CLEAN LONG ENOUGH

And so to sayings on the subject of cleanliness and tidiness. The chapter heading comes from John Craster of Market Lavington, Wiltshire who wrote (1993), 'My mother, Jean Craster, not infrequently said, "Darling, that jumper (or whatever else) has been **clean long enough**.*" I find myself saying it to my children and grandchildren.'*

all done and dusted Meaning 'that task has been completed'. Heard in a Yorkshire hotel in 1996, but without doubt much, much older.

all Sir Garnet Meaning 'all correct', this phrase alludes to Sir Garnet Wolseley (1833–1913), a soldier noted for his organizational powers, who led several successful military expeditions from 1852–5 and helped improve the lot of the Other Ranks. The expression was known by 1894. Wolseley is also celebrated as 'The Modern Major-General' in Gilbert and Sullivan's *Pirates of Penzance* (1879). From the same source, *Sir Garnet* is the name of a boat in *Coot Club*, a novel (1934) by Arthur Ransome.

as right as ninepence Very right, proper, correct, in order. But why ninepence? Once again, the allure of alliteration led to the (probably) earlier phrase 'as nice as ninepence' and then the slightly less happy phrase resulted when someone was coining an 'as right as' comparison. In any case, the word 'ninepence' occurs in a number of proverbial phrases ('as like as nine pence to nothing', 'as neat as ninepence'), dating from the time when this was a more substantial amount of money than it now is.

you could grow potatoes in there 'Said to children with dirty ears' – *Wickenden*.

'After a hard day at work I would sometimes come home to find Mum had done the housework for me. She would say, **"The fairies have been in"'** – *Wickenden*.

to give something a lick and a promise The *OED2* finds this in use about hasty cleaning of the body by 1860. It can also be applied to hurriedly completed and slapdash work.

'Dirty hands looked **"like the colour of Old Nick's nutting bag"'** – Mrs Jean Wigget, Kent (1995), reported her mother's turn of phrase. This is remembered elsewhere as 'You're black as the Devil's nutting bag.' *Apperson* has that by 1866.

a place for everything and everything in its place A prescription for orderly domestic arrangements. The writer Charles Osborne (born 1927 in Australia) recalled being an untidy child and his mother's nannyish admonition, when he appeared on *Quote ... Unquote* (24 May 1994). Samuel Smiles quotes it in *Thrift* (1875), but he had been preceded by the illustrious Mrs (Isabella) Beeton in *The Book of Household Management*, Chap. 2 (1861). One feels that Mrs Beeton was probably more interested in domestic order than in making delicious food. The saying was not original to her, however, as is plain from even earlier uses.

George Herbert had the basic idea in his *Outlandish Proverbs* (1640): 'All things have their place, knew we how to place them.' Captain Marryat in *Masterman Ready*, Bk 2, Chap. 1 (1842) has: 'In a well-conducted man-of-war ... everything in its place, and there is a place for every thing.'

Then there is this Wellerism from *Yankee Blade* (18 May 1848): '"A place for everything and everything in its place", as an old lady said when she stowed the broom, bellows, balls of yarn, cards, caps, curry-comb, three cats and a gridiron into an old oven.'

'A family saying that I did not resolve for almost fifty years was why, if I came in untidy or windswept, my mother always said, "**You look like the Wreck of the Hesperus!**"' – Janet M. Carr, Isle of Wight (1997).

In fact, this used to be a common expression for 'in a mess, in a sad state'. The reference is to the title of Longfellow's poem (1839), much recited in Victorian days and relating the actual shipwreck of a schooner off the coast of New England. It contains such immortal lines as 'The skipper he stood beside the helm,/His pipe was in his mouth.' The skipper has unfortunately taken his daughter along with him and when a hurricane blows up, he lashes her to the mast – and that's where she's found washed up the next morning.

Partridge/Catch Phrases dates the use of this saying to the late 19th century. 'He looked and behaved like the Wreck of the *Hesperus*' – P.G. Wodehouse, *The Code of the Woosters*, Chap. 10 (1938). 'The Wreck of the *Hesperus*' is also referred to in the song 'Lydia, the Tattooed Lady' – lyrics by E.Y. Harburg, music by Harold Arlen (1939) – as though it were commonly known as a picture.

you must wear clean underwear in case you get run over On *Quote … Unquote* (7 November 1989), the actress Jean Boht recalled advice that has been given to many a young person – in her case, from her grandmother, in the form, 'Always wear a clean pair of knickers, dear, in case you get run over.'

Chapter 3

HUNGER IS THE BEST SAUCE

Cooking and eating and food in general produce our next subject area. 'A notion is that good plain food is best for a child, so when he asks for sauce or pickles he is told, **"Hunger is the best sauce"***'* – Widdowson. *This is a venerable proverb.* Apperson *finds it in Latin (Cicero) and in English by the late 14th century.*

almost good enough to eat A simple compliment when something (*not* food) looks attractive or appetizing. It could be said about a dishy man or woman, for example.

However, the broadcaster Sir David Attenborough was once on a ship ploughing its way through the South China Seas and being served with the worst food he had ever tasted in his life: 'There was a Cockney steward and when you got up every morning for breakfast, you'd go down to the cabin and the ship would be rolling around, and he'd plonk this thing down in front of you which looked absolutely disgusting, and every morning without fail, this steward would say, "There you are! That looks almost good enough to eat!"' Related on *Quote ... Unquote* (6 April 1993).

always buy your own cherries! Susan Williams started us off on a merry trail in 2005 when she asked about a saying of her father's that she suspected was one he had made up himself. But no. There was a silent film entitled *Buy Your Own Cherries* (Scotland, 1904) of which a plot summary on the internet is: 'A barmaid plies a swell with smiles and with cherries from a box that's just been delivered. When she refuses a cherry to a roughly dressed tradesman who runs a tab at the bar, he pays off his debt in a huff, using all his week's pay. He then storms penniless and without provisions into his ill-furnished house where his wife and two children, ill-clad and ill-fed, cower. Is there any hope for him and for his family? If he does realize how low he's sunk, what help is there to lift him up? Will the family ever know the taste of cherries?'

This film, it then transpired, was based on a best-selling 16-page temperance tract of 1863, written by John William Kirton. As it was published in *The Athenaeum* in October of that year, I take it that Kirton was British, but editions were soon published in the US. Marian Bock summarized her findings thus: 'It's the story of a drunkard who reforms and stops abusing his loved ones. "Buy your own cherries" is something said to him during his drunken days, when he tries to join a group of people who are sharing the fruit together. I conclude that the tract was known wherever temperance organizations were active and its title might easily have become a temperance slogan. I believe it meant something like "Take responsibility for your own life".'

'My father maintains that one of his silly sayings, "**Always eat a kipper with the skin side up**" was actually a serious piece of advice during the Second World War. Any evidence?' – Pam Tomlinson (2003). Not to date. Pam said that another favourite saying of her father's was '**Never clean the window with a soft-boiled egg.**' This is easier to source. Rendered by its initials – 'N.C.T.W.W.A.S.B.E. – this was a joke uttered by Tommy Handley in the 300th edition of the BBC radio show *ITMA* (28 October 1948).

that's another meal the Germans won't have A dismissive catchphrase on finishing a meal. 'When my (French) wife arrived in this country some thirty years ago, she surprised me by remarking, after a particularly good meal, *"Voilà, un autre repas que les Allemands n'auront pas."* This saying apparently derived from her mother, or indeed her grandmother, who suffered in the Occupation. To my astonishment, on a trip to Avignon ten years ago, after an exceptional banquet, a young French lad aged about 25 turned to my wife and made the same remark. It would seem that this has now become a French proverb' – Raymond Harris (1995).

Confirmation came from *The Sunday Times* (23 March 1997): 'Older Frenchmen admitted they sometimes still use the toast, when raising their glasses, of "This is one the *Boches* won't get".'

And from even further back: 'On his first visit to Germany nearly forty years later, [Matisse] told one of his students that ... he never forgot his mother repeating like a grace at meals: "Here's another one the Germans won't lay their hands on". The phrase would become a familiar refrain throughout the region during the incursions of the next seventy-five years and more' – Hilary Spurling, *The Unknown Matisse*, Vol. 1 (1998), referring to the Prussians who passed through north-eastern France during the 1871 Franco-Prussian war.

apples don't grow on trees 'A remark of my mother's which became a family saying. She had bought some particularly delicious apples and my brother and I (children at the time) were eating these at such a rate that she felt obliged to point out, "Apples don't grow on trees, you know!" I should add that my mother was an intelligent and witty woman and knew what she was saying.' – Tony Bremner, London N3 (1992).

as long as you get some good food inside you, you can't complain An everyday saying, quoted in Richard Hoggart, *The Uses of Literacy* (1957), which adds the comment: 'The insistence on food which is both solid and enjoyable is not difficult to appreciate.'

back teeth submerged/B.T.S. Replete after a meal. 'I was amused to hear of the quote "Back teeth submerged" quoted by Nick Higham on *Quote ... Unquote* [31 March 2003]. My family had a similar one: "Back teeth awash." Was this slightly less over-eaten?' – Rose Glennie, Waterlooville, Hants (2003).

'Our family had a similar: "BTF – Back Teeth Floating". But I suppose that coming from a naval family, we would expect them to be floating rather than submerged. Submerged hazards are a threat to life and limb' – Nigel Blanchford, Peterborough (2003).

'My maternal family (which has a military background) uses "BTUW", i.e. "Back teeth under water", after a particularly satisfying repast but, as children, we were actively discouraged from ever repeating this in polite company. I wonder why?' – Liz Hampton (2003). Compare GO AND SPLASH ... (page 349).

a bad cheese needs butter and a good cheese deserves it Informal proverb – 'from my grandmother who died in 1955' – Joan Whitworth, Cumbria (1995). Compare the saying attributed to Napoleon regarding champagne: 'In victory you deserve it: in defeat you need it.'

'Our family, especially my father, were (are!) very keen on food. Luckily, my mother was an excellent cook for us four children and any others who happened to be staying with us. There was always loads of food and the main quote that our house echoed to was **"better belly button burst than good things waste"**. My parents died several years ago but the quote is still to be heard by the current generation!' – Fen Marshall, Wotton-under-Edge, Gloucestershire (2001).

'My Victorian grandmother brought up six children in poverty on her own between 1895 and 1910. When a feast time such as Christmas came round, the well-laden table was not to be wasted. As she tucked into the meat, she invariably said, "Better belly busted than good food wusted." When all was cleared, she then finished with, **"Carry I out but bend I not"**' – Ralph W. Harrison, Stroud, Gloucestershire (2004).

black as the devil, hot as hell ... A recipe for coffee. 'Black as the devil,/Hot as hell,/Pure as an angel,/Sweet as love [*Noir comme le diable,/Chaud comme l'enfer,/Pur comme un ange,/Doux comme l'amour*]' – is attributed to the French politician Talleyrand (1754–1838) and, as

Bartlett's Familiar Quotations still tells us, is to be found as an inscription on many old coffee pots.

a boarding house reach Reprimand to child who leans too far across the table at dinner. 'My parents had a range of differing phrases used for most occasions, like this one' – Matthew Hind, Buckinghamshire (2002).

the boy stood in the supper-room Mike Hallsworth sought a particular parody of Mrs Hemans's 'The boy stood on the burning deck' (i.e. the poem 'Casabianca', 1849). David Pocock turned it up in *A Century of Humorous Verse* (1959) – though it is also to be found in Iona and Peter Opie's collection *I Saw Esau* (1947). Either way it appears to be by Anon:

> The boy stood in the supper-room
> Whence all but he had fled;
> He'd eaten seven pots of jam
> And he was gorged with bread.
>
> 'Oh, one more crust before I bust!'
> He cried in accents wild;
> He licked his plates, he sucked the spoons –
> He was a vulgar child.
>
> There came a hideous thunder-clap –
> The boy – oh! where was he?
> Ask of the maid who mopped him up,
> The bread-crumbs and the tea.

brewed, saucered and blowed A drink of tea that is now ready for drinking – because it has been brewed, poured into a saucer and blown on to cool it a little. A British expression, probably in use by the mid-20th century.

'I had an uncle who used to amuse my little friends at tea parties by saying he was so hungry he could "eat the dates off a calendar". He called my mother's fancy cakes "ooja-ka-pivs" for want of a special name and would say such things as "**Can I press you to a jelly?**" which made the small guests collapse in mirth' – Helen Rudge, Hampshire (1994).

I warrant cheese won't choke her 'As to the saying, "Butter wouldn't melt in his/her mouth", have you come across the second line, as it were, which has certainly been current in the West Midlands area, "... and a brick wouldn't choke him!" I write "him" advisedly, as I am more familiar with the saying being applied to a male rogue coming the innocent, which is how I recently heard it used in a production of Somerset Maugham's *The Constant Wife*' – David Matthews, West Malvern, Worcestershire (2004). Actually, Maugham, Act 2 (1926) only has: 'Yes, I kept on saying to myself, I wonder if a pat of butter really would melt in his mouth', without the continuation. But Swift's *Polite Conversation* (1738) does have: '... but I warrant Cheese won't choak her.'

I've come to Stokes' bridge 'My mother (b. 1883, Stafford) had this saying for the moment in a meal when she felt she had had enough and wouldn't be able to eat another morsel from her plate. Now adopted by most of the family, especially in restaurants when faced with a plateful designed to satisfy the largest possible appetite' – Lloyd Storr-Best, Chichester, West Sussex (1998). Origin unknown.

custard boiled is custard spoiled Informal proverb. Told to me on a London News Radio phone-in (December 1994).

'This is a quotation which I heard from my elder brother about 65 years ago. I have never read or heard it since' – A.C.J. Scott, Llanddarog, Carmarthen (1999):

> **Dearly beloved brethren: is it not a sin ...**
> **When we peel potatoes, to throw away the skin?**
> For the skin feeds the pigs, and the pigs feed us;
> Dearly beloved brethren, is it not thus?

Well, the Opies in *The Oxford Dictionary of Nursery Rhymes* (1980) print an almost identical verse in their comments on the 'finger game':

> Here is the church, and here is the steeple;
> Open the door and here are the people.
> Here is the parson going upstairs,
> And here he is a-saying his prayers.

The Opies say, 'School-children then make the parson deliver an oration on potato peeling ...' Both the verses may go back to the 19th century and also seem to have been known in the US.

'Fifty years ago I was employed as Nanny to the children of an ex-MP and historian who had led a very colourful life. He was writing his memoirs at the time and had completed the first part, covering his eventful youth. This he called *With One Swift Glance* and said the title was taken from a book of nursery etiquette – "**Do not fumble with the cakes** – with one swift glance select the best"' – Margaret Pattison, King's Lynn, Norfolk (2002). I have been unable to trace any book with this title.

'My father was renowned within the greater family for his skill at carving the dinner joint, for which duty he brought his own knife and undertook slowly and deliberately. Before he sat down to eat himself he would always ask, "**Does anyone want any more before I start?**"' – Bob Dean, Walsall (2003).

Theo Beamish told me (2000) that a favourite expression in his mother's family – when, say, soup was too hot – was '**Don't blow on it, 'Erbert – fan it with yer 'at**'. But where did that originate? Chris Daniells suggested that Arthur Askey said, 'Don't blow on it, Harold, fan it with your hat' in one of the several films of *The Ghost Train* (UK 1941), but this has yet to be confirmed. Then Theresa E. Lynch, who listens to the radio show via the web in North Carolina and heard our discussion on this topic, said that a similar line occurs in the Judy Garland movie *The Harvey Girls* (US 1946).

As so often, however, the origin seems to lie with *Punch*. Lucy Baldwin sent me a copy of F.H. Townsend's cartoon from the issue of 9 May 1906. Two young women are seated, for no apparent reason, in front of a labelled bust of Hogarth (which locates it in Leicester Square, London, where Joseph Durham's 1875 bust is still in place), and one says, 'Such a nice young man took me out to dinner last night – such a well-mannered man. D'you know, when the coffee come and 'e'd poured it on 'is saucer, instead of blowing on it like a common person, 'e fanned it with 'is 'at!'

I think the instruction to Herbert may have been inserted later in a music-hall song.

'If a child fails to eat all that is set before him, he is told to clean up his plate, with the constant adjuration, "**Don't leave a saucy plate**"' – *Widdowson.*

eat it or leave it ... 'My mother had her own version of "Take it or leave it" – "Eat it or leave it, as dogs do dumplings"' – E. Mary Watson, Wendover, Buckinghamshire (2004).

'My great grandfather was a farmer in Co. Wicklow, Ireland. Whenever they slaughtered the family pig, they used to make various cuts and preparations from its body. Nothing was wasted. My father told me that when he visited the house, he was told, "**Eat up. The pig don't care who ates it**"' – Dermod Malley (2004).

'I can still remember when as a child in the 1950s and my parents were entertaining their friends, as we sat down at the table to begin our meal, my father would always say, "Eat up – your auntie's in the store. The more you eat, the bigger the dividend." The store referred to was the North Eastern Co-Operative Store which my mother did *not* use as she considered it to be "working class". However, despite her reprimands, my father continued the practice' – Hilary M. Reynolds, Tynemouth, Tyne and Wear (2004).

Partridge/Catch Phrases has 'Eat up, you're at your auntie's'.

eat well, work well, sleep well, and — well once a day Informal proverb, probably seen as graffiti and quoted (from the 1890s) by Flora Thompson in *Lark Rise*, Chap. 1 (1939).

'My grandmother – early 1940s – if you had your elbows on the table, would say, "You don't want anything to eat – **you're having elbow pie**"' – William W. Bishop, London SE24 (1998).

every time a sheep bleats it loses a nibble Sometimes rendered as 'Every time a sheep baa's it loses a bite'. H.L. Mencken's *Dictionary of Quotations* (1942) has this as an English proverb in the form 'Every time the sheep bleats it loses a mouthful' and states that it was 'apparently borrowed from the Italian and familiar since the seventeenth century'. In this form it certainly appears in Thomas Fuller's *Gnomologia* (1732). *ODP* finds a version in 1599 and seems to prefer, 'A bleating sheep loses a bite', explaining this as 'opportunities are missed through too much chatter'. 'My uncle at mealtimes, if us kids were talking, would say, "Every time you speak, you will miss a mouthful"' – Pip Checksland (2002).

'In Newcastle-upon-Tyne, a lady we knew would say, "**I feel like a bus on a wet day – full up inside**"' – Mrs Monica Nash, Nottinghamshire (1995). Presumably after she had eaten a meal.

fish is good for brains Nannyism. *Casson/Grenfell* has 'fish is good for the brain'.

'My wife's family have a charming way of indicating that they can eat no more. The phrase is "**I'm full to dolly's wax**". This derives from the wax-headed dolls that the children had at one time. The head ended at the top of the chest and the sawdust-filled body was inserted at this point. The dolls also had wax hands – but no cogent saying has emerged from this fascinating fact!' – Barry Wilsher (2003).

'A saying of my late mother-in-law's – which has become a habit in our family. It is used when dividing something into portions, e.g. pudding at mealtimes. She would invariably say, "**Shall I do the gezinters, or will you?**" Coming from a teaching family, this went back to lessons in simple division – "one gezinter four" etc.!' – Robin Wager, Cheltenham, Gloucestershire (1997).

'As we tucked into a big meal, my grandmother used to say, "A good 'oss con ate" – dialect for "**a good horse can eat**", i.e. a healthy person can eat a lot. Exercise wasn't mentioned ...' – Rob Barratt, Lostwithiel, Cornwall (2003).

stupid bird, goose – too much for one and not enough for two The grandfather of Antony Jay, the writer, would always say this whenever goose was served. Related on *Quote ... Unquote* (20 November 1990).

hard in, soft out A slogan of the Campaign for Real Bread. I was interviewing a spokesman for the campaign on the BBC Radio 4 *Today* programme on 19 December 1977 and commented that the brown rolls he had brought along with him were, well, a bit on the tough side. This was his reply. I haven't forgotten it, obviously.

'Before the war, my late father, being of a kindly disposition, used to visit a number of pensioners in a row of almshouses,' wrote David Hine of Temple, Buckinghamshire (1994). 'To his surprise, one of the old ladies invited him to lunch. He duly attended and, as they sat down, she said, "Now, Sir, **have plenty of vegetables ... the meat cost sixpence.**"

'This became a family joke and, with wartime rationing, often did much to cheer a meal when in fact the meat was often non-existent – or cost less than ninepence.'

Compare: 'My parents-in-law were born and brought up in Exeter. When sitting down for the main meal of the day, my Mother-in-Law always said, "Help yourself to teddies [potatoes] and greens, but a little piece of meat costs ninepence"' – Mrs B. Penberthy, Cullompton, Devon (2002).

here am I, slaving over a hot stove all day (while all you do is ...)
The housewife's lament, since the early 1900s. A catchphrase when used ironically or as a joke. Compare the caption to a drawing (*circa* 1912) by Art Young: 'Here am I, standin' over a hot stove all day, and you workin' in a nice, cool sewer!'

here's to the Lord in whom we trust – if it wasn't for our bottoms, our bellies would bust 'My mother would say this after a good meal' – Mrs H. Acklin (aged 82), Essex (1998).

'In my childhood, prewar, when the family planned a day out in the car and Dad couldn't get the engine to start, my mother would say, "Never mind, we have the sandwiches and **I can always run up a rice pudding**." This saying was used as a standby in any emergency!' – I. Mayhew, Ashstead, Kent (1996).

'My father, in the Black Country, when asked if he liked a certain type of food (which he really wasn't too keen on – e.g. pasta), would say, **"I can eat it."** We never thought anything of this until my wife, from the South-East, asked me what else he might do with it. It always made us smile after that' – Rob Barratt, Lostwithiel, Cornwall (2003).

I love it but it doesn't love me What people say to soften their refusal of what they have been offered – usually food or drink. Jonathan Swift lists it in *Polite Conversation* (1738):

Lady Smart: 'Madam, do you love bohea tea?'
Lady Answerall: 'Why, madam, I must confess I do love it; but it does not love me ...'

'When my brother was young, he said, "Have I got time for porridge?" When told he had, he said, **"I'll have a boiled egg, then."** I always remember that when having porridge or boiled egg' – Sally Boakes, Deal, Kent (2003).

I'll just have to kill a tin 'One of my mother's sayings (she was born in 1895) that I have not heard anywhere else. This was if there was no fresh food in the house' – Margaret Jones, Newcastle upon Tyne (2002).

I'm so hungry, my back is sticking to my front 'Said by my wife, Diana, who does not claim originality' – Richard Toeman, London N6 (1995). Just as well. There are a number of 'I'm so hungry . . .' phrases, of which the other nearest to this is 'I'm so empty, I can feel me backbone touching me belly button.' 'I used to have a much-loved elderly great aunt in my youth, who when feeling the need for sustenance used to say, "I'm so hungry – I could wipe my nose with the skin of my belly"' – Jacqueline Cottle, Southsea (2002).

if you don't take the eyes out, they might see us through the week 'Wry stoicism from my mother, when peeling a few potatoes' – Peter Ellis, Market Bosworth (2002).

that should keep body and soul together What you say when you have kept yourself going, chiefly by eating properly. 'In my late husband's family, a great saying when serving up a substantial snack or full meal was, "There you are, that will keep B. and S. Tog"' – Joan Bell, Cambus, Clackmannanshire (1993).

'Keeping body [*or* life] and soul together' is, of course, an old phrase. According to the *OED2*, 'Tate' in *Dryden's Juvenal* (1697) has:

> The Vascons once with Man's Flesh (as 'tis sed)
> Kept Life and Soul together.

Jane Collier, *The Art of Tormenting* (1753) has: 'By never letting him see you swallow half enough to keep body and soul together.' *The Century Illustrated Monthly Magazine* (November 1884) has: 'How on earth they managed to keep body and soul together.'

makes old men young, young men strong A Lancastrian saying, used when recommending food, by the father of Joan Bakewell, the broadcaster, as she related on *Quote ... Unquote* (24 May 1994).

'My father's pre-Christmas Dinner toast was, "**May this be the worst of our lives!**" I still inflict it on my family, and by my son's enthusiastic response, it seems a fair bet that he will in the fullness of time repeat it to his three children' – Charles F. Garvey, Peacehaven, East Sussex (1996).

may you never meet a mouse in your pantry with tears in his eyes 'A saying of my late grandfather' – John O'Byrne, Dublin (1998). Presumably the wish here is that your cupboard should never be bare.

Mr Gladstone chewed every mouthful of food thirty-two times before swallowing W.E. Gladstone, several times Liberal Prime Minister in the late 19th century, was held up as an example to countless generations of children as the man who did this tedious thing.

However, in the BBC TV programme *As I Remember* (30 April 1967), Baroness Asquith (Lady Violet Bonham Carter) gave an eye-witness account of the Grand Old Man's jaw in action. She recalled having had a meal with Gladstone, when she was a little girl, but – horrors! –

he did no such thing. Quite the reverse in fact: *he bolted his food.*

Confirmation of this deplorable fact also came in a lecture given by George Lyttelton at Hawarden (Gladstone's old home) on 24 June 1955: 'More than one lynx-eyed young spectator [has discovered] that Mr Gladstone did *not* chew every mouthful thirty-two times ... though I am not sure that Mr Gladstone himself might not have made some weighty and useful observations on the common and deplorable gap between principle and practice.'

A little oddly, Mr Gladstone does not make an appearance in *Casson/Grenfell.*

a moment on your lips, a lifetime on your hips This is a dieter's slogan that I recorded in November 1987, but presumably it is much older. 'Back in the 1960s/70s, my late mother-in-law had a more dietetically precise version: "**A moment on the lips, a lifetime on the hips** – that's chips"' – Michael Grosvenor Myer, Haddenham, Cambridgeshire (1999).

Compare: 'Back at school, about 1960, "A minute in your mouth, an inch on your waistline"' – Veronica M. Brown, Wigston, Leicestershire (2002).

the mountain sheep are sweeter ... Proverb sometimes recalled at mealtimes, though actually a quotation – from Thomas Love Peacock, *The Misfortunes of Elphin*, 'The War-Song of Dinas Vawr' (1829):

> The mountain sheep are sweeter,
> But the valley sheep are fatter,
> We therefore deemed it meeter
> To carry off the latter.

mustard on mutton is the sign of a glutton Proverb. From my wife (1995). The nearest *Apperson* has to this is 'Mutton is meat for a glutton', dating from 1611.

my stomach thinks my throat's cut 'I'm hungry' – as in Peter Nichols, *The Freeway*, Act 1, Scene 1 (1974). As 'My belly thinks my throat's cut', *Apperson* finds this in Palsgrave, *Acolastus* (1540).

'"**The nearer the bone the sweeter the meat**" ... they used to say' – Flora Thompson, *Lark Rise*, Chap. 1 (1939). We must take Flora's word for it, as I have been unable to find any other record of this expression.

'When I was a lad, my family regularly ate Sunday lunch together – that lunch consisting of the traditional "roast and two veg". On one particular Sunday, however, my mother produced a different main course – possibly steak and kidney pie. Having finished and obviously thoroughly enjoyed the meal, my aunt put down her knife and fork, sighed and said, "**Nice dinner – for a change.**" Now, if any out-of-the-ordinary meal is served, someone in the family is bound to say, "Nice dinner – for a change"' – C.J. Misselbrook, London SE6 (1994).

'When using jam we always say this rhyme:

Oh, look, Mama, what have we here that looks like strawberry jam?
Hush, hush, my dear, 'tis your papa – run over by a tram!

– Gail Cromack, Carmarthenshire (1998).
  Linda Addison, Northamptonshire (1999), sent the slightly different:

> Oh, mother dear
> What is this here
> That looks like raspberry jam?
> Hush, hush my dear
> It's poor papa
> Run over by a tram.

Now, along comes Althea Lydon to point out that this rhyme is featured in R.C. Sherriff's play *Journey's End* (1928) about life near the Front in the First World War. In Act 2, Sc. 2, the character Trotter recites the rhyme thus:

> Tell me, mother, what is that
> That looks like strawberry jam?
> Hush, hush, my dear, 'tis only Pa
> Run over by a tram.

We must ascribe it to Anon.

the pigs will love you A remark addressed to someone who does not finish his food – because scraps are traditionally fed to pigs. Laurence Boswell, the theatre director, quoted it on *Quote ... Unquote* (29 November 2004) as 'If we had a pig, he'd love you.'

'My father would never drink all of his cup of tea. If he was asked if he would like a fresh cup, he would say, "**Just put a half on top of this one**"' – Mrs K.Y. Williams, Herefordshire (1998).

same thing, different gravy 'When comparing dishes in a restaurant, my father always used to make this complaint' – Dave Hopkins, Kent (1998).

'As a boy in the Thirties, I used to be reprimanded for my appalling table manners with the rhyme:

> Only men in rags
> And villains old in sin
> Treat their insides like carpet bags
> **And shoot the wittles [vitals] in.**

– Wilfred Baker (2003). I have not traced this anywhere else.

'My father, who was in the army for much of his life, always enjoyed a cup of tea but didn't like it too strong. If it was, he would remark that it was "**strong enough to trot a mouse on**"' – J.G. Hills, Hampshire (1994).

The film director Bryan Forbes remembered this in 1998 from Lincolnshire as 'strong enough for a mouse to skate on'.

Compare from Neville & June Braybrooke, *Olivia Manning: a Life*, Chap. 13 (2004): '[In Athens, 1941] "The tea was so sweet a fly could trot on it," was Reggie's verdict.'

tea at five, supper at nine ... A 19th-century litany, here at full-length: 'Tobias Liversedge was a man of substance, but in domestic habits he followed the rule of the unpretentious middle-class. Breakfast at eight, dinner at one, tea at five, supper at nine – such was the order of the day that we had known in boyhood, and it suited him well enough now that he was at the head of a household' – George Gissing, *Denzil Quarrier* (1892).

that's gone where they don't play billiards 'My grandmother used to say this on seeing my nice clean plate after a meal (this was in the 1930s!)' – C.H. Filbey, Dorset (1995). 'My wife's family from around Liverpool and Lancashire (originally publicans) have a wonderful expression for when something is lost – "Gone where they don't play billiards"' – David Barham (2005).

that's the stuff to give the troops 'I remember people saying this in the 1940s when sitting down to eat ration-book food at home' – Norman Beaumont, Ropley, Hampshire (1993).

Partridge/Slang actually dates the saying from the First World War but defines it simply as 'that's the idea, that's what we want', not necessarily referring to food. There is an obvious allusion in P.G. Wodehouse, *Carry On, Jeeves*, 'Jeeves and the Spot of Art' (1930): 'Forgive me, old man, for asking you not to raise your voice. A hushed whisper is the stuff to give the troops.'

tinker, tailor, soldier, sailor ... 'As an evacuee during the war, I was introduced to an alternative rhyme for counting cherry pips. Can anyone complete it, please?' – Sheila Dodwell, Taunton, Somerset (2002). Here is a pretty full version, as given by the Opies in *The Oxford Dictionary of Nursery Rhymes* (1980):

> Tinker,
> Tailor,
> Soldier,
> Sailor,
> Gentleman,
> Apothecary,
> Plough-boy,
> Thief.
> Soldier brave, sailor true,
> Skilled physician,
> Oxford blue,
> Learned lawyer,
> Squire so hale,
> Dashing airman, curate pale.
> Army, Navy,
> Medicine, Law,
> Church, Nobility,
> Nothing at all.

water bewitched and tea begrudged 'This is what my mother used to say on being given a weak cup of tea' – Gareth Howells, Anglesey (2002).

you should eat to live, not live to eat 'The grandfather in a Sheffield family deprecates greediness by saying, "You should eat to live, lad, not live to eat"' – *Widdowson*. The idea behind this proverb goes back to classical times and is found in Old English by the early 15th century.

your hair won't curl 'If I didn't eat my crusts' – Alison Adcock, Oxford (2004).

Chapter 4

SEEN AND NOT HEARD

'This asking of questions teased their mother and made them unpopular with the neighbours. **"Little children should be seen and not heard"**, they were told at home' – Flora Thompson, Lark Rise, Chap. 1 (1939). The origins of this venerable saying are somewhat complicated. Thompson was writing about her childhood in the late 19th century but, at one time, it was thought that the first dated citation was from Bernard Shaw, Parents and Children (1914): 'And impudently proclaim the monstrous principle that little children should be seen and not heard.'

However, the reason for this is that originally the saying applied only to little girls or young women. An old English text dating from about 1400 has (with modern spelling): 'A maid should be seen, but not heard' – and describes it even then as 'an old English saw [saying]'. The change to 'children' does not seem to have taken hold until the 19th century. Here now are the expressions used when parents (and nannies) have to interact with children.

act daft and I'll buy you a coal yard 'I was born and brought up in
Birkenhead [on the Mersey] in the 1930s. This was one my mother used
to say if we were being silly. We knew what she meant but it really
makes no sense at all, does it?' – Patricia Valetich, Tasmania (2003).

act your age (also **be your age**) Grow up, behave in a manner more
befitting your years. Probably from the US and in use by the 1920s.
An elaboration heard in New Zealand in the late 1960s and in the UK
in 1985 is **act your age, not your shoe size** (normal shoe sizes in the
UK are in the range 4–12).

'In my young days in Northern Ireland, when I started to grow quite tall,
a grumpy old aunt of my mother's said to me, "**All ill weeds grow tall**"'
– Mary J. Price (2001).

always tell the truth – the truth tells twice 'It means: if you tell a lie, in
court for example, you may forget this lie. If you tell the truth, however,
you'll be able to tell it twice, or more. You won't forget. It's always better
to tell the truth. My Grandmother, who is 93 years old and from
Scotland, told me and her mother told her' – Gregor Milne (2004).

and when it stops ... Judith Smith of Felthorpe, Norwich, recalled,
in 1992, an interesting family use of a stock phrase from BBC radio's
Listen With Mother broadcasts for small children. Apart from 'Are you
sitting comfortably? Then I'll begin', another familiar phrase from the
programme was the story-teller saying, 'And when the music stops,

Daphne Oxenford [or A.N. Other] will be here to tell you a story...'
Judith Smith felt sure, however, that the phrase was, rather, '... and
when it stops ...' 'Our surname being *Stopps*, my late husband always
vowed that if we had a son he should be called "Wennit". Fortunately,
perhaps, we only had daughters.'

another dress for Mrs Colman! 'When I was a child, my grandmother
would always say this when I left any unconsumed mustard on my plate
– presumably implying that the Colman's Mustard fortunes were
founded on what was left, rather than what was actually consumed'
– Malcolm Bull, Brighouse, West Yorkshire (2002).

ask your father what he's doing, and tell him to stop it A frequent
injunction, apparently, from the mother of the poet Michael Rosen,
as he recalled on *Quote ... Unquote* (24 May 1994). Her saying was
probably extrapolated from two quotations: 'Go directly, and see what
she's doing, and tell her she mustn't!' – caption to cartoon entitled
'EXPERIENTIA DOCET' ['experience teaches'] in *Punch*, Vol. 63
(16 November 1872). Drawn by George du Maurier, French-born British
artist, cartoonist and novelist (1834–96), it shows Emily, an 'Elder of
Fourteen', asking a younger girl, 'Where's baby, Madge?' Madge replies,
'In the other room, I think, Emily.' And then Emily comes up with this
pronouncement. And compare this from A.P. Herbert's poem 'Let's
Stop Somebody from Doing Something' (1930):

> Let's find out what everyone is doing,
> And then stop everyone from doing it.

back in the knife-box, little Miss Sharp A nannyism addressed to a small person with a sharp tongue. Compare **you're so sharp you'll be cutting yourself**. *Casson/Grenfell* also has: 'Very sharp we are today, we must have slept in the knife box/we must have slept on father's razor case/we must have been up to Sheffield.'

Paul Beale (1994) found a homely example of the knife-box version in Donald Davie's autobiographical study *These the Companions* (1982): 'More than twenty-five years ago I [composed] a poem which has for epigraph what I remember my mother [in Barnsley, Yorkshire] saying when I was too cocky as a child: **"Mr Sharp from Sheffield, straight out of the knife-box!"**'

Earlier than all this, see MR BROOKS OF SHEFFIELD (page 254).

'As a child growing up in the early sixties, if I and my brothers and sisters were making too much noise, my late grandfather would say, **"Be quiet, there's a man sick in Birkenhead."** I've mentioned this to colleagues at work and nobody has heard of it' – Jim Poole, Liverpool (2006).

be quiet, you lot – do you think it's outside you're in? 'This is a saying my father used when I was young and lived in Airdrie, near Glasgow. When I was playing with my friends indoors and making a lot of noise, he would turn round and say it' – Jim Kennedy, Watford, Hertfordshire (2006).

better than a slap in your belly with a wet fish Nannyism. What you say to someone who may be hesitating over accepting something. 'I have a friend in her eighties whose Nanny always used to say this to her little charges, whenever one or other was complaining about something' – Anon, Surrey (1998). *Partridge/Slang* has 'slap *in the* belly' and *Partridge/Catch Phrases* has 'slap across the kisser'. The art critic Brian Sewell revealed on *Quote . . . Unquote* (12 April 1994) that his nurse, when bathing him, would not only inquire, 'Have you done down there?', but also command him to stand up at the conclusion of the proceedings and whack him with a sopping wet flannel, saying, 'There's a slap in the belly with a wet fish.'

bless his little cotton socks! A pleasant (but also rather irritating) remark to make about a child, meaning, 'Isn't he sweet, such a dear little thing'. As 'bless *your* little cotton socks', it just means 'thank you'. *Partridge/Slang* dates the expression from *circa* 1900 and labels it heavily 'middle-class'.

Boney will get you A curiously enduring threat. Although Napoleon died in 1821 (and all possibility of invasion of Britain had evaporated long before that), the threat was still being made in the early 20th century. In 1985, the actor Sir Anthony Quayle recalled it from his youth and, on *Quote . . . Unquote* (4 December 1990), John Julius Norwich remembered the husband of his nanny (from Grantham, interestingly) saying it to him in the 1930s.

John Julius added, 'And a Mexican friend of mine told me that when she was a little girl her nanny or mother or whoever it was used to say, "*Il Drake* will get you" – and that was Sir Francis Drake!'

Compare: 'When Laura was a child, some of the older mothers and the grandmothers still threatened naughty children with the name of Cromwell. "If you ain't a good gal, old Oliver Crummell'll have 'ee!" they would say, or "Here comes old Crummell!" just as mothers of southern England threatened their children with Napoleon' – Flora Thompson, *Lark Rise*, Chap. 14 (1939).

boys will be boys! This proverbial comment on the inevitability of youthful male behaviour seems to have begun life as, rather, 'youth will be youthful' in the 17th century. Then came 'girls will be girls' and only then, finally, 'boys will be boys'.

We've had a bit more luck finding out who originated the continuation of it that goes, '"Boys will be boys – " "And even that," I interposed, "wouldn't matter if we could only prevent girls from being girls."' That's from Anthony Hope's little book, *The Dolly Dialogues*, Chap. 15 (1894).

P.G. Wodehouse has it, combined with another such phrase, in *Frozen Assets*, Chap. 3 (1964): 'I tried to tell him that boys will be boys and you're only young once.'

has the cat got your tongue? Question put to a person (usually young) who is not saying anything, presumably through guilt. Since the mid-19th century and a prime example of nanny-speak, as in *Casson/Grenfell*. The *OED2*'s earliest citation is H.H. Harper, *Bob Chadwick* (1911): 'I was so angry at her that I ... made no answer ... Presently she said, "Has the cat got your tongue?"'

'When my grandmother became annoyed by noisy, bad behaviour or rude children (often we grandchildren!) she would remark, **"Dan'l, light the kid(s)."** I have never understood the logic, but presume "Dan'l" to be Daniel of biblical fame' – M.W.G. Skinner, Coulsdon, Surrey (1995).

In 2003, Mike Brett wrote, 'For many years when a child said to me, "Don't care" my reply has been: "**Don't care was made to care**/Couldn't care was shot/And [something else] care was put in a pot and boiled till they were done." This is clearly not what it should be ...' Not quite. Iona and Peter Opie in *The Lore and Language of Schoolchildren* (1959) have only what they describe as a 'Hackney version' (i.e. from London):

> Don't care was *made* to care,
> Don't care was hung,
> Don't care was put in a pot
> And boiled till he was done.

This was definitely in circulation by 1933/4 and is also the version included in *Casson/Grenfell*. A number of people pointed out that there is a verse sometimes quoted *in front of* the above:

> Don't care didn't care,
> Don't care was wild:
> Don't stole plum and pear
> Like any beggar's child.

This is also included in *The Annotated Mother Goose*. Another version of the main verse was remembered from her grandmother by Rosie Cullen (2001):

> Don't care was made to care,
> Don't care was beaten,
> Don't care was put in a pot,
> And boiled till he was eaten.

Margaret Martin of New Malden, Surrey, wrote (1993), 'As a child, how my heart sank when I heard, **"Don't do as I do, do as I say."**' *ODP* manages to find a version of this in Anglo-Saxon dating from 1100. By 1546, the proverb had become 'It is as folke dooe, and not as folke say'.

In John Selden's *Table Talk* (1689), on 'Preaching', he remarks, 'Preachers say, "Do as I say, not as I do".'

don't do that – that is how Nelson lost his eye 'When we were children we would make drinks and leave the spoon in the cup while we were drinking from them. My mother always said ...' – Marian Jarvis (2001).

'I was the thorn between two female roses in my pre-teens in the 1920s. Any misbehaviour, tantrums, etc. on the part of my sisters or myself would be met by the rebuke from Mother, **"Don't put your parts on with me!"'** – Alan Beckerlegge, Lincolnshire (1996). I suspect this was an adaptation of 'to play a person any of one's parts', meaning 'to play a nasty trick on a person', known by 1887.

don't rush so, you'll be there before you start off 'My own grandmother would say this to slow us down' – Mrs Stella Mummery, London sw14 (1995).

don't stand there like one o'clock half struck; do something 'My mother would say this when we (her five children) were mooning around' – Miss L. Williams, Greater Manchester (1993). *Partridge/Slang* defines 'like one o'clock half-struck' as 'hesitatingly' and finds it in use by 1876.

a dry bed deserves a boiled sweet A nannyism – *Casson/Grenfell*.

'When a child chatters inconsequentially, he is told sternly and scornfully that "**an empty cart makes the most rattle**"' – *Widdowson*. Obviously, a variant on 'empty vessels make the most sound', known since 1579.

Fred Ritchie of Pickering, North Yorkshire, wrote (1994), 'When a child was naughty, a friend's mother (a real Yorkshire woman) would say, "**Fetch me something to hit you with.**" I use it myself now, I'm afraid, quite often.'

goody two-shoes The name given to an unpleasingly well-behaved child. There is a precise origin for this. A nursery tale, possibly written by Oliver Goldsmith in 1765, was called *The History of Little Goody Two-Shoes*. The heroine had only one shoe and when she got hold of a pair, she went round showing them to everyone, saying 'two shoes'. Obviously a child to be avoided.

In my *Cassell's Humorous Quotations* (2003), I included under 'Penises', the age-old remark from a little girl to a little boy when he dropped his trousers – '**My, that's a handy little gadget!**' I dated it 'by 1941', but then Alison Parker related that her husband John heard it from his father in about 1922. 'John remembers his father telling him that two small children were taken on a picnic, and the rugs etc. were laid out in a corner of a field. After a while the little boy and girl wanted to spend pennies, so they walked over to some long grass at the edge of the field.

The little girl squatted in it and discovered, too late, that it was full of nettles. The little boy had no such problems, and the little girl remarked, "My, that's a handy gadget to have on a picnic."'

I first included my version in a collection I made of children's remarks entitled *Babes and Sucklings* (1983) and I mentioned 'handy little gadget' as coming from the common stock of 'traditional' sayings which – as I had found when compiling my earlier *Eavesdroppings* – does not prevent people from claiming it as their own. It had, I said, reached me from several sources. One said that it involved 'the daughter of a friend', another that 'it was told me by a friend who was a teacher about the local primary school at which he taught', and a third specifically said it concerned 'our two-year-old son'.

My explanation for this phenomenon was that 'personalizing' stories is an accepted way of making them – and jokes – more compelling. Why else does the comedian frequently say, 'My wife, she's so fat ...' when he may not have a wife at all, let alone a fat one?

hold your chin chocker up, Billie-o-lair-o 'My mother, when bathing us children and wishing to wash our necks, would say this' – Henry Nichols, Yardley, Birmingham (1996). Is 'Billie-o-lair-o' a rearrangement of 'Lillibulero', the name of a traditional folk song?

how many hundred times have I told you not to exaggerate! In *The Guinness Book of Humorous Irish Anecdotes,* ed. Aubrey Dillon-Malone (1996), this is given with the comment that 'the Irish penchant for exaggeration is captured in the father's admonition to his son ...' But I am not sure it is necessarily an Irish coinage. Compare HAVEN'T I BEEN (page 291)

I lift up my finger and I say 'tweet-tweet' Bryan Magee, the philosopher and broadcaster, remembered that when, as a little boy, he wanted to do something and went to ask his father if he could, his father would say, 'I lift up my finger and I say "tweet-tweet"' – '. . . and that meant I couldn't do it.' Recalled on *Quote . . . Unquote* (26 April 1994). The song whose title line this is was written by Leslie Sarony in 1929.

I've taught you all I know and you still know nothing 'My paternal grandfather said this' – Denis Sharp, Arundel (2002). He was not alone. Could this be related in a schoolmasterly way to 'Every time I open my mouth, a fool speaks' – one of the teaching profession's most popular foot-in-mouths and delighted in by Gervase Phinn, the former schools inspector and now author?

it fits like a stocking on a chicken's lip i.e. 'it is no damn good, it doesn't fit at all'. 'My Yorkshire mother-in-law would say this if an article of clothing was badly made' – Mrs Phyllis Jessop, Hampshire (1993). Paul Beale glossed this as 'a traditional carpenter's catchphrase which I first heard from a Loughborough College carpenter and joiner in 1990'.

'When I was growing up in the late 50s/early 60s, our dad had a saying that he used whenever any of us – I had six brothers and three sisters – felt hard done by. When any of us argued, our dad would decide which one was in the right. If the loser said, "**It's not fair!**", our dad would reply, "**Neither is a pimple on a black man's arse.**" Of course, you couldn't say that nowadays . . .' – Desmond Dwyer, Birmingham (2004).

lift her up, lower her down, cock, goose or hen 'My Irish grand-mother would say this when lifting and dandling a child on her lap' – Elizabeth Seager, Witney, Oxfordshire (2000).

like an old woman with a worsted leg 'As a child, if I was making a clumsy effort at carrying out a simple task, my father (who came from Aberdeen) would say, "You're like an old woman with a worsted leg"' – Andrew G. Forsyth, Hertfordshire (1996).

'When I was young, eighty years ago, I lived with my grandmother on the Suffolk coast at Aldeburgh. When I did anything silly or inept she would say, "You are like the man on the beach with a worsted nose who has never seen the sea"' – George Goldsmith-Carter, Kent (1989).

'If one had misbehaved, the usual reprimand from my mother would be, "If you do that again, you will be **like Billy Gibbons' cat, you will know all about it**"' – Marjorie E. Weston, West Sussex (1998). As to how and why the Billy Gibbons cat was punished and held up as an example, we may never know.

'My father (and I'm now an old lady of 81) used to say, if as a child I had stomach ache, "**You've a pain in your little Mary**" – any connection with the Virgin Mary?' – Dorothy Flann, Edgware, Middlesex (2004).

No, I don't think so. This euphemism for a child's stomach arose from J.M. Barrie's play with the title *Little Mary* (1903).

'My grandmother, whenever we had a family gathering, of which there were many, and a meal was included, would busy herself in the kitchen preparing the meal. When all was ready, she would come to us and announce, "**Little pigs** ..." We, that is the grandchildren, would then finish the invitation with "... **come to supper/Come and get your bread and butter**"' – Bob Dean, Walsall (2003).

little pitchers have big ears 'A warning that children are around who may hear what they should not' – Marjorie Wild, Crediton, Devon (2000). *Apperson* finds this in Heywood's *Proverbs* (1546), as 'Auoyd your children: small pitchers haue wide eares'. *Casson/Grenfell* has the nannyism 'Little pitchers have long ears, so have donkeys'. 'Our version of *pas devant les enfants*' – Alison Adcock, Oxford (2004).

Originally, the saying was probably just 'pitchers have ears' – a warning that people might be listening, young or old. The allusion is obviously to the handles on a pitcher that look like its ears.

little things please little minds A dismissive remark addressed to someone engaged in an activity of which one disapproves. *Apperson* finds it in Lyly's *Sapho and Phao* (1584) , with 'catch' for 'please', while *ODP* pushes it back to 1576 as 'a litle thyng pleaseth a foole' and also suggests that Ovid had the gist of it in *Ars Amatoria* in the first century AD: '*parva leves capiunt animos* [small things enthral light minds]'. The actress June Whitfield, quoting it on *Quote ... Unquote* (13 June 1995), added, 'Little trousers fit little behinds.'

'At school the reply was "while lesser minds look on"' – Veronica M. Brown, Wigston, Leicestershire (2002).

'My Yorkshire mother used to say, "If you don't behave, **I'll look over your heads and see your nose.**" I never understood this, but it always had the desired effect!' – Jean Findlay, Northumberland (1996).

'As children we were told to **"make a noise quietly"**' – Mrs D.M. Broom, Berkshire (1996).

Miles's boy told me 'As a small child, many years ago, I used to be puzzled as to how my mother knew about all my dark deeds – when I'd told a fib, for example; and she always knew where I'd been and who I'd been with *and* what I'd been up to. When I asked, she always replied this. How I grew to hate that boy!' – Anon (1998).

Partridge/Slang has 'Miles's boy is spotted' as a printers' catchphrase, meaning 'We all know about *that,* addressed to anyone who, in a printing office, begins to spin a yarn: from *c.* 1830. Ex Miles, a Hampstead coach-boy celebrated for his faculty of diverting the passengers with anecdotes and tales.'

at one's mother's knee At an early and formative stage of one's life, when one learned useful things from one's mother. Known by 1855. 'Mother's Knee' was the title of a story (1920) by P.G. Wodehouse.

my mother said, I never should, play with the gypsies in the wood From the old children's rhyme that takes various forms and dates back well into the 1800s. There is a clapping version that goes:

My mother said
That I never should
Play with the gypsies
In the wood
Because she said
That if I did
She'd smack my bottom
With a saucepan lid!

And one which goes on:

... The woods are dark, the grass is green,
Here comes Sally with a tambourine.

Charlotte Keatley's play with the title *My Mother Said, I Never Should*, about the mother-daughter bond, was first put on in 1989.

'When I was a young teenager, I asked my Father for permission to stay out until the small hours. My Father refused and when I asked why he said that, "**There is nothing that you could want to do after midnight** that you could not do at nine or ten o'clock the previous evening"' – R.F. Harvey, Hinckley, Leicestershire (1996).

his/her parents would have been better off with a set of jugs 'When a child said something unintelligent' – W.E. Kaye (1998).

play with fire, pee in the bed A taunt to a child. My wife remembers it from Buckinghamshire in the 1950s and still finds it inexplicable.

you'd laugh to see a pudding crawl 'My mother-in-law would say this to children who were having a fit of the giggles for no reason' – Mira Little, Somerset (1999). 'Said [by my wife's grandmother] when someone laughs at something silly or for no apparent reason' – Arthur Haseler, London N22 (2000). 'My mother, when referring to someone who was "intellectually challenged" would say, "He would laugh to see a pudding crawl' – Alan Smith, Sidcup (2002).

Compare: 'What would shock me would make a pudding crawl = it would take an awful lot to shock me (a female)', by 1900, according to *Partridge/Catch Phrases*.

come on, put your bonnet and draws on – we're going out 'In spite of the difficulties of bringing up a family of nine children with an uncertain income, my grandmother always retained her dignity and poise and sense of humour. This saying always amused younger members of the family – duly shocked that such an utterance could come from their grandmother' – Jean Evershed (2001). Compare GET YOUR HAT (page 105).

remember Belgium! 'My mother used to say this to me in the 1930s when, as a small boy, I showed signs of being about to do something she disapproved of. The meaning was clear – "remember what happened to *them*" – presumably in 1914' – Guy Braithwaite, Middlesex (1998).

Indeed, 'Remember Belgium!' was an actual recruiting slogan referring to the invasion of Belgium by the Germans at the start of the First World War. It eventually emerged with ironic emphasis amid the mud of Ypres, encouraging the rejoinder, 'As if I'm ever likely to forget the bloody place!' – *Partridge/Catch Phrases*.

save your breath to cool your porridge i.e. stop talking at table. A nannyism in *Casson/Grenfell.* A proverb in similar form existed by the late 16th century – *ODP.*

shake yourself and give the hens a feed i.e. get a move on. 'From my Dad' – Anon.

smack both – you'll get the right one then 'On kids squabbling' – *Wickenden.* The broadcaster Sir David Attenborough recalled on *Quote . . . Unquote* (6 April 1993), 'I had two brothers and we used to have a room in which we sort of, I suppose, used to *carry on.* We used to make a hell of a row, and we used to quarrel and one thing and another, and when it got too bad, my mother used to come in and she used to hit all three of us round the ear, "Clip-clip-clip". And then she used to say, "There you are. I've got one of the right ones this time!"'

'I grew up in Middlesbrough in the 1950s. If me and my brothers had "nothing to do" and were being a general nuisance, my dad would say, **"Stop hanging about like a smell on the landing"** . . .' – Steve Budd, Ban Chang, Thailand (2003).

there are three sorts of Sin – Little Ones, Bigger Ones, and Taking Off Your Shoes Without Undoing the Laces! Nannyism – included in Jonathan Gathorne-Hardy, *The Rise and Fall of the British Nanny* (1972).

time to skin a rabbit 'When undressing the children at bathtime' – Tony Malin, Blandford Forum, Dorset (2003).

whistle and ride 'My mother's hurrying-up phrase' – Joan Martin, Hampshire (2000). This is rather a puzzle, as *Partridge/Slang* has 'to whistle and ride' as a phrase used by tailors meaning 'to work and talk at the same time'. Eric Partridge wondered whether it derived from a rider's 'whistling as he journeys'.

Chapter 5

IT FITS WHERE IT TOUCHES

*According to Wickenden, '***it fits where it touches***' is a consolatory remark about loose clothing.* Partridge/Catch Phrases *has 'they fit where they touch' as applied originally to* loose-fitting *trousers (with a 1932 citation) and, since the 1960s, to suggestively* tight *clothes, especially trousers. Here is a suit of phrases about clothes and clothing.*

all dressed up like a Christmas tree Gaudily attired – not a compliment. Since the late 19th century.

looked as if they'd been learning Hebrew A description of wrinkled and untidy clothes – an expression used by the mother of Mrs Jean Wiggett, Kent (1995).

'When I was at school in the sixties, "**Charlie's dead**" was the cry used to indicate that a girl's petticoat was showing below the hem of her dress. It is obsolete now, by virtue of the fact that the underwear in question does not seem to be commonly worn any more. Is it anything to do with Bonny Prince Charlie or Charles I?' – Christine Bishop (2000).

Well, it was a cry known by the 1940s at least. Could it be that it looks like a flag flying at half-mast because whichever Charlie it is, is dead?

rock-of-eye and rule of thumb 'My mother was trained to be a tailoress and in the work-rooms they always referred to things cut out without a pattern as "rock-of-eye". This word is also used in our family when cakes etc. are made without a recipe' – Betty Butcher, Wiltshire (1995).

This is more widely known in the full expression (as in the head phrase). *Partridge/Slang* explains that it describes guessing instead of measuring precisely and suggests it originated in the tailoring trade in the mid-19th century. 'Rock' here means 'a movement to and fro'.

'I was a young schoolgirl soon after the First World War and lived near the Portobello Road in London. Most of the stallholders wore rough clothes and caps and mufflers – and had very Cockney cries, but one man wore collar and tie, a proper suit and bowler hat. He had a stall full of needles, pins, tape, elastic, press fasteners, and his cry, in a very high-falutin' voice, was, "**Everything a lady needs for sewing I have.**" We youngsters (and our parents too!) took up this cry – and if *anyone* in my family and amongst our circle of friends ever asked anyone for anything, be it for sewing or not, we would hand the article over, and in our best rendition of the stallholder's voice, say, "Everything a lady needs for sewing I have!" Sadly, I now live alone, but to this day, if I can't immediately find something I want – a knife, pen, scissors etc., after hunting about and finding the article I will still say, in that same voice, "Everything a lady needs for sewing I have!"' – Miss F.M. Laughton, London N21 (1994).

first up ... best dressed! 'My mother came from a large family and this was always her saying' – Mrs Smitten, Kent (1994). *Partridge/Catch Phrases* confidently asserts that this is an Australian phrase for circumstances 'where members of a family use each other's [or one another's] clothes'.

get your hat and knickers on 'My father telling my mother to get ready to go out' – Doreen Casey, Buckinghamshire (1998). Compare COME ON, PUT YOUR BONNET ... (page 100).

you need a good bed and a good pair of shoes – if you're not in one, you're in the other 'One of the sayings I use both at home and at work' – George Kerr, Horndean (2001).

Molly St P. Swords of Barton-on-Sea, Hampshire, wrote (1993) of her 'very Wessex' mother that she used to say, **'That was good stuff for backs of westcots'** [waistcoats] – meaning, presumably, of material that because it was not visible it did not have to be very good.

if you can't fight, wear a big hat *Partridge/Catch Phrases* has this as a taunt made to someone who has just bought a new hat. Presumably the implication is that they have bought a big hat, somehow of the type that would intimidate potential opponents. A 1930s starting point is suggested.

'My husband's mother was a very talented dressmaker/tailoress whose services were much in demand. She occasionally made an outfit for her sister who, at the final fitting, would often pay her the compliment, **"Oh, well, it'll be a covering"'** – Lynne Carter, Buckinghamshire (1996).

it's snowing in Paris 'Meaning that your petticoat is showing below your skirt' – Gisela Lehmann, Herefordshire (1995). Iona and Peter Opie include this in *The Lore and Language of Schoolchildren* (1959) as a 'juvenile corrective', along with **'SOS [Slip On Show]'** and **'Is your name Seymour?'** [i.e. 'see more']. To which one might add another, **'It's snowing down south.'** Compare CHARLIE'S DEAD (page 104).

'My wife's Yorkshire grandma, when she saw a man with a shiny trouser seat, would remark, **"Joe Plush – man wi't velvet bum!"'** – Paul Thompson, Scone (2004).

neither shape nor make to it 'Clothes criticism' – Stella Richardson, Essex (1998).

'Rooted in a large, close-knit Scots family, [Mary Ure, John Osborne's first wife] was the daughter of a retired engineer who lived modestly in Kilcreggan above the Clyde. One of the dour family sayings – Osborne noted with perverse pleasure – was **"Put another woolly on"'** – John Heilpern, *A Patriot for Us*, Chap. 21 (2006).

In 2003, Mamie Carson of Crieff, Scotland, wrote that she had tried in vain to find the origin of the saying **'Red and green should never be seen except when worn by an Irish Queen'**.

Well, I doubt if we'll ever find the origin of this, but St Clair Stewart underlines its Scottishness: 'My father (we are all Scots and have all been for many generations), who, whatever his other failings, had better taste than any other man of his generation I saw in the flesh, used to say, "Blue and green should not be seen, except upon a highland queen"; I have always thought it was a traditional Scots saying and that my father meant that the two colours ought not to be worn together, at least by gentlemen, although he was in the Black Watch until the end of WWII.

'That regiment's tartan – also called "the government tartan" because it consisted of a conventional tartan without any foreground so that it would not excite any clan allegiances – was black, blue and green. While the Black Watch wore the tartan in a very dark and a medium-sized setting, the Argyll and Sutherland Highlanders wore it in a much lighter-coloured version and a larger setting. De gustibus non est disputandum.'

So, whether red/green or blue/green, it is just one of those bits of sartorial advice – like never wear brown shoes with a dark suit.

sewn with a hot needle and a burnt thread 'Clothes criticism' – Stella Richardson, Essex (1998). 'If a job was badly done, my grandmother would say, "That was sewn with a red hot needle and a burning thread." This became a family saying for any shoddy workmanship' – Jean Evershed (2001). 'My mother used "hot needle and burning thread" specifically to refer to the way buttons are sewn on bought clothes' – Veronica M. Brown, Wigston, Leicestershire (2002).

suit the wearer, bugger the starer 'Clothes criticism, when one wears what one likes' – Stella Richardson, Essex (1998).

tear away! – my mother's a dressmaker What you say to someone who is being rough with clothing, for example. Recalled by the broadcaster Terry Wogan on *Quote . . . Unquote* (17 April 1998).

a tear is an accident of the moment – but a darn is premeditated poverty 'Poverty was something my grandmother knew about in the late 1800s and this is what she used to say. During my grandfather's bouts of ill health when he was unable to go to sea, she would take in "piece work", sewing buttons on shirts at a penny a shirt' – Jean Evershed (2001).

'When I was a conscript in the late forties, doing infantry training, we had a platoon sergeant who would say to a recruit who was incompletely dressed, "**Do your flies up, lad, this isn't a circus**". After more than fifty years, I am still baffled' – Geoffrey Langley (2004).

Chapter 6

WOULD IT WERE BEDTIME ...

Beds are not just for sleeping in ... as will now be confirmed.

put another dog on the bed What you do when it is cold. I first encountered this expression in an overheard remark collected by Cherry Lavell of London NW1 and broadcast on *Quote ... Unquote* (28 November 1989): 'She said, "It's going to be very cold tonight, so I've put another dog on your bed, dear."' I have heard this saying repeated elsewhere, but I am not sure how widespread it is.

have you/is there any more, Mrs Moore? A common jest about an obviously pregnant woman. From the music-hall song 'Don't have any more, Mrs Moore', known by 1930:

> Don't have any more, Mrs Moore,
> Mrs Moore, please don't have any more;
> If you have too much, you can't stop, they say,
> And enough is as good as a feast, they say,
> And enough is as good as a feast, they say;
> If you have any more, Mrs Moore,
> Then you'll have to take the house next door;
> Too many double gins give a woman double chins,
> So don't have any more, Mrs Moore.

The singer and composer Betty Roe told me (1994) that her mother when talking of someone who had 'slipped up' (i.e. become pregnant) would say, '**She must have caught her foot in the sheet.**'

The American model and actress Jerry Hall gave her version of how a married woman should comport herself in living room, kitchen and bed, in 1985: 'My mother said it was simple to keep a man – you must be a

maid in the living room, a cook in the kitchen and a whore in the
bedroom. I said I'd hire the other two and take care of the bedroom bit.'

Presumably predating this is the well-known Welsh version: 'What are
the attributes of a Welsh wife? She should be **shrewd in the market,
fervent in chapel and frantic in bed**' – John Walker, Hampshire
(2006).

'I (a Welsh woman) was brought up to know that we are "Devout in
Chapel/Shrewd in the market/and Frantic in bed' – Jean Bayliss (2006).

we found him under a/the gooseberry bush Explanation for the
arrival of a baby and known by 1903. In *Lore and Language* (July 1980),
J.B. Smith noted that such expressions 'probably reflect ancient beliefs
according to which babies had their prenatal abode in trees, rocks
or watery places and could be brought thence by a stork or another
creature.'

Whereas, in Britain, babies that are not delivered **by the stork** are
found under a gooseberry bush, in the US, they are found in 'cabbage
patches'. Both 'stork' and 'cabbage-patch' theories of childbirth were
known by 1923.

all hands above the bedclothes, girls! 'I overheard the most senior of
three women in their late twenties who were in a tea-shop in Kensington
on their way to an old girls' reunion. As they were sitting down, she
said, "We haven't seen each other for some time so let us hear what has
been happening to us since last we met. There were giggles galore as
they all chorused in recollection' – Edward V. Marks, Surrey (1994).
Compare:

hands off cocks, on with socks As though delivered as a wake-up
call to a men's dormitory (in the army, the Scouts or wherever). I first
encountered this cry in a play called *Is Your Doctor Really Necessary?*
at the Theatre Royal, Stratford East, in 1973. *Partridge/Catch Phrases*
suggests an early 20th-century British Army origin and the slightly
more elaborate form 'Hands off your cocks and pull up your socks!'

happy dreams and sweet repose/half the bed and all the clothes!
A rhyme before bedtime. Other versions are: 'Good night, sweet
repose ...' and 'Pleasant dreams, sweet repose'. 'This goes back to
shared beds for children and wishing the child the stolen delights of
all the blankets!' – R.W.D. Coupe, Wing, Buckinghamshire (2006).
'The significance of this will immediately be obvious to anyone who
has had to share a bed with a blanket snatcher!' – Brian Huxley (2006).
'The meaning is that it's the most comfortable way to sleep, occupying
half the bed but having pulled all the bedclothes on top of you' –
Kate Gartside (2006). 'My aunt's take on this was: "Goodnight, sweet
repose – lay on your back and you won't hurt your nose." I have to
say, it was equally soothing to my sister and me when we were small'
– Jaquie Conway (2006). 'My father used to say this to us at night,
followed by the line, "Lie on your back and don't break your nose"'
– Ted Fenton (2006). 'My mother used to say, "Happy Dreams and
sweet repose/Keep you safe, under the clothes./Night, night, God
bless." I am now 63 with children and grandchildren of my own,
and this brings childhood memories rushing back!' – Kay Courts,
Cornwall (2006).

Quite often the couplet is wrongly remembered as ending: '... all the
bed and all the clothes.'

Iona and Peter Opie in *The Lore and Language of Schoolchildren* (1959)
recorded yet another version: 'A Dulwich girl, giving the rhyme, "Good
night, sweet repose,/Mind the mosquitoes don't bite your toes," added,

"That's how I was told it, but I always says "reposes" and "toeses" because I like it better.'

See also NIGHTY-NIGHT (page 116).

how's your father? Originally, this was a catchphrase associated with the British music-hall comedian Harry Tate (1872–1940). Apparently, he would exclaim it as a way of changing the subject and in order to get out of a difficult situation (compare 'Read any good books lately?'). One account tells of a sketch in which he was on a sofa with a young woman. He was just saying something like, 'Let's get together for a bit of . . .' when he saw her father enter the room and hastily said to the girl, 'And how's your dear father?' Possibly this was what gave rise to the phrase's use as a euphemism for sexual activity (as, 'indulging in a spot of how's-your-father'). Mark English tipped me off that a comic song entitled 'If a Grey-haired Lady Says "How's Your Father?" (That'll Be Mademoiselle)' was performed during the Second World War by Flanagan and Allen.

Indeed, the duo sang it in the characters of a First World War veteran and his newly enlisted son. Obviously, the suggestion is that the lady in question had indeed been up to some 'how's your father' with the father long ago. In turn, the 1939/40 number refers to the First World War song 'Mademoiselle from Armentiers', which, however, in its many versions, does not actually contain the expression 'How's your father?' Whatever the case, the phrase has also taken on a third use, meaning the same as a 'thingummy' or anything the speaker does not wish to name.

I think I shall be easing off to the great pit now 'These words would be faintly slurred when my father would announce his retirement to the bedroom, having consumed a fair amount of cheap wine' – Nick Cartwright (2002).

'My late grandfather, Fred Broughton, always said every night before he went to bed, **"I'm lighting the blue end."** When I was older, I questioned this phrase and he explained that the instruction on old fireworks was to "Light the blue end and retire immediately ..."'
– Liz Smith (2004).

'When confronted by a man who indecently exposed himself to her, my grandmother, after a minute or so's awkward silence, made this remark: **"I've seen better on my mantelpiece."** This then entered the annals of family history and whenever any object of a phallic appearance was in use, my father always made the comment: ''Ere, missus, I bet tha's got nowt like this on your mantelpiece' – H.D. Dowling, Rotherham (1998).

keep your hand on your ha'penny Advice to woman or girl to fend off sexual advances, with the implication that she should 'save' herself 'until the right man turns up'. *Partridge/Catch Phrases* dates it from the 1880s. A letter dated 20 October 1969 from the actor Kenneth Williams, commiserating on the death of a friend's mother, contains this: 'Mine is still going strong, and leaves on the 25th for a cruise in the Med. I told her to be careful "Keep your hand on your ha'penny dear" I said, "they're all after a bit out there" and she retorted "Don't worry yourself, I want nourishment, not punishment" so I think she knows what she's doing. Certainly at 69 she ought to ...' – from *The Kenneth Williams Letters* (1994).

nighty-night sleep tight/mind that the fleas don't bite Or 'Good night ... mind the fleas and bugs don't bite.' A nursery bed-time valediction. *Casson/Grenfell* has:

> Good-night, sleep tight,
> Mind the fleas don't bite.
> If they do,
> Get a shoe
> And crack their little heads in two.

'My Aunt Kate used to say':

> Night night
> Sleep tight
> Mind the bugs don't bite.
> If they do
> Grab a shoe
> And beat the blighters black and blue.

– Janet Spencer-Knott (2003).

> Night night,
> Sleep tight,
> Mind the fleas don't bite,
> Pleasant dreams and sweet repose,
> Lie on your back and you won't hurt your nose,
> Half the bed and all the clothes,
> Mind the mice don't nibble your toes.

– grandmother of Chris Gamble, Norfolk (2003). This appears to be an amalgam of various such lines – see, for example, HAPPY DREAMS (page 114).

On the use of the word 'tight': 'I was told on a visit to the American Museum in Bath that early settlers in America built traditional wooden bed frames and then "strung" them, rather like tennis racquets. The most comfortable sleep was deemed to be likely on a bed that had been *tightly* strung. Presumably if a bed were slack, then the occupant might well drop to the floor through the meshing!' – Brian Adams, Berkshire (1997).

ah, well, I'm off to have a bath in a teacup Mrs Anne Hill of Innsworth, Gloucestershire (1994), remembered that this is what her Gran would say as she went off to bed. 'When you realize she was a dumpy little woman who wore long dresses and looked as if she moved on casters, you can imagine what a lovely picture it conjured up.'

putting an equal strain on all parts i.e. going to bed – 'an expression my dear old mother used' – T. Braun, London sw3 (1996).

up the wooden hill/stairs to Bedfordshire Originally a nursery euphemism, this has now become part of grown-up 'golf-club slang', as someone once termed it – i.e. a conversational cliché. *Casson/Grenfell* include it as a nannyism, together with 'Come on, up wooden hill, down sheet lane'.

'Up the Wooden Hill to Bedfordshire' was the title of the very first song recorded by Vera Lynn, in 1936. The 'bed – fordshire' joke occurs in a synopsis of *Ali Baba and the Forty Thieves; or, Harlequin and the Magic Donkey* staged at the Alexandra Theatre, Liverpool, in 1868. Indeed, as so often, Jonathan Swift found it even earlier. In *Polite Conversation* (1738), the Colonel says, 'I'm going to the Land of Nod.' Neverout replies: 'Faith, I'm for *Bedfordshire.*' But then again, the poet Charles Cotton had used it in 1665 and *Apperson* finds 'Bedfordshire' = 'bed' in a play by Middleton in 1608.

Jim Sweeney, the comedy performer, recalled on *Quote ... Unquote* (10 May 1994) that not only would his mother say the above, but his father would set off early to bed with the words, 'I will arise and go now, and go to Innisfree' (courtesy of W.B. Yeats).

you don't look at the mantelpiece when you poke the fire 'A woman doesn't need to be pretty to make sexual intercourse with her enjoyable' – quoted in Richard Hoggart, *The Uses of Literacy* (1957). In that same year, the saying had another outing in John Osborne's play *The Entertainer.*

Chapter 7

MONEY AND FAIR WORDS

On Quote ... Unquote *(20 April 1993), the actress Diana Quick said that her grandmother (clearly an honorary nanny) came from Suffolk. When asked how much anything cost, she would reply, 'Money – and fair words.' Here are the fair words on that topic.*

all contributions gratefully received As with **please give generously/ all you can**, this is a standard phrase from charitable appeals for money. But it is also used jokingly when accepting gifts of almost anything – another helping of food, even a sexual favour. Probably since the first half of the 20th century.

all curtains and kippers 'A phrase for a fine, well-appointed house but with only a frugal "table"' – Harold E. Stock, Staffordshire (1999). Compare PLUS FOURS AND (page 259–60).

all is fish that comes to the net Meaning 'don't be choosy, everything can be used to advantage' – as a fisherman makes use of anything that he catches. Related by Barry Cryer on *Quote . . . Unquote* (5 December 1989). This dates back to about 1520, when he probably first heard it.

as free of money as a froggie of feathers 'A wonderful old Surrey saying' – Cherry Norman, Tadworth (2001)

ash, when green, is fire for a queen . . . This saying may have nothing to do with money but it is about the value of something that may have an important contribution to housekeeping. It is one of several quotable lines from a poem – or as it turns out, *poems* – examining the burning properties of various woods. The earliest appearance of such a poem – exalting the ash above all others – was as an appendage to a letter in *The Times* (1 March 1929). Lionel James of Five Ashes (*sic*), Sussex, was commenting on a leading article of a few days before on the subject of

'Wood Fires'. He wrote, 'You may like to print the enclosed country commentary in verse', but he does not say whether it was an old rhyme or whether he had written it himself (one assumes he had not):

>*Beechwood* fires are bright and clear,
>If the logs are kept a year;
>*Chestnut's* only good, they say,
>If for long it's laid away;
>Make a fire of *Elder* tree,
>Death within your house shall be;
>But *Ash* new or *Ash* old
>Is fit for Queen with crown of gold.
>
>*Birch* and *Fir* logs burn too fast,
>Blaze up bright and do not last;
>It is by the Irish said
>*Hawthorn* bakes the sweetest bread;
>*Elmwood* burns like churchyard mould –
>E'en the very flames are cold;
>But *Ash* green or *Ash* brown
>Is fit for Queen with golden crown.
>
>*Poplar* gives a bitter smoke,
>Fills your eyes and makes you choke;
>*Apple* wood will scent your room
>With an incense-like perfume.
>*Oaken* logs, if dry and old,
>Keep away the winter's cold;
>But *Ash* wet or *Ash* dry
>A King shall warm his slippers by.

The Times Index gives this poem the title 'In Praise of Ash'. Gordon Le Pard has found a slightly later printing in an essay by the Hampshire archaeologist Heywood Sumner in 1930. Sumner ascribes the poem to a certain Celia, Lady Congreve, and states that it had first appeared in *Country Life*. He says it is the subject of 'frequent misquotation'. Pamela Vandyke Price recalls singing a musical setting (with a bouncy tune) in the early 1930s.

Apperson, as ever, finds an even earlier reference to the poem. In George Borrow, *Lavengro,* Chap. 3 (1851): 'That makes good the old rhyme ... "Ash, when green, is fire for a queen".' He also gives the couplet:

> Burn ash-wood green,
> 'Tis fire for a queen;
> Burn ash-wood sear,
> 'Twill make a man swear.

And Muriel Smith points out that 'Ash, when green,/Is fire for a queen' is given as an 'old saying' in *Benham's Book of Quotations* (1948) under the listing for 'Green wood makes a hot fire', which is taken from George Herbert's *Outlandish Proverbs* (1640).

Another poem on the same theme (and with some similar touches) has also come to light. Bob Dutton remembered it from an appearance in the Ministry of Agriculture journal, *Agriculture* (December 1952), where it was described as 'an old rhyme':

> Logs to burn; logs to burn;
> Logs to save the coal a turn.
> Here's a word to make you wise
> When you hear the woodman's cries;
> Never heed his usual tale
> That he has splendid logs for sale,
> But read these lines and really learn
> The proper kind of logs to burn.
>
> Oak logs will warm you well
> If they're old and dry;

Larch logs of pinewood smell
But the sparks will fly.
Beech logs for Christmas time;
Yew logs heat well;
'Scotch' logs it is a crime
For anyone to sell.

Birch logs will burn too fast,
Chestnut scarce at all;
Hawthorn logs are good to last
If cut in the fall.
Holly logs will burn like wax,
You should burn them green;
Elm logs like smouldering flax,
No flame to be seen.

Pear logs and apple logs,
They will scent your room;
Cherry logs across the dogs
Smell like flowers in bloom.

But ash logs all smooth and grey,
Burn them green or old;
Buy up all that come your way,
They're worth their weight in gold.

Ian Forsyth also found this 'old rhyme' printed a year or two earlier in Herbert L. Edlin, *Woodland Crafts of Britain*, Chap. 24 (1949).

And then we have Juliet Burnand. She is of the family of Sir F.C. Burnand, who edited *Punch* until 1906, and believes the second poem was composed by her grandmother, who wrote under the name of E.W.A. Goodhart or possibly Honor Goodhart (another correspondent named her as 'H. Goodheart') and that it appeared anonymously in *Punch* during the coal strike preceding the General Strike of 1926. This has not yet been confirmed in *Punch,* but would seem plausible and appropriate.

A complication is that in *The White Goddess* (1948), Robert Graves describes a version of the above as 'current on Dartmoor' and as an 'emasculated' version of the Irish Ossianic 'Song of the Forest Trees' to be found in E.M. Hull's *The Poem-Book of the Gael* (1912), in a translation by Standish O'Grady. In fact, having seen the Irish poem, I do not think it is connected with either of ours but merely on the same subject. Further, as Ross Baxter informs me, 'Logs to burn' is substantially the version set to music by Robin Williamson (who called it traditional) and published in the 1970s.

(it would be) cheap at half the price i.e. cheap, very reasonable. Not a totally sensible phrase, dating probably from the 19th century. Presumably what it means is that the purchase in question would still be cheap and a bargain if it was *twice* the price that was being asked. Some consider that the expression does make sense if 'cheap' is taken as meaning 'of poor quality', in other words, 'It would still be a poor bargain if it was only half the price.' Another interpretation is that the market trader means that his product is 'cheap, at half the price it ought to be'. The rest of us are not convinced by such arguments. In his *Memoirs* (1991), Kingsley Amis comments on phrases like this that perform semantic somersaults and manage to convey meanings quite the reverse of their literal ones. He cites from a soldier: 'I'd rather sleep with her with no clothes on than you in your best suit.'

Christmas has come early this year Meaning 'we have had some good fortune or welcome [usually financial] news'. A relatively recent expression, I would say.

Beginning a report in *The Guardian* (8 April 1988), Michael Smith wrote of the Volvo purchase of the Leyland Bus operation: 'Christmas has come early for management and staff at Leyland Bus, the sole UK manufacturers of buses, which changed hands last week' – they stood to enjoy a windfall of £19 million. The previous week, Lord Williams had said of another sale – that of Rover to British Aerospace – 'Christmas has come rather early this year.'

From McGowan & Hands's *Don't Cry for Me, Sergeant-Major* (1983) (about the Falklands war): 'De briefings afterwards ... related that the SAS "thought Christmas had come early". They couldn't believe their luck. There were at least eleven Argentine aircraft virtually unguarded.'

every little helps – as the old lady said when she piddled into the sea A Wellerism – and, indeed, perhaps the most famous such. 'My old Gran used to say it,' remembered Jack O'Farrell, Cleveland (1994). In fact, lots of people did/do. In 1590 there was this French one: 'Every little helps, said the ant, *pissant en mer en plein midi*.' As '"Every little helps," quoth the wren when she pissed in the sea' it occurs in William Camden's *Remains Concerning Britaine* (1605). In 1623, Camden also had the slightly different version: 'Everything helps, quoth the wren when she pist i' the sea.'

The slightly politer '"Every little bit helps," said the lady, as she spit in the ocean', is in John Dutton, *Letters from New England* (1867). There are many different variations.

I am prompted to include this saying by a *Quote ... Unquote* listener who drew my attention to the fact that in 2005 the Tesco supermarket chain was using 'Every little helps' as a slogan on the back of its till receipts. Did they know what they were doing? she inquired. Then I was sent a photograph of the slogan as displayed in one Tesco store, just outside the ladies' loo ...

give me a kiss and lend me tuppence 'My grandmother has always said this to me at bedtime and she says her father used to say it to her at her bedtime when she was a child' – Pauline Sinclair (2000). 'My grandmother (1888–1981) used this expression, but the money was threepence, not tuppence' – Phil Rees, Bedford (2000). 'In my family we say, "Give us a kiss and lend us a shilling"' – Carole-Anne Davies (2000). Put it down to 20th-century inflation.

hang the expense – throw the cat another kipper 'My grandfather would say this if he or anyone else was contemplating a mild extravagance' – Jane Klemz, North Yorkshire (1994). 'I have always heard this as "hang the expense, throw the cat another goldfish" (the tie-up being the inclusion of expense and gold)' – Owen Friend, North Devon (1996). 'One that my late husband inherited from his grandmother: when she was deciding if something was affordable or not, she would say, "Hang the expense, fry another herring" – this was when herrings were about one penny each' – Sheila Jacques, Halstead, Essex (2003).

to have a Hezekiah's Palace 'In my family, this means to display all you have bought on your return from a shopping trip – not ordinary shopping like food, but clothes etc. This saying was used by my grandfather, a clergyman who died in 1937, but the saying lives on!' – Mary Calwell (2001). The allusion here would seem to be to 2 Kings 20:13.

how much are fourpenny haddocks? 'My mother used to say this if she saw someone wearing and flaunting a particularly handsome ring, or when family members arrived waving their hand in the air, wearing a new engagement ring. I have often wondered where the saying comes from?' – Evelyn Baigrie, Dartmouth, Devon (2002).

Compare: 'When describing anyone (usually a woman) who was overdressed, my grandmother would say they were "all got up like a fourpenny rabbit". As I remember, she used to say that the origin lay with butchers hanging rabbits in the windows of their shops. The twopenny rabbits would be undressed but the fourpenny ones would be dressed with frills etc.' – Jane Foster, Goodrich, Herefordshire (2005).

'When the conversation turns to money and legacies, my mother always says, **"I shall leave all my money to the doctor who saves my life"**' – Joan Perry, Christchurch (2000).

I'm on t'Bridlington trip 'This means that you have no money with you and are thus dependent on the bounty of others. It refers to an outing to Bridlington taken by my father and his brothers and sisters many years ago, when one of them was in that position. We all use it. It's very useful as a light-hearted, embarrassment-free way of admitting to being broke' – Gerald Haigh (2001).

in my days, you could get a tanner's worth for thruppence! 'Those who still remember "old" money will understand the relevance of my grandmother's saying, indicating value for money' – Tony Alston, Enfield, Middlesex (2002). Those who don't will need to be told that a 'tanner' was worth sixpence, whereas 'thruppence' was threepence.

it was cheaper than not having it On *Quote... Unquote* (11 February 1992), the theatre director Patrick Garland said that his mother was a great searcher out of second-hand book bargains. This meant that she would often buy a book she already had or that she didn't really want at all. But, as she rationalized it, 'It was cheaper than not having it.'

'A saying from my maternal grandfather who died in the early 1960s: **"A little goes a long way, the monkey said, as he spat over the cliff"** '– Ann Bamford, Cumbria (2006). Another Wellerism. This has been found in the US by 1914, in the form '"A little will go a long way," said the man, as he spit off the Woolworth building.'

'When younger, I was questioned by my grandfather about a spending spree. In justification, I said, "Oh, Grandad, **it's made round to go round**." He replied, "Aye, lass, **but it's made flat to pile up**"' – Hylda M. Ball, Cheshire (1995).

Another version from Yorkshire: 'Money is made round to go round' – 'Nay, lad, it's made flat to stack.' Neither of these versions is much recorded in proverb books.

'My mother, Lilian Rose Rees, born 1901, left school at 14 and worked in a fruiterer's, becoming shop manageress at 18. She would say, **"Money makes money"** – ruefully: we were poor' – George Rees, Swansea (2001).

Originally, this proverb was in the form 'Money begets money' and *Apperson* has it by 1587.

'She would also say, **"Parting is such sweet sorrow"** on taking money from someone.' So she also knew a bit of Shakespeare, it would seem:

Good night, good night. Parting is such sweet sorrow
That I shall say good night till it be morrow.

Juliet to Romeo in Act 2, Sc. 2 of *Romeo and Juliet* (1594).

money, money, money Phrase emphasizing the lure of money, as in
'All she is interested in is money, money, money!' Date of origin
unknown. 'Money-money-money – we are all crying for money and
might as well cry for the money' – J.B. Fagan, *And So To Bed*, Act 1
(1926); 'I'll be thankful if she sells it [a newspaper] … because apart
from wearing her to a shadow it's costing me a fortune. Money, money,
money, there's no end to it' – P.G. Wodehouse, *Jeeves and the Feudal
Spirit*, Chap. 11 (1954).

'Money Money Money', the title of a song recorded by Abba (1976),
undoubtedly reinforced the phrase's place in the language.

'Round here, over-competitive players of whist or snooker are frequently
reproved by the admonishment, **"We're not playing for the town-hall
clock!"** Why anybody would *ever* have wanted to win this as a trophy
baffles me' – Keith Ellel, Rishton, Lancashire (2003).

Paul Beale (1994) recorded, '**Not for a big clock**: *I* wouldn't do it –
not for *any* inducement', as in, "I don't know how these mortuary
technicians put up with it every day," [the Liverpool policeman] said,
"I wouldn't have their job for a big clock"' – quoted in James McClure,
Spike Island: Portrait of a Police Division (1980).

'Whenever anyone offers me anything, or asks if I could make use of this or that, I offer them this family saying: "Like me granny said to the bookie, **"Owt to come, glad of it."**" I am 65 and remember her saying it to the bookie's runner when he used to call at the house for her daily threepence each way' – Ron Farley, Selby, North Yorkshire (1994).

'My grandfather believed money was for hoarding, not spending. When budget discussions were about to become arguments, my grandmother would look him straight in the eye and with total conviction say, "George, **there are no pockets in shrouds**." This saying has become a household word' – Ena Constable, London N20 (1991).

ODP has this as 'Shrouds have no pockets'. R.C. Trench, *On Lessons in Proverbs* (1854) refers to an Italian proverb: 'With an image Dantesque in its vigour, that "a man shall carry nothing away with him when he dieth", take this Italian, *Our last robe . . .* is made *without pockets.*'

'My mother – born and bred a Lancastrian, but all Welsh forebears, was a great one for sayings. Although I've heard many variations of one of her remarks, I first heard this aphorism in my own home: "**Poverty's no disgrace but it's a damn nuisance**"' – Miss L. Williams, Greater Manchester (1993).

Indeed, this is a popular saying. As 'Poverty's no disgrace, but 'tis a great inconvenience', it was said to be 'a common saying among the Lark Rise people' in Flora Thompson, *Lark Rise*, Chap. 1 (1939).

'Poverty of course is no disgrace, but it is damned annoying' is attributed to William Pitt, British Prime Minister (1759–1806) in *The Treasury of Humorous Quotations*, ed. Evan Esar & Nicolas Bentley (1951). 'Poverty is no disgrace to a man, but it is confoundedly inconvenient' has also been ascribed to Revd Sydney Smith and is supposedly in his *Wit and Wisdom* (1860).

Before any of this, *Apperson* finds it in John Florio, *Second Frutes* (1591), in the form 'Poverty is no vice but an inconvenience'.

'As a child of the 1930s, money was very scarce. Whenever I asked my mother for something – sweets, clothes, bus ride, shoes, etc. – her answer was always the same: **"I shall have to see how the cat jumps."** Needless to say, I was always watching the cat' – Mrs I.N. Knight, Surrey (1998).

Partridge/Slang defines this as 'watching the course of events before committing oneself to decision or action' and dates it from about 1820. *Apperson* finds it in Sir Walter Scott's *Journal* (7 October 1826).

that's taken a shilling off its value 'This would be used should my father hear, for example, a waiter dropping a tray of plates in a restaurant' – Nick Cartwright (2002).

we have wall-to-wall carpets – they have wall-to-wall money 'An old work colleague had some excellent phrases which caused me endless amusement to brighten up the working day. This one referred to a well-off family!' – Mike Bailey (2002).

the war's over, you know Said to someone who is being noticeably and unnecessarily careful about not wasting food, electricity, etc. Current since the Second World War and a natural replacement for '**Don't you know there's a war on?**', a reproof delivered in response to complaints and used by (Will) Hatton and (Ethel) Manners portraying a Cockney chappie and a Lancashire lass in their British variety act of the 1940s.

Somehow or other it found its way into the script of the US film *It's A Wonderful Life* (1946), where it is exclaimed by James Stewart.

Partridge/ Catch Phrases has the similar 'Remember there's a war on' dating from the First World War. In a letter to Cyril Connolly on 19 October 1939, John Betjeman wrote, 'We must all do our bit. *There's a war on, you know.*'

Chapter 8

ONLY FOOLS AND HORSES WORK

The title of the BBC TV comedy series Only Fools and Horses
*must have puzzled many people. Written by John Sullivan, it has
been on the air since 1981 and concerns itself with a pair of 'wide boy'
brothers sparring together in London. The title, although almost
unrecorded in reference books, apparently comes from an old Cockney
expression, 'Only fools and horses* work*' – though this is also a proverb
recorded in the US. It has been suggested that it makes more sense
if you say, 'Only fools and horses work* for nothing.' *A version
remembered from the 1930s goes: 'Only fools and horses work and
horses turn their backs on it.' In the book* An tOileánach [The
Islandman] *written in Irish by Tomás Ó Criomhthain (1856–1937)
and published in 1929, an inhabitant of the Great Blasket island in
Kerry is quoted as saying* circa *1911, '* – ná raibh ag obair sa tsaol seo
ach capaill agus amadáin *[only horses and fools work in this world].'*
    *In a television documentary (2002) about his show, John Sullivan
explained that much of his comic inspiration came from his father,
whose family was from County Cork. He has only mentioned 'only
fools and horses work' as the reason for the title. But an Irish origin
of this 'Cockney' saying now seems more than likely.*

if you had a boy working for you, he was as good as a man ... 'My grandfather said, "If you had a boy working for you, he was as good as a man; if you had two boys, then you only had half a man; and if you had three boys, then you might as well not have one at all"' – Ted Cotterill (2001). In other words, the more boys you have, the less work they do. Known by 1930.

The Scottish critic Joyce McMillan gave her version in 2001 as 'A boy's a boy, two boys is half a boy, but three boys is no boy at all'.

'My father, a hard-working man, was always on the go, muttering such things as, "**Must soldier on**" or "**Sell the pig**" or "**Dear mother**, it's a bugger". He told me that when men became soldiers they had to serve a minimum time and if they wanted out sooner, they had to pay to leave the army: hence the following correspondence from unhappy son (in army), "Dear mother, sell the pig and buy me out." And from mother to son, "Dear son, pig's dead. Soldier on"' – Mrs Jay Carlyle, Edinburgh (1998).

Partridge/Catch Phrases dates this saying to about 1910. Hence, the title of W.F.N. Watson, *Sell the Pig and Buy Me Out: Humorous Aspects of Military Life, History and Tradition* (1998).

'My mother was born in Bradford in 1906. After doing any particular job of hard work, or after some other physical exertion, she would sit down in a chair, give a big sigh of exhaustion and exclaim, "**The Death of Nelson**!" I don't think she originated this phrase. She had certainly seen reproductions of the painting with that title. Have you any idea if this was some Victorian catchphrase? She used it all her life – it was certainly deeply ingrained in her repertoire of phrases!' – Heather Thorn, Edinburgh (2002).

This is indeed the title of a painting (1857–63) by Daniel Maclise

(1806–70). The large canvas shows Horatio Nelson lying mortally wounded on HMS *Victory* during the battle of Trafalgar. Much earlier, 'The Death of Nelson' was the title of a song from the opera *The Americans* (1811) by John Braham and S.J. Arnold. It became one of the most popular songs of the 19th century and contained the phrase, 'England, home and beauty'. The incident itself was of enormous iconic (as we would now say) significance, but the phrase 'the death of Nelson' also appears to have caught on in various ways.

Vernon Rogers of Bath wrote to say (1994) that he came originally from near Land's End where, because unemployment was always a fact of life, the younger members of the family traditionally had to leave home to seek employment. 'As a result of so many of us doing quite a range of jobs in so many parts of the world, we agree on one thing – our family saying, "**Even digging ditches is some lot easier than having to work with people.**"' Mr Rogers also pointed out that 'some lot' is a West Cornwall expression.

hard work pays off in the end, laziness pays off now A modern proverb quoted by the actor John Bird on *Quote . . . Unquote* (3 November 1998), but it is hard to find when and where it originated.

I have a lot on my slop chit 'I am very busy.' Wilfred Granville, *A Dictionary of Sailors' Slang* (1962) defines a 'slop chit' as a 'form made out by the Supply rating, which enables a man to buy "slops" in the stores'. Then he gives the expression as 'I can't do that job, I've enough on my slop-chit already' – 20th-century Royal Navy usage.

'When a task long put off finally has to be tackled: "Right! **I'll have to dive into the turnips**"' Mary Coghill, Bristol (1994).

I'm like Barney's bull, I'm buggered 'What you say after a hard day's work' – Stella Richardson, Essex (1998). Presumably this refers to the same creature as in the expression listed under I'M ALL BEHIND LIKE ... (page 290). In my book *The Gift of the Gab* (1985), I included, 'Bitched, buggered and bewildered (like Barney's bull)', though I can no longer recall the circles I had been moving in and where I heard it ...

I've only got one pair of hands The cry of hard-pressed mothers (especially), through the ages. Meaning 'One person can only do a certain amount of work, there being physical limitations on this' – *Chambers Dictionary of Idioms and Catch Phrases* (1995). Hence, *One Pair of Hands*, the title of a book (1939) by Monica Dickens about life as a cook and general servant. In the first series of the BBC radio show *Round the Horne* (1965), the character Sandy says to Julian, 'I've only got *two* pairs of hands.'

it's a poor house which can't afford one lady 'My Irish mother would say this, when I was reading but knowing I should be helping in the house' – Kate Cunningham, Hampshire (2000).

my work here is done In 2005, June Lashmore inquired as to the origins of an expression she had suddenly found herself using at the conclusion of any little task she had accomplished about the house or in the garden.

There is little doubt of its general usefulness and I told her that it probably originated in showbiz, where it is often to be found. It has been spoken by the character Josh Lyman in TV's *The West Wing* and Buffy Summers in *Buffy the Vampire Slayer*, also in *The Simpsons* (1990), *Third Rock From the Sun* (1996), *Will and Grace* (1998) and the film *Idle Hands* (US 1999). But what, if anything, were they all referring to?

Jack Foster recalled (accurately) that in Shaw's *St Joan*, Scene 5, Joan says to King Charles VII, formerly the Dauphin, 'I have made you king: my work here is done. I am going back to my father's farm.' Charles G. Francis of IdeaBank wondered, 'Could the inquirer possibly mean the suicide note left by George Eastman (1854–1932), the American inventor and founder of Eastman Kodak, on March 14, 1932, which read, "To my friends, my work is done. Why wait"?'

Then, somewhere along the line, the Lone Ranger was mentioned. Marian Bock declared, 'I am absolutely certain that the Lone Ranger did *not* say it (at least, not on a regular basis), but I have contacted Clayton Moore's daughter (aka my friend Dawn) for a more official denial.' But no denial was forthcoming.

For my part, I had been rather excited by the Lone Ranger mention, as it seemed to me just the sort of thing the wooden-voiced Moore would have said to Jay Silverheels (Tonto) at the end of the TV episodes (1949–67). Then Joe Kralich tracked down the script of Season 1, Episode 35 (11 May 1950) in which, indeed, at the end of the show, the Lone Ranger said, 'Our work is done here.'

Now Joe has presented me with 18 episodes of the TV *Lone Ranger* on DVD. I have examined the endings of all of them and can report a voice-over saying, 'And now their work was done' and the Lone Ranger himself saying, on various final occasions, 'Our job has just begun', 'We have work to do elsewhere, Tonto', 'Come, Tonto, we have more work to do' and 'Tonto, time to go on.' So there we are: ample but not conclusive evidence that the saying might have originated with this show.

Whether you believe the Lone Ranger ever said, 'My work here is done', may depend on which manifestation of the character you are familiar with. Richard Twight in Idaho emailed: 'I listened to nearly every radio broadcast of the Lone Ranger during the 1940s and early 1950s when I was a kid. I never saw the television actor who played the Lone Ranger, for which I am very glad. The heroic image of the Lone Ranger on radio was far better in the imagining than the mere mortal that I would have seen on television. I have firmly emblazoned in my "voice memory" the sound of the Lone Ranger saying the words "Our work here is done, Tonto" and possibly saying those words to the people he had just saved from the evil-doers as he and Tonto started to take their leave. In my recollection it is safe to say that it was used many times on that radio show.'

Well, whether the Lone Ranger did or he didn't, Mark English has been googling away and come up with plenty of people who did so 'in an atmosphere of Victorian high-mindedness'. Just three instances: 'Something has been done here, and very much more than I had any right to expect, still I firmly believe and am persuaded that my work here is done' – Henry Alford, in a letter to a parishioner on his decision to seek another parish (1848) – *Life, Journals and Letters of Henry Alford, D.D., late Dean of Canterbury* (1873); 'When I expressed a hope that he would recover, he replied, "You ought not to wish it. Why should I outlive my usefulness? My work here is done"' – 'In Memoriam. Testimonials to the Life and Character of the late Francis Jackson' (1861) (Jackson was an American anti-slavery campaigner); '"Now my work here is done, and I must go," thought Christie, when the waves of life closed over the spot where another tired swimmer had gone down' – Louisa May Alcott, *Work* (1873).

Comments Mark: 'I always knew the Lone Ranger was just a vicar in a stetson.'

Talking of which, a number of people also considered that it all started with Cardinal Newman in his poem *The Dream of Gerontius* (1865), as used by Elgar in his oratorio of the same name (1900). The Angel proclaims these words over the sleeping soul of Gerontius in her first utterance:

My work is done,
My task is o'er,
And so I come,
Taking it home,
For the crown is won,
Alleluia,
For evermore.

never show a fool half-finished work *ODP* glosses this proverb as '[because fools] may mistakenly judge the quality of the finished article from its awkwardness while it is being produced' and finds a version in a Scottish proverb book by 1721.

'My father said, "Never show a fool half-finished work" – always used as a retort to someone who came along and offered comment (or worse still criticism) while you were grappling with a job like cooking, sewing or DIY' – Robert Craig, London N12 (1996).

Also: 'Only fools and children criticize a job that's half-finished'. '"Fools and bairns should no see half-done work" (my father if I hung over him while he did DIY)' – Alison Adcock, Oxford (2004).

'When I was a young Management Trainee at Ford of Dagenham, a gnarled old hand on the line said to me, "So, always remember that in life, **it's not so much a question of starting at the bottom, it's more a question of starting at the *right* bottom**"' – Paul Cloutman, London SW11 (1995).

Paul Beale recalled (1994), 'My wife's family had a nice family saying that alluded back to an early 20th-century dialogue that is supposed to have taken place between her maternal grandfather, who was a master cabinet-maker in North Finchley, and one of his craftsmen:

Grandfather: Is that job finished yet?
Craftsman: It's near enough.
Grandfather: Near enough's not good enough. It's got to be just right.
Craftsman: Well, now, it *is* just right!
Grandfather: **That's near enough then.**

'So now, two generations later, "that's near enough" covers the whole thing. Actually, although the family was convinced of its authenticity, it has the look of one of those long drawn out late 19th-century *Punch* captions.'

'My mother, Yorkshire born and bred, when taking a break from her work, would always say, **"This, and better, might do; this, and worse, will never do."** "Do" of course means "be sufficient". Then she would resume her work' – June Fuller, Essex (1997).

'Years ago we had a neighbour who had a (as far as I know) unique saying. If you were sitting having a cup of tea in the middle of the morning and there was work still to be done, she would stand up and say, "Well, this and better *may* do; this and worse'll never." I still say it' – Gwyneth Harwood, North Yorkshire (1996).

'One day at the cotton mill, two men were carrying heavy beams of cotton and my father said to one of them, "Why are you only carrying one, when Charlie can carry two?" He got the logical reply, **"He's too idle to go twice"**' – Graham Whitehead, Aughton, Lancashire (1998).

Chapter 9

HE DRINKS LIKE A FISH

On Quote ... Unquote *(2 February 1982), I included a story from
a listener in Coventry, of which I said that it 'may be an old chestnut
but none the worse for that': 'A small boy was taken out to tea by
his parents at a neighbour's house. Also present at the meal was the
neighbour's lodger. As soon as the meal began the small boy started
to stare at the lodger. In spite of several words of correction, he
continued to stare. Finally, the boy's father asked, "Why on earth
are you staring at Mr Jones?" The boy answered, "***Well, I can't see
that he drinks like a fish ...***" This line has certainly entered my
family's store of oft-repeated jokes.'*

*It was as well that I supplied the caveat. I have since found the
source of this story and, as so often, it came as the caption to a
George du Maurier cartoon with the title 'Enfant Terrible' in* Punch
*(1 November 1890): "'I've brought you a glass of wine, Mr Professor.
Please drink it!" "Vat! Pefore tinner? Ach, vy?" "Because Mummy
says you drink like a fish, and I want to see you – !"' And so to
drink-related sayings ...*

and what's the drink situation? Anthony Thwaite, the poet and literary editor, recognized that in his household this was a phrase always used prior to a dinner party. So much so that when his daughter Alice was aged about five and was asked what she had done at Sunday School, she replied – apropos the water-into-wine miracle at Cana – that she had been learning about 'Jesus and the drink situation'. Related on *Quote* … *Unquote* (1 June 1993).

An Edwardian toast that the painter Francis Bacon (1909–92) acquired from his father – according to Daniel Farson, *The Gilded Gutter Life of Francis Bacon* (1993) – was, '**Champagne to our real friends, and real pain to our sham friends.**' But it is of earlier provenance. In R.S. Surtees, *Jorrocks's Jaunts and Jollities* (1838), the famous fox-hunter Mr Jorrocks gives a dinner party during the course of which he comments on champagne and Surtees has him pronouncing it 'shampain'. 'Mr. Jorrocks then called upon the company in succession for a toast, a song, or a sentiment. Nimrod gave, "The Royal Stag-hounds"; Crane gave, "Champagne to our real friends, and real pain to our sham friends" … and Mr. Spiers, like a patriotic printer, gave "The Liberty of the Press", which he said was like fox-hunting – "if we have it not we die" – all of which Mr. Jorrocks applauded as if he had never heard them before, and drank in bumpers.'

'"**Hard liver, hard worker**" was a sound old country maxim, and the labouring men did well to follow it' – Flora Thompson, *Lark Rise*, Chap. 3 (1939), recalling the 1890s, when she was growing up.

here's to it and to it again, and if you get to it and don't do it, may you never get to it to do it again A toast (spoken quickly) from Northern Ireland brought along to *Quote* ... *Unquote* by the entertainer Nuala McKeever (4 October 2004). I have also seen this described as 'an old Welsh toast'.

here's to the Pope and his paraffin lamp 'My maternal grandmother had a great fund of sayings dating from about 1880 onwards, including this toast' – Vivien Rees, Bristol (2002). I don't understand this ...

'My wife's wonderful mother was a codes and cipher officer in the RAF during the Second World War. Amongst the many sad and funny stories of people, places and events that she relates is one about a commanding officer – a person she was none too fond of and who would regularly hog his officers' meagre cheese rations. However, she – and I – have adopted a toast with which he would often drive her mad ... "**I looks towards you and I suffers accordin'**." Sounds a bit Dickensian to me' – Geoff Goodwin (2004).

Partridge/Catch Phrases has 'I look towards you' and its response, 'I catches your eye', suggesting they are 'drinking conventions' rather than true catchphrases. Both of them occur, for example, in Nevil Shute's novel *Pastoral* (1944). They are probably Cockney in origin and may go back to 1850 or earlier.

I'll pee over nine hedges 'My maternal grandmother, born and bred in Essex, had a number of colourful and often quite earthy sayings. Offered a refill of liquid refreshment (whether alcoholic or not), she would say, invariably accepting it, "Oh, I shouldn't really. I'll pee over nine hedges!"' – Graham Sparrow, Bunwell, Norfolk (2004).

may you live long and die rectangular – oblong, if you can't manage that 'My late father had this rather fine toast' – Lewis Conquer (2002).

oops, save a sailor 'When my mother inadvertently "clinked" two glasses together – for instance, when putting them away after use – she would say, "Oops, save a sailor." Can you give an explanation for this?' – Penny Mortimer, Watford, Hertfordshire (2002). 'My cousin, who died two and a half years ago at the age of 96 and was a captain of a minesweeper during the war, would never chink his glass when raising a toast. He said, "Every time you chink a glass, a sailor dies"' – Richard Winch (2004).

The origin of this superstition – recorded first at the end of the 19th century – lies in the fact that, to a sailor, ringing bells are equated with a sinking vessel and therefore signify death. Because of this, if a struck glass makes a ringing sound or chime, it should be silenced.

An anonymous, drunken parody of 'Twinkle, twinkle, little star', goes:

> **Starkle, starkle, little twink,**
> Who the hell you are, you think?
> I'm not under the alcofluence of incohol,
> Though some thinkle peep I am.
> I fool so feelish. I don't know who is me
> For the drunker I sit here, the longer I get.

This is said to have been published in the small magazine *Argosy* in about 1943. A musical version was recorded by the English comedian Charlie Drake in 1959.

In 2002, Deirdre Lay asked about something that her mother always says instead of 'Cheers!' or 'Bottoms up!' before taking a sip: '**Up she goes and down she goes, and wallops Mrs Cox!**' This led to an examination of the last three words in particular.

'Wallop' is an old word (possibly Australian) for beer, or for alcohol in general – which may be relevant – but 'to wallop' something is to give it a blow. 'To wallop' has also had the meaning 'to keel over and die'. My wife says her father used to say, 'Wallop Mrs Cox!' when there was a bang or a loud noise. Indeed, it would seem to have been an exclamation popular particularly in the English Midlands in the mid-20th century.

Hence *Wallop Mrs Cox,* which was used as the title of a musical celebration of life in Birmingham, written (2000) by Euan Rose and Laurie Hornsby. I asked Euan why they called it that and he said because it means 'fall down dead'. Indeed, the principal character is called Mrs Cox and the show starts with her funeral. There is even a song entitled 'Wallop Mrs Cox'. But where did the phrase originate? Who was the original Mrs Cox (apart from it being a common working-class name in the Birmingham area)?

Well, Julian Fellowes, the Oscar-winning scriptwriter of *Gosford Park,* was appearing on *Quote ... Unquote* on the occasion when I mentioned this matter. His instant reaction was to say that it referred to a notorious unresolved Victorian murder mystery, the Bravo case.

In 1876, a London barrister called Charles Bravo died of poisoning and his wife, Florence, was the chief suspect, although she was neither charged nor convicted. Florence had a companion who lived in the Bravo household and her name was Mrs Jane Cannon Cox. She was present in the house when Charles cried out for help and she went to his aid, although it was later revealed that she had had many arguments with him. At a second inquest into the poisoning – virtually a trial of Florence and Mrs Cox – a verdict of wilful murder was returned, but there was insufficient evidence to proceed to a proper trial. The whole case is described in James Ruddick's book *Murder at the Priory* (2001).

Could this possibly be the origin of a phrase that brings together a Mrs Cox and a situation where someone does drop down dead?

Chapter 10

ALWAYS LOOK ON THE BRIGHT SIDE

A proverb is a saying that embodies some general truth. Where I have not been too sure that the saying has wide circulation and does not have the force of a full-blown proverb, I have labelled it 'informal'. An example would be '**always look on the bright side**', *which is a common expression, encouraging another to take a positive attitude. It is quoted in Richard Hoggart,* The Uses of Literacy *(1957) and the OED2 has the expression by 1839. In 1784, Samuel Johnson talked of 'looking on the* best *side of every event'.*

Latterly, the phrase has been elevated to super-catchphrase status through 'Always Look on the Bright Side of Life', a song performed by crucifixion victims in the film Monty Python's Life of Brian *(UK 1979).*

So what we are dealing with in this chapter are pieces of advice and homely wisdom that may sound like proverbs but may not be fully fledged ones.

As always, I would draw attention to the fact it is perhaps unfortunate that a 'proverb' and a 'proverbial expression' are two very distinct forms of words. A proverb is as above, but a proverbial expression may not contain any truth. It may simply be an old turn of phrase that is still popular.

all cats are the same in the dark This proverb would appear to have begun life as 'When all candles be out, all cats be grey. All things are then of one colour' – modernized spelling – according to Heywood's proverb book of the 1540s. In fact, *Apperson* and *ODP* do not give the modern version as here. Nor do they seem to be aware of the similar 'all women look the same in the dark'.

all the world's queer, save thee and me – and I'm not too sure about thee 'My paternal grandfather said this' – Denis Sharp, Arundel (2002). It is based on the remark attributed to Robert Owen, the Welsh-born socialist reformer (1771–1858), when he broke up with his business partner, W. Allen, at New Lanark (1828): 'All the world is queer save thee and me, and even thou art a little queer.'

he/she is as God made him/her A proverbial expression. Hence, Sancho Panza's comment: 'Every man is as God made him, and often even worse [*Cada uno es como Dios le hizo, y aun peor muchas veces*]' – Miguel de Cervantes, *Don Quixote*, Pt 2, Chap. 4 (1615). 'My Lord, I am as God made me' – Swift, *Polite Conversation* (1738). '[On the horribleness of jellyfish] They are as God made them, Mr Reeve' – Henry Reed, *The Primal Scene, As It Were...* (1958).

On *Quote... Unquote* (18 June 1996), John Cole, the former BBC Political Editor, related how his grandmother had used 'She is as God made her', censoriously, of Margaret Thatcher.

well, it's better than a poke in the eye with a sharp stick What you say to someone who is hesitating over accepting something – a small tip, say, or an equivocal compliment. In other words, it is better than nothing.

Certainly an established usage by the time it was uttered on BBC radio, *Round the Horne* (15 February 1967). Indeed, *Partridge/ Catch Phrases* dates it and other similar phrases to '*circa* 1920', and adds, 'Most seem to have originated late in C19.' Compare Grose's *Dictionary of the Vulgar Tongue* (1788): 'This is better than a thump on the back with a stone.'

An English Midlands variant, dating from the mid-20th century, is: 'Better than a poke in the eye with a hedge stake' (which is, of course, a sharp stick).

'My mother, who will, please goodness, reach the age of 102 years in January, will say about people who try to change their religion, "**A cat can have kittens in a dog kennel, but it doesn't make them puppies**"' – H.M.B. Fisher, London NW8 (2001). I find this echoic of the Duke of Wellington's alleged remark, when chaffed for being an Irishman: 'Because a man is born in a stable that does not make him a horse.' This is quoted in Elizabeth Longford, *Wellington: The Years of the Sword* (1969). Compare the proverbial 'Truly a man does sometimes become a horse by being born in a stable' (known by 1833).

From the theatre director Sir Peter Hall's memoir *Making an Exhibition of Myself* (1993): 'My mother was alert to my temperament from my beginnings to the end of her days. She was a Suffolk country woman who lived by precept and aphorism. Her vocabulary was packed with comforting phrases like "**a change is as good as a rest**".' The earliest citation so far found for this is, 'One of our greatest statesmen has said that a change of work is the best rest. So it is' – Arthur Conan Doyle, in *Lippincott's Monthly Magazine* (February 1890). Who could this have been – Disraeli, Gladstone?

'Christmas comes but once a year' – thank God! The allusion is to a 16th-century rhyme ('... and when it comes it brings good cheer'); the sour additional comment – presumably from someone objecting to the commercialization of the season or the exhaustion of having to organize the festivities – was known by the 1940s.

(we'll) cross that bridge when we've burnt it 'One of my mother's favourite sayings' – David Shenton, Poole, Dorset (1998). Ah, the joy of mangled proverbs.

'My mother taught me that if anyone ever teased me, I should respond, **"Do you insinuate that I should tolerate such diabolical impudence from a youngster like you? The audacity of your vulgarity simply shocks the sensibility of my natural modesty. You are the concentrated essence of asinine stupidity."** It might not trip off the tongue, but I could quote it from the age of about five, and it now forms part of the oratory taking place in my own children's primary school playground' – Katie Jarvis, Minchinhampton, Gloucestershire (2003).

'When I was a child, my mother would often say, "How dare you insinuate that I should tolerate such diabolic insolence from a microscopic individual creature like you? If it were not for the inconvenience of removing my white kid glove ..."' – Pauline Jenkins, Polegate, East Sussex (2006).

don't do anything for nothing, and do very little for sixpence Written by Mrs Keppel (mistress of Edward VII) to Nancy Astor on the occasion of her marriage in 1906. Quoted in James Lees-Milne, *Beneath a Waning Moon* (2003) – entry for 7 July 1987.

Mrs S.J. Stevens of Barnacle, near Coventry, asked me (2003) to find a source for (and any more text to) '**Don't hurry, don't worry, and don't forget to smell the flowers**'. She had seen this attributed to a certain 'G. Rice' (sports journalist/poet Grantland Rice?) and on the internet there were mentions of a 'T. Rice' (surely not Tim Rice of musicals fame?)

My first reaction was to recall something that Len Murray, leader of the Trades Union Congress, said in May 1984 when he unexpectedly announced his retirement: 'There are a number of things I have wanted to do for a long time. There are places to go, books to read, flowers to smell and trees to look at.' But I also remembered something from a little Hallmark-type book of American quotations that I picked up in Boston, Mass. in 1972. And surely wasn't it in song, too? Yes, indeed: 'Don't Forget to Smell the Flowers (Along the Way)' was the title of a record made by (among others) Bobby Lord and dating from 1969.

Finally, all fell before what is probably the original – which is in *Bartlett's Familiar Quotations* – 'You're only here for a short visit. Don't hurry. Don't worry. And be sure to smell the flowers along the way.' This comes from *The Walter Hagen Story* (1956) by the US pro-golfer Walter C. Hagen (1892–1969). The only question is, how did he manage to win the US Open twice and the British Open four times if he stopped to smell the flowers along the way ... ?

don't get your knickers in a twist! 'Don't make a drama out of a crisis; don't get worked up or confused about something; don't get excited or you'll make the problem worse.' As 'knickers' (for female underwear) is mostly a Britishism, this popular phrase has not travelled, I don't think. The *OED2* describes 'to get your knickers in a twist' as a jocularism, meaning 'to become unduly agitated or angry' and gives the earliest citation as from 1971. I have a feeling that it was around in the 1950s but have no confirmation of this, nor any date for the cod Latin version, *Ne pantalorum torqueis.*

David Critchlow points out, however, that the phrase does occur in essence in George Eliot's novel *Romola*, Chap. 63 (1863), which is set in the 15th century: "'Nay, Goro,' said a sleek shopkeeper, compassionately, 'thou hast got thy legs into twisted hose there.'"

When I asked Marian Bock to find out how well-known the expression was in the US, she confirmed that it was 'not very' and only really known from its use in imported British sitcoms. She did, however, uncover these supposed American equivalents in the 'don't get your X in a Y' stakes: 'Don't get your panties/tights/undies in a bunch/bind/knot/snarl/wad'. And then there is the magisterial 'Don't get your panties in an uproar'. She also produced this fine citation from Fox News on 7 March 2006 when Vice-President Cheney accidentally shot one of his friends: 'The White House press corps has just got its panties bunched up about it.'

don't meet trouble half-way An everyday saying quoted by Richard Hoggart in *The Uses of Literacy* (1957).

'My mother, born in 1872, once told me that *her* mother, whenever a family member said something like "Well, every dog has his day", would mutter this response, "**Every dog has its day – and a bitch two afternoons!**"' – Clare Meadmore, Cornwall (1994). *Apperson* finds this addition to the proverb occurring by 1896 and earlier – by 1864 – the 'Essex saying', 'Every dog has his day, and a cat has two Sundays.' Patricia Nielsen, Aalborg, Denmark (2000), had, from her Derbyshire father, 'Every dog has its day and every cat its Saturday afternoon.'

Another version that I encountered before 1985 was 'Every dog has its day and every cat its night out.' Perhaps the original was '"Every dog has his day and every man his hour", inscribed on a Royal Doulton biscuit barrel' – Veronica M. Brown, Wigston, Leicestershire (2002).

everything comes to those who listen I encountered this proverbial-sounding line in Neville and June Braybrooke's biography of the novelist Olivia Manning (2004). In the form 'Never speak too much, for everything comes to those who listen', it is given as a saying of Olivia Manning's mother. But, given its non-appearance in the main proverb books, I suspect that it may have been her re-working of EVERYTHING COMES TO HE WHO WAITS (page 300).

fine words butter no parsnips This standard proverb, known since the 1630s at least, tends to get rattled off with little regard for its meaning or point, which is that 'fine words won't achieve anything on their own'. Or, as the other saying has it, 'Deeds not words'. Quite why parsnips are singled out is a puzzle, except that they are traditionally buttered up before serving. However, John Taylor, *Epigrammes* (1651), has this verse which shows that parsnips were not the only food mentioned in this regard:

> Words are but wind that do from men proceed,
> None but Chamelions on bare Air can feed:
> Great men large hopeful promises may utter;
> But words did never Fish or Parsnips butter.

Sometimes the word 'fine' is replaced with 'fair' – as in *Casson/Grenfell* – or 'soft'.

'My (very) late father had quite a varied selection of sayings that he would trot out on occasions – and a quotation he could never attribute. Have you ever come across the adage "**Gaze not on swans**"?' – Geoff Wilde, Great Crosby, Lancashire (2004).

Now that is interesting. It was written by either Henry Noel or

William Strode and is from a poem entitled 'Beauty Extolled'. In Henry Lawes's *Ayres and Dialogues* (1653), it is attributed to Noel:

> Gaze not on swans, in whose soft breast,
> A full-hatched beauty seems to nest
> Nor snow, which falling from the sky
> Hovers in its virginity.

Even more interestingly, Samuel Pepys wrote in his diary (11 February 1662) of setting the poem to music – though someone else had to finish it off for him – and then on 14 March he records playing the lute to accompany the song.

God helps those who help themselves. But God help those that help themselves 'My mother used to say this' – Colin Le Bachelet (2006).

'My grandmother always used to say, "God helps those who help themselves, but God help those caught helping themselves"' – P.J. Walter, Tiverton, Devon (2006).

Also in the form '**the Lord helps those who help themselves …**' – 'My grandmother used to say, "The Lord helps those who help themselves – but the Lord help those that I catch helping themselves." She was much given to obscure sayings and would encourage guests at table by saying, "Be like the Scots lad: help yourself, but dinna pinch!"' – Ian Forsyth, Durham (2002).

In 2002, Gillian Bockley asked about a motto or mantra that she had heard for getting one through difficult situations. We found that it seems to have originated with a Mrs Cornish, who was the wife of a master at Eton College in the late 19th century. If ever tempted by depression, she would repeat three things to herself: '**I am an Englishwoman. I was born in wedlock. I am on dry land.**'

The immediate source for this is a rather obscure little book *Bensoniana & Cornishiana* (1999), although Joyce Grenfell in *In Pleasant Places*, Chap. 15 (1979) has this as 'said to her [Mrs Cornish's] daughter Charlotte, "Even after a Channel Crossing, I say to myself, 'I am English; I was born in wedlock; and I am on dry land.'"'

I thought of this recently when reading what John Osborne wrote in his Notebook for 1964: 'Whatever else, I have been blessed with God's two greatest gifts: to be born English and heterosexual.'

if it *looks* good/right, then it *is* good/right I remember hearing some desk-bound BBC wallah passing judgement on the Concorde 002 supersonic airliner after it had flown over the Queen's Birthday Parade in June 1969: 'If it looks good then it probably is good.' But where did this view originate? Michael Lewis commented (2006), 'I suspect that this is a truism of engineering and that no single point of origin will be found. But it does seem to have particular currency among aviation engineers, not least because it certainly was one motto of Clarence "Kelly" Johnson (the other was "Be Quick, Be Quiet, And Be On Time"). Johnson was responsible for a series of revolutionary aircraft, culminating in his direction of the legendary Skunk Works that produced the U-2 and the A-11/SR-71 Blackbird. Ben Rich of Skunk Works said, "All of us had been trained by Kelly Johnson and believed fanatically in his insistence that an airplane that looked beautiful would fly the same way."'

Where the relevance to the domestic scene occurs is in the parallel injunction from William Morris: 'Have nothing in your houses that you do not know to be useful, or believe to be beautiful' – *Hopes and Fears for Art*, 'Making the Best of It' (1882).

if we had ham, we could have ham and eggs – if we had eggs 'This was a "joke" my late father quoted as typical of the despairing, mordant humour among his sad companions in muddy trenches while waiting to go over the top during the Great War' – Douglas Cornelissen (2006). 'It can be found in Joe Corrie's play *In Time of Strife* (1930) about the General Strike and its effect on a mining family. This is a quote from a young boy who is dreaming of a proper meal' – Christine Hamilton, Glasgow (2006).

'I remember this well from my childhood in Devon in the 1950s – which I assumed was a local saying. It was said as follows in a Devonshire dialect: "If us 'ad some ham, us could 'ave some ham and eggs, if us 'ad some eggs ..."' – Dave Walter (2006).

An undated seaside postcard by 'D. Tempest' (probably from the 1950s) shows a middle-aged couple at breakfast. He says, 'If we'd been able to get some bacon yesterday, we'd have had bacon and eggs for breakfast, if we'd had any eggs!'

if wishes were horses, beggars would ride A nannyism (*Casson/Grenfell*) – or rather a proverb that nannies were once much inclined to quote. In this form, the proverb has been in existence since the 18th century – *ODP*. 'In response to any sentence beginning "I wish ...", my mother would always recite: "If wishes were horses, beggars would ride,/If turnips were watches, I'd wear one by my side"' – Ian Forsyth, Durham (2006).

if you can't say anything nice about someone, then don't say anything at all Evelyn Zisch, who listens to *Quote ... Unquote* in Austria, told the programme (2005) that her mother always used to say this, as did her mother before that. It is a proverbial saying and some claim it is to be found in Aesop's fables. The earliest citation to hand –

and we are probably looking at a North American origin here – is from the *Gettysburg Times* (20 September 1922), in the form, 'If you can't say anything good about people, don't say anything.' In the film *Bambi* (US 1942), Thumper is taught by his mother, 'If you can't say anythin' nice, don't say nuthin' at all.'

On the other hand, Alice Roosevelt Longworth, the American political hostess (1884–1980), had this embroidered on a cushion: 'If you haven't got anything nice to say about anyone, come and sit by me.'

it is better to light a candle than to grumble about the dark Bryan Magee, the philosopher and broadcaster, said on *Quote ... Unquote* (22 January 1991) that when he has to bestir himself, 'I give myself little talkings to' – and quotes this Jewish proverb. Another notable user was Adlai Stevenson, who said on the death of Eleanor Roosevelt, the former First Lady, in November 1962, 'She would rather light a candle than curse the darkness, and her glow has warmed the world.' Possibly he had been inspired to do so by what Mrs Roosevelt herself had written in *My Day* (based on her newspaper column): 'Even a candle is better than no light at all.' However, Stevenson was merely quoting the motto of the Christopher Society (an American organization that honours authors and creative personnel who produce uplifting work), which came, in turn, from a supposedly *Chinese* proverb. 'Better to light a candle than curse the darkness' was also quoted by Peter Benenson, the founder of Amnesty International, at a Human Rights Day ceremony on 10 December 1961 and provided Amnesty International with its symbol of a burning candle (encircled by barbed wire).

it will all come out in the wash 'The truth will be revealed, a problem will be resolved, as dirt and stains are removed from clothing by washing.' This expression seems to have been established by about 1900.

P.G. Wodehouse delightfully mixes it with another proverbial expression in *The Man With Two Left Feet*, Chap. 2 (1917): 'Heredity, and so forth. What's bred in the bone will come out in the wash.'

'If one was at all worried by any aspect of one's appearance – from shoes to hair – my mother would say, **"Oh, well, it won't show with your hat on"'** – Jean Ruthven (2001).

'My Mother had a saying, **"Keep on keeping on** – whatever you do will be sure to be wrong"' – Ron Shuttleworth, Coventry (2006).

Well, the first part of this has an interesting background, although the origin and date of the injunction remain unknown. It may have been used as a Salvation Army slogan at some time and in 1906, a song by George Bastow (recorded by Arthur Gilbert), 'Wire in My Lads', had a verse about trying to seduce a young lady and being rejected: 'Don't 'e take no notice, boys, but keep on keeping on.'

George Orwell used the phrase in a 'London Letter' to *Partisan Review* (5 June 1945): 'In the face of terrifying dangers and golden political opportunities, people just keep on keeping on, in a sort of twilight sleep in which they are conscious of nothing except the daily round of work, family life, darts at the pub, exercising the dog, mowing the lawn, bringing home the supper beer, etc. etc.' The phrase also appears in Bob Dylan's song 'Tangled Up in Blue' (1974).

laugh and the world laughs with you ... The original of this well-known rhyme is 'Solitude', by the American poet Ella Wheeler Wilcox (1855–1919), published in *The New York Sun* (25 February 1883):

Laugh and the world laughs with you;
Weep and you weep alone.

As the *ODP* points out, this is an alteration of the sentiment expressed
by Horace in his *Ars Poetica* in the first century BC: 'Men's faces laugh
on those who laugh, and correspondingly weep on those who weep.'

Another alteration is: '... weep, and you sleep alone'. In this form it
was said by Anne, Countess of Rosse, to the architectural historian James
Lees-Milne and recorded by him in his diary for 6 June 1945 – published
in *Prophesying Peace* (1977).

In the form '... snore and you sleep alone', it occurs in Anthony
Burgess, *Inside Mr Enderby* (1963), though he did not claim it as original.

'My wife's Yorkshire grandma had a stoical attitude: "Laugh, and the
world laughs with you. Cry, and you wet your muffler"' – Paul
Thompson, Scone (2004).

As was only appropriate in a former head of BBC Radio Entertainment,
Jonathan James-Moore was keen to learn about the expression '**Laughter
is the best medicine**' (in 2002). At first I mistook this for the title of
an Irvin S. Cobb joke and anecdote collection from 1921, *A Laugh a Day
Keeps the Doctor Away*. Then I began to come across the correct saying
labelled as a proverb but with no supporting dates or sources. Wolfgang
Mieder & Co.'s *A Dictionary of American Proverbs* has it, together with
'Laugh and be well', which states the same thing.

Going back a bit further there are other similar proverbs, like 'Time
is the best medicine' (Ovid) and 'Patience is the best medicine' (John
Florio). The nearest I have got to a sourced version of this one is 'Mirth
is God's medicine', which is in *Proverbs from Plymouth Pulpit* by Henry
Ward Beecher, the American Congregationalist minister and writer
(1813–97). I don't know, but I take it that, like Benjamin Franklin's *Poor
Richard's Almanac*, this work was a collection rather than an original
composition. Still, it confirms the proverbial nature of our target remark.

Odd that 'Laughter is the best medicine' is not more specifically recorded before the 20th century and before *Reader's Digest* began running its 'Laughter, the Best Medicine' feature (whenever that was). Of course, there have been a number of studies to show that laughter can have a very positive effect on patients' health, especially where conventional medical methods have failed. I don't think this extends to the Robin Williams film *Patch Adams* (US 1998) about an excruciating man who entertains terminally ill kids in clown costume (or something – I could hardly bear to sit to the end of the trailer, let alone watch the movie).

I came across the following remark (which is a bit suspect) ascribed to a 17th-century British physician: 'The arrival of a good clown into a village does more for its health than twenty asses laden down with drugs.'

least said, soonest mended Quoted in Richard Hoggart, *The Uses of Literacy* (1957) as a common advisory saying. *Apperson* has it by 1776, but *ODP* fields this in about 1460 (modern spelling): 'Who saith little, he is wise ... And few words are soon amended.'

a little help is worth a lot of pity Sometimes 'a little help is worth a deal of pity' and sometimes 'an ounce of help is worth a pound of pity'. Clearly, the meaning is much the same as 'actions speak louder than words'. I suspect this is a modern coinage. It is not much recorded in proverb books, except in the US.

a little of what you fancy does you good A nudging point of view from a song by Fred W. Leigh and George Arthurs:

I always hold in having it, if you fancy it,
If you fancy it, that's understood.
And suppose it makes you fat,
I don't worry over that
Cos a little of what you fancy does you good.

The song was popularized, with a wink, by the music-hall singer Marie Lloyd (1870–1922) in the 1890s. Hence, *A Little of What You Fancy*, the title of a novel (1970) by H.E. Bates.

'When I told my Mum I'd repay her in a couple of days for the tights/perfume/whatever I'd "borrowed", she'd say (wryly, I now know), "Och aye, **live horse and you'll eat corn**"' – Morag Becker, London SE22 (1996). Presumably derived from: **live horse and you'll get grass** *Apperson* has, rather, 'Live, horse! And thou shalt have grass' and finds it, in that form, in Swift's *Polite Conversation* (1738).

On *Quote... Unquote* (11 February 1992), the actor Bernard Bresslaw said his mother-in-law used the saying in response to people saying if you do such and such, everything will come all right.

Partridge/*Slang* has, rather, 'Live horse! And thou shalt have grass' and glosses it as, 'Well, let's wait and see! Later on, we'll see!'

I think a comma between 'live' and 'horse' is rather important.

'I should like to know the origin of a quotation of my father's – long since dead. After some minor calamity in the family, he would say, "Ah, well, more was lost at Moax Hill." I do not know the correct spelling of Moax – this is how it sounds and has two syllables' – Joy Troughton, London N12 (2002).

Here we go: in the middle of the 15th century, the Ottoman Turks began to raid Hungary. Then, in 1526, on the plains near Mohács, the

Hungarian army suffered a total defeat. According to one website, even today, Hungarians, when pressed, will say jokingly, 'Don't worry, **more was lost at Mohács.**'

never go anywhere for the first time Words of wisdom sent to *Quote ... Unquote* by Miss M.K. Hinds of Bracknell (22 March 2004). 'Many years ago,' she said, 'I had an elderly aunt who drove a small car along the winding lanes of Suffolk. She had two useful pieces of advice for drivers. The first requires a little thought to see its meaning: 'Never go anywhere for the first time.' And the other more obvious one was: **'If in doubt, follow the white line.'**

'If ever one of the family received a less than delightful present, or bought something which, when brought home, did not quite match, my mother would say, **"Well, never mind – it won't eat anything"**' – Margaret Coles, Leeds (1994).

'One of my great-aunts, who lived in Lincolnshire, had a saying to us small children when we were being reluctant over food or little jobs: "Never let your mother know she bred a jibber", spoken very rapidly so the words coalesced into one long incomprehensible word. As a child, I often wondered what a "bredajibber" was. A jibber is a horse which refuses a fence or refuses to pull a load, a much-unloved animal' – Ted Clark (2002).

In 2006, Dame Margaret Anstee, the former British diplomat, came to me with an interesting query somewhere on the axis of book titles and domestic catchphrases: 'What is the origin of the saying, **"Never say your mother had a jibber"**? This was the title I wanted to give to my autobiography, because it was the saying I had been brought up on by my own mother, but my publishers objected that no one would know what it meant.

'In vain I explained that it meant a horse that jibs at a fence and that it had served as a motto for me during the whole of my chequered life, resulting in my trying to leap over metaphorical fences that could much more easily have been circumnavigated. Even twenty years after her death, when I was leading a doomed UN peacekeeping mission to Angola, I would face each day and its new catastrophes muttering the familiar words between gritted teeth. It was no good: in the end I had to settle for *Never Learn to Type.*

'I had always thought that the full phrase on which my mother brought me up had a close connection with the Welsh Marches (Radnorshire and Herefordshire) where she was born and spent her youth. In local speaking engagements I find it always has a resonance with those whose families have long lived here. This was certainly the case when I was addressing the Wye Valley Grasslands Society, to an audience entirely made up of hill farmers and their wives whose families have lived thereabouts for generations and intermarried. Afterwards one of them came to talk to me and gave me some interesting information.

'I had always thought that the phrase meant a horse that jibbed at a fence but according to him it more generally refers to a horse that refused to haul a heavy load. He illustrated this with a gruesome account of how waggoners in earlier times used to cure a jibber: they would smoke their clay pipe until it was red hot and then insert it under the unfortunate horse's tail. Apparently this cruel (and no longer current) practice had 100% success in all cases, with no recurrences.'

This is how I responded to Dame Margaret: '*Jibber*, meaning a "horse that jibs", has been known since 1847 and as "one who jibs" since 1936. Eric Partridge mentions your phrase in his *Dictionary of Catch Phrases*, in the entry headed "never let it be said your mother reared a jib," which he describes as an Australianism (but he was often rather shaky in his attributions).'

So, other people do know the phrase. Dame Margaret's book *Never Learn to Type: a Woman at the United Nations* (2003) was published by John Wiley.

'When I was a child my father would squash any unnecessary prattle with the remark, "**It is a wise man who, having nothing to say, does not proceed to demonstrate the fact**' – Erica Smale (2003).

This observation has an interesting pedigree. 'Better to keep your mouth shut and appear stupid than to open it and remove all doubt' is attributed to Mark Twain in *The Sayings of Mark Twain*, ed. James Munson (1992). It has also been ascribed to Abraham Lincoln in *The Golden Book* (November 1931). 'It is better to be silent and be thought a fool than to speak out and remove all doubt' is a proverb that has so far not been dated. The late Sir Denis Thatcher, husband of the former British Prime Minister, was fond of quoting this form.

Compare Proverbs 17:28: 'Even a fool, when he holdeth his peace, is counted wise: and he that shutteth his lips is esteemed a man of understanding.'

'If anyone mentioned patience, or the lack of it, one of my aunts used to say this' – Sylvia Dowling, Lancashire (1998):

> **Patience is a virtue**, virtue is a grace.
> Grace was a little girl who wouldn't wash her face

'Patience is a virtue' was a proverb by the 15th century. *Casson/Grenfell* has, rather:

> Patience is a virtue, virtue is a grace.
> Put them both together, and you get a pretty face.

Another version (known by 1960):

> Patience is a virtue, possess it if you can;
> Seldom found in woman and never in a man.

'When, as a small child, I was very energetic around her house, my grandmother would make use of this somewhat "lateral" saying: **"Remember – three much is too much, but two much is just enough"**. But once it sinks in, it does make sense' – Tony Alston, Enfield, Middlesex (2002).

you could ride bare-arsed to London on that 'Referring to a blunt knife' – *Wickenden*. 'My old nanny – who rejoiced in the name of Mary Anne Hannaford Pulleyblank – when given a blunt knife to use, would say in a strong Devon accent, "You could ride to London on this and not tear your breeches"' – Mrs Diana Barber, Kent (1995). *Casson/Grenfell* has: 'These knives are so blunt you could ride to Romford on them', and this is obviously a development of Swift's *Polite Conversation* (1738) version: 'Well, one may ride to *Rumford* upon this Knife, it is so blunt.' Why Romford, one wonders?

'In my family, York is the place to which to ride on blunt knives/scissors' – Veronica M. Brown, Wigston, Leicestershire (2002).

rules is rules A semi-proverbial saying. Peter Williams asked (2006) whether it was from Dickens. Apparently not. Patricia M. Guy proffered this from Ellis Parker Butler's famous story 'Pigs Is Pigs' (first published in *The American Magazine*, September 1905): '"Do as you loike, then!" shouted Flannery, "pay for thim an' take thim, or don't pay for thim and leave thim be. Rules is rules, Misther Morehouse, an' Mike Flannery's not goin' to be called down for breakin' of them".'

Then Mark English found a much earlier example – though with a significant change in the wording. This is from Charlotte M. Yonge's novel *The Clever Woman of the Family* (1865), in which one character says, 'But, Mrs Kelland, rules are rules.'

speak as you find *Apperson* finds a proverb 'Speak of a man as you find him' by 1875. 'He was a man incapable of repressing anything. "Speak what you feel," was [John] Osborne's byword, "not what you ought to say"' – John Heilpern, *A Patriot for Us*, Chap. 43 (2006).

As for 'Speak as you find, that's my motto': in a 1950s BBC radio series *Hello Playmates!* featuring Arthur Askey, this catchphrase was spoken not by him but by Nola Purvis (Pat Coombs), the daughter of the studio cleaner (Irene Handl). It was her smug excuse for the appalling insults she hurled. Perhaps she just meant, 'I say what I have to say according to circumstances.'

In 1955, *Hello Playmates!* won the *Daily Mail* Radio Award as the year's top show and the catchphrase was inscribed on the presentation silver microphone – which didn't go down too well with Askey, the show's star, who had never uttered it. The source for this information was Bob Monkhouse, who with Denis Goodwin wrote the show. Bob told me in May 1980, 'That [catchphrase] was a very big laugh for us. We didn't know why. We put it in because it amused Denis. Someone he knew, a relative, said it.'

'At the bottom of my prep. school daily menu was printed "Manners maketh man" and underneath that, the words, "**Talk quietly, eat slowly, and sit up!**" As a consequence, today, in my mid-fifties, I have permanently to repeat myself, am always the last to finish eating at dinner parties (irate stares from the impatient "scoffers" of this world, and my back is set rigidly in the vertical position' – Bryan Taylor, Liskeard, Cornwall (2001).

tell me the time, not how the watch works 'My parents had a range of differing phrases used for most occasions, like this one for those taking too long to get to the point in a story' – Matthew Hind, Buckinghamshire (2002).

'When I was called up into the navy in WW2, new recruits joined up at HMS Royal Arthur, which was really Butlin's holiday camp at Skegness. We had to parade for divisions (morning parade), sharp at seven thirty. I hurried up one morning with only a few seconds to spare. The elderly Chief Petty Officer growled, "You're late." "No, chief," I protested, pointing at the clock, "half a minute to go." He fixed me with a steely eye: "**Them as is keen gets fell in previous.**" This has become a regular catchphrase in our family' – Paul Diamond, Woodford Green, Essex (2001).

they don't open t'oven for one loaf 'A middle-aged mother to a young wife expecting her first baby, who had said that she would be happy to have only one child' – quoted in Richard Hoggart, *The Uses of Literacy* (1957).

In his memoir *Making an Exhibition of Myself* (1993), the theatre director Sir Peter Hall recalled that some of his mother's precepts 'induced alarm in a small boy' – like "**They're always out to get you**" and "**They'll get you if they can**". In later years she was much given to pronouncing these mantra grimly, usually after she had heard me sounding off on television or radio on censorship, or the teaching of Shakespeare, or the iniquities of the government's art policy … She became most anxious if I discussed politics. In her opinion, they would indeed then be out to get me. She was right in a sense: in the Thatcher years, they nearly did.'

'The notion, for instance, that waste is a sin, handed down from Victorian times and reinforced by the privations of the Depression and the two World Wars, is constantly reiterated in the proverbial saying, "**Waste not, want not**." This was used with trenchant effect apropos of children wanting food, for example' – *Widdowson*. The saying has been proverbial since the mid-16th century.

A saying of the grandmother of Pat Stimpson, Keston, Kent (2001) was:

> **A whistling woman and a crowing hen**
> **Is neither loved by God nor men.**

This was being discussed in *Notes & Queries* by 1850 with the second part '… are neither fit for God nor men'.

An even earlier version emphasizes, rather, the unluckiness of what is listed: 'A crooning cow, a crowing hen, and a whistling maid boded never luck to a house.'

'Cynicism towards the newspapers: A.P. Ryan supports my rough chronology of the change. He says that "**You can't believe what you**

read in the newspapers" became a current phrase after the First World War' – Richard Hoggart, *The Uses of Literacy* (1957).

you must suffer in order to be beautiful A nannyism, as in *Casson/Grenfell.* The origin of this statement has not been determined. It is usually regarded as a French saying: '*Il faut souffrir pour être belle*' – and that is how it is given as the title of a George du Maurier cartoon in *Punch* (29 May 1880). The caption explains: 'The scene depicted above is not so tragic as one might suppose. It merely represents that best of husbands, Jones, helping the lovely Mrs J. to divest herself of her jersey.'

The French phrase occurs earlier in a review in the *London Quarterly*, reprinted in *The Eclectic Magazine* (New York) (September to December 1847).

Chapter 11

I LIKE YOUR COMPANY, BUT ...

Sir Bill Cotton, the TV producer and executive – and son of bandleader Billy Cotton – recalled on Quote ... Unquote *(17 November 1998), that when a party went on too long, his mother would say to guests,* **"Here's your hat, what's your hurry?** *Also:* **'I like your company, but your hours don't suit.'** *Here is a selection of phrases and sayings on the subject of guests and hosts, manners and social niceties. By 'initial code', I mean the coded way of passing on advisory messages.*

as welcome as a fart in a spacesuit 'On the arrival of an unwanted guest' – Anonymous correspondent from an East Kent Women's Institute (2003).

'Some years ago, an arrogant and pushy home improvement salesman asked to view the back of our house. He was shown out over a patio where our pet geese had spent a long afternoon doing what geese do. On hearing my wife warn him to step carefully, my young daughter muttered, **"He'll blend in nicely."** This phrase has become a family euphemism for "What an unpleasant chap". If the comment is overheard by the subject, we feel reasonably safe it will be taken as a compliment' – Anonymous, Water End, Hertfordshire (1996).

both arms the same length This is said of someone who arrives *not* bearing a gift. Robin Wrote-Brown of Colchester (2003) told of something said by 'my wife's great aunt, from Oldham, who was convalescing in hospital. She complained of another relative who had visited her without taking a present, by saying, "And she came to see me **both arms the same length.**"'

'In Ireland in the 1950s, we used to say about anyone who didn't bring an expected present or contribution, **"One hand was as long as the other."** I think the saying was quite general' – Toni McCabe, Mitcham, Surrey (2003).

'My wife Pauline knows a very Northern phrase which her father-in-law used to say every time she visited with her children: **"Eh, Toots, tha's brought tha pigs to a bonny market"**' – Tony Eivers, Flint (2002). *Apperson* finds the expression 'He has brought his pigs to a fine (or fair)

market' going back to 1600. I am not sure what, if any, inference is contained in this remark. I assume it is complimentary.

June Hennessy of Lohitzun Oyhercq, France, wrote (1993), 'Whenever my grandmother opened the door to an unexpected visitor before she was properly dressed (but without a hair out of place), she always complained of being "**caught in my disbil**". It wasn't until I came to live in France that I realized she must have anglicized the word *déshabillée . . .*'

cold hands, warm heart A forgiving little phrase when shaking hands and finding the other person's to be cold. A proverb first recorded in 1903 – *ODP*.

he doesn't know pussy from a bull's foot 'My father used to say this when referring to someone who didn't know what they were talking about. Is this (a) attributable and (b) rude?' – Richard Paul-Jones, East Sussex (1998). To which the answer in both cases is no. 'My (Bedfordshire) mother always used to repeat a saying of her own mother's to denote someone's ignorance – "He/she doesn't know A from a bull's foot". In recent years I said to her, "Surely it must have been *hay*, that would make more sense, but she insisted her mother had always pronounced it A' – Faith Moulin, Somerset (2000).

Partridge/Slang has 'doesn't know a great A from a bull's foot' and 'does not know A from a battledore/windmill/the gable-end' (these last two versions known since 1401). There is also 'doesn't know B from a bull's foot' (1401), 'battledor' (1565) and 'broomstick' (undated). So we are definitely talking about the letter A rather than hay. I think all this means is that somebody cannot distinguish between the letter in a child's alphabet book and the object in question.

'A saying I recall is from an uncle who offered me the last slice of bread and butter, with the promise of a handsome husband, with £1,000 a year, if I ate it up. Then he'd utter the words, "**Don't say 'No', if you'd rather not!**"' – Mrs M.M. Lockyer, London SE9 (1998). See also A THOUSAND A YEAR (page 186).

don't thank me, thank the Duchess I don't know where this duchess came from, but I was given the expression by Bob Hart of Powys (2000). There is a precedent for referring to some unnamed duchess as a figure of benevolence or at least authority in the two sayings 'Ring up the Duchess!' and 'I must ring up the Duchess!' *Partridge/Catch Phrases* states that these sayings, 'applicable to the resolution of a doubt or to the solution of a problem', caught on for a while following their use in the play *Young England* (1935) by Walter Reynolds.

E.B.B. (eyes bigger than belly) Initial code, for a greedy person – reported by Janet M. Carr, Isle of Wight (1997).

When declining an offer of more food, my father (1910–89) would often say, 'No, thank you, I have had **an *excellent* sufficiency**.' I have also heard people say, '… I have had **an *ample* sufficiency**' – as in the second episode of the TV *Forsyte Saga* (1967) – but neither of these is quite right. Paul Beale's *Concise Dictionary of Slang and Unconventional*

English (1989) has the correct form, rather, as 'an **elegant sufficiency** . . . Jocular indication, mocking lower-middle-class gentility, that one has had enough to eat or drink, as "I've had an elegant sufficiency, ta!" since *c.* 1950.'

In truth, 'elegant sufficiency' is the commonest of the three versions. Mary B. Maggs, Conwy, drew my attention (1998) to the fact that it is, after all, a quotation: 'My paternal grandmother, who died in 1956 aged almost ninety, would not, I think, have acquired anything that was possibly slang – she tended to model herself on Queen Mary and made a very creditable job of it. I remember it from the 1930s. Later I traced it to James Thomson, *The Seasons,* "Spring" (1746): "An elegant sufficiency, content,/Retirement, rural quiet, friendship, books".'

Even if they don't know this provenance, most people know one or other version of the saying. 'I once heard two elderly ladies trying to piece together a much longer version of this, which went something like "I have had an elegant sufficiency of the appetising comestibles which you in your gracious hospitality so generously have provided", but I doubt if that is an accurate version as the only thing they could agree on was that it ended, "In other words – I'm full!"' – Sylvia Dowling, Lancashire (1998).

Indeed, there would seem to be other jokey and verbose variations. 'From Wakefield in the 1890s, an aunt would say, "I've had quantum sufficio, an elegant sufficiency, and if I have any more I shall bust"' – Miss D.F. Rayner, Surrey (1999). 'My mother would say, "I have had an elegant sufficiency. Any more would be an abundant superfluity"' – Lorna Cooper, Oxshott (1999).

'It has been suggested that "Ma'am, I've had elegant sufficiency – any more would be an indulgence of my exasperated appetite" was what Lord Palmerston replied to Queen Victoria' – Deirdre Lewis, London W11 (2000). Another version I have heard of this is: 'Adequacy is sufficiency, thank you. Any more would be an over-indulgence on the part of my already exasperated appetite.' 'My mother used to say, "I have had an excellent sufficiency and any more would be superfluous to my palate"' – S.A.F., East Sussex (2000). 'My Welsh grandmother always said on finishing a meal, "I have had an eloquent sufficiency, more would be superfluity and render that obnoxious of that which I have already partaken"' – Helen van Oostayen-Thomas (2003). "'I've had an elegant sufficiency of the delicacy and any more would be superfluous to my already satiated appetite"' – Valerie Pate, Loppington, Shropshire (2003). 'My grandfather, the late Alexander James Wells (1883–1967) had a much longer version: "Thank you, I have had an elegant sufficiency. A little more would be a great indulgence to an exaggerated appetite. Gastronomical satiety admonishes me that I have arrived at the utmost state of deglutition consistent with dietetic integrity." As a five-year-old, it made a great impression there for almost 60 years' – Dr Peter Borrows, Amersham, Buckinghamshire (2005).

'My father after a meal when offered "seconds" would say that he had "ample sufficiency of plenitude"' – Pat Murphy, Bolton, Lancashire (2005). 'My father (Jack Silver) when asked if he had enough to eat frequently replied, "Elephants and fishes eggs." When pressed, he explained it served for "an elegant sufficiency" – Marion Ellis, Lincolnshire (1996). 'On the subject of strange family sayings, my late father would say after a meal either that he had had "an *ample* sufficiency" or "that's enough, no more, as it's not so sweet now as it was before"' – John Harrison, East Sussex (1995). This last alludes to a line from the opening speech of Shakespeare's *Twelfth Night* (1600) – "'Tis not so sweet now as it was before.'

I have also been told of the phrase being used not at the table: 'My mother, Lilian Rose Rees, born 1901, would say, "I've had an elegant sufficiency" – [meaning] that's enough from you' – George Rees, Swansea (2001).

excuse stinkers A smokers' phrase from the 1920s/30s, when lighting up an inferior brand. As Robert Graves and Alan Hodge explain in *The Long Week-End* (1940), cigarettes made from Virginia tobacco were, at that time, considered by fashionable women to be a little vulgar.

A common catchphrase when offering them was 'I hope you don't mind; it's only a Virgin', or, more pointedly, 'Excuse stinkers'.

F.H.B. (family hold back)/ F.H.O. (family hold off)/ F.K.O. (family keep off) Initial code. Meaning that certain food in short supply is not to be eaten by members of the family when guests are present. Mentioned in Ian Hay's *Safety Match* (1911). Compare the opposite codes **M.I.K.** and **P.M.K.** (page 183).

Margaret Hines of Lymington, Hampshire, wrote (1993), 'My Granny was staying to look after the family while my Mother was confined for my birth. She had cooked fish for lunch and asked the cleaning lady to lay the tray for the patient. "Where are the fish-knives?" demanded the charlady. Granny replied that we had none and ordinary knives would do. The job was completed in tight-lipped silence. When she presented the tray to my mother, the charlady announced, "My sister's got a lovely house in Bedford. **Fish-knives an' all!**" Mother was somewhat puzzled by this until Granny related the earlier conversation and for ever afterwards we used "Fish-knives an' all!" to describe superior people.'

'In Norfolk, if someone thought you were staring at them, they'd say, **"Got yer eye full?"** (which sounded like "got yer rifle?")' – Mrs Monica Nash, Nottinghamshire (1995).

horses sweat, men perspire – and women merely glisten/glow A saying used to reprove someone who talks of 'sweating'. *Casson/Grenfell* (1972) lists it as a nanny's reprimand in the form 'Horses sweat, gentlemen perspire, but ladies only gently glow.' J.M. Cohen includes it in *More Comic and Curious Verse* (1956) as merely by Anon, in the form 'Here's a little proverb that you surely ought to know:/Horses sweat and men perspire, but ladies only glow'.

I was first alerted to the question of what a man should say when surprising a woman in the bath or with no clothes on when, in 1980, C.D'O. Gowan of Ulverston contributed a snippet of overheard conversation to *Quote . . . Unquote*. He said he had picked it up when a housemaster at Eton and he and his wife were walking round Agar's Plough there on 4 June: '. . . And as he'd had a long run down, he asked for the bathroom. When he was shown into it, he suddenly looked and there was his hostess in the bath. He couldn't think what was the correct thing to say, so he said, "You *are* looking well."'

In that same year, the story also appeared in a collection of after-dinner stories entitled *Pass the Port Again*, told by Sir Peter Mursell, about a plumber intruding upon 'my wife', similarly positioned.

But what does etiquette dictate that either of these men should have said? I decided to consult Douglas Sutherland, author of the *English Gentleman* series of books. He advised that the correct reply in that situation was: '**I beg your pardon, *sir!***'

This sounded much better, and I subsequently found confirmation of it when reading a 1932 novel, *Charming Manners* by John Michaelhouse (a pen name of the Revd Joseph McCulloch). In the story, a group of Oxford undergraduates happen upon half-a-dozen naked nymphs dancing in the sunlight on the banks of the River Cherwell. 'We all collapsed in the punt at once, there being no chance of saying, "Sorry, gentlemen" in the approved style.'

In François Truffaut's film *Baisers Volés* (1968), the character played by Delphine Seyrig says that she was taught the difference between tact and politeness – if a man surprises a naked lady in the bathroom, politeness is to say 'Sorry', tact is to say, 'Sorry, *sir.*'

The boot is on the other foot, so to speak, in a glancing comment from E.M. Forster's *A Room with a View* (1908): 'Mr Beebe [the clergyman] was not able to tell the ladies of his adventure at Modena, where the chambermaid burst in upon him in his bath, exclaiming cheerfully, "*Fa niente, sono vecchia*" [It doesn't matter, I'm an old woman].'

Mary Collins from Cowbridge, South Glamorgan (1977), said that her father, on meeting one of the opposite sex for the first time, would invariably inform her, '**I don't know your age, madam, but you don't look it**.' Mrs Collins added that every woman took it as a compliment.

if you can't behave nicely, don't behave at all Margaret R. Jackson of Chipping Campden, Gloucestershire, quoted (1994) the useful instruction given by a small hostess to a notoriously disruptive guest at a children's Christmas party. This anecdote would seem to have originated in a *Punch* cartoon, of which the idea has appeared at least twice. In the issue of 24 April 1897, Bernard Partridge drew one with the title 'An Admonition' and the caption: *Bridget:* 'Now then, Miss Effie, you must behave yourself properly, or not at all!' In the issue of 27 April 1932, a cartoon by George Belcher was captioned: *Indignant Young Lady:* 'If you can't behave properly, you'd better not behave at all.'

if you're as soon in my grave as you are in my seat, you won't be long after me 'From my grandmother when you sat in *her* chair' – Pat Stimpson, Keston, Kent (2001).

if your father had been a glazier, he'd have fitted you with windows What you say to someone standing between yourself and a source of light. Swift's *Polite Conversation* (1738) has the short version: 'I believe your Father was no Glazier', which Grose's *Dictionary of the Vulgar Tongue* (1788) glosses: 'If it is answered in the negative, the rejoinder is – I wish he was, that he might make a window through your body to enable us to see the fire or light.'

Compare the nannyism in *Casson/Grenfell:* 'You make a better door than window.'

let the dog see the rabbit 'Said to others when crowding around a fire' – Stella Richardson, Essex (1998). *Partridge/Catch Phrases* gives a less specific meaning – 'Get out of the way, get out of the light', from dog-track frequenters.

'My grandfather kept me quiet during family mealtimes when I was a child with the words, "**Let your meat stop your mouth**", advice which was apparently given to him by his own grandfather many years before' – Emma Hodgson, Co. Durham in a letter to *The Independent* (10 August 1994).

M.I.K. (more in kitchen) Initial code. In other words, 'Go ahead and eat it.' *Partridge/Slang* has this by 1939. M.S. Peebles, Glasgow (1999), recalled the variation **P.M.K. (plenty more in kitchen)**.

milk? [pronounced *'mil-uck'* on a rising inflection]. Adopted in many households from Drusilla (Hermione Gingold) making tea for her husband Edmond (Alfred Marks) in a feature called 'Mrs Doom's Diary' on the BBC radio show *Home at Eight* (first broadcast 21 April 1952).

According to *The Independent*'s obituary of the show's scriptwriter Sid Colin (28 December 1989): 'Sid ingeniously combined Mrs Dale with Charles Addams in a series of sketches ... [The Dooms] lived in a suburban castle with Fido, their pet alligator, and Trog, their giant speechless servant. At tea-time, people all over Britain were parroting the words that closed every Dooms sketch: **"Tea, Edmond?"** "Yes, thank you, dear – thank you." **"Mil-uck?"**'

When the sketches were included in another radio show, *Grande Gingold* (1955), the phrase became '**Tea, Gregory?** ... Milk?'

'A man renowned as a wit and raconteur often visited us and kept us in fits of laughter. But one day my mother and I found it hard to enjoy a long, hilarious anecdote over tea as a drip of honey on the narrator's chin slowly, slowly moved tie-wards. Thereafter, the family could always discreetly warn a member who had a similar disaster impending (rather like IT'S SNOWING IN PARIS/DOWN SOUTH page 106). **"Mr Dyson,"** we would murmur, and remedial action would instantly be taken' – Alison Adcock, Oxford (1998).

'My mother used to use an expression which sounds as if it ought to be a quotation. When she wanted, for example, an item of food passed to her, she would say, "**Pass the biscuits, M'randy.**" I wonder whether the source may be a film' – Stephen Lamely (2001).

Jim Bartlett found the answer. '"Pass the biscuits, Mirandy" was the title of a cartoon short released in 1943, in the series "Swing Symphony". The title came from a song by Spike Jones and his City Slickers, published the previous year.' The song was based, in turn, it seems, on the advertising jingle for "Pappy" O'Daniel's [American] radio show ("Please pass the biscuits, Pappy").'

already saucered and blowed 'Said by my late Uncle Percy who was a true Black-Countryman, living all his life in Tipton, when serving you with a cup of tea' – Marion Brennan, Trowbridge, Wiltshire (2001).

A variation on this description of tea that is ready to drink is 'brewed, saucered and blowed'.

The expression also seems to be known in the US: 'Have you ever heard the old Texas expression "saucered and blowed"? If a cowboy's coffee is too hot, he puts some in a saucer and blows on it. A cowboy will say to a friend, "Take mine, it's already saucered and blowed". Jim needs to get the energy bill saucered and blowed' – *The New Yorker* (9 January 1978).

'My Grandmother's favourite saying at the dinner table, when she only wanted a small portion, was "**a slightest suspicion**". No one ever asked why she said it but it still brings a laugh when all the family are together twenty-five years after her death' – Mrs W. Morton, Surrey (1996).

T.T.T. (tummy touching table) Initial code. This was either a parental instruction not to eat more or an indication that one was so full that one could not eat more. Recalled by the broadcaster Joan Bakewell, from her Stockport childhood, on *Quote . . . Unquote* (24 May 1994).

'"**T.P.T.**" (**tummy** *pushing* **table**) was well known in my family, and at College, in the late 1940s' — Jean Beattie, Bugbrooke, Northants (2003).

In 2001, Suzanne Hinton asked about an expression used by her mother (then in her eighties), in response to the slightest gift or good deed – 'Thank you, Mrs Loudborough-Goodbeam.' Joyce Rubin of American *Vogue* rightly surmised that this was a mishearing of Cole Porter's 1934 song '**Thank You So Much, Mrs Lowsborough-Goodby**', in which the narrator imagines, instead of the conventional thank-you note he had sent, an honest letter telling Mrs L-G what a miserable weekend he had actually spent at her house. Porter himself recorded the song, but it does not appear to have been used in any of his shows. It was found among the unused lyrics for *Anything Goes*.

think of all the poor starving people in Africa/China/India A nannyism. Wasn't it also advised that it was polite to leave a little food on the side of the plate 'for the starving in India' if not for 'Mr/Miss/Captain Manners'? Paul Beale in *Partridge/Catch Phrases*, commenting on the American expression 'Remember the starving Armenians', notes: 'The one used to exhort me as a child, late 1930s, to clear up my plate or to tackle something I found unpalatable was "Think of all the poor starving children in China!"'

As for 'When people are starving in India . . .', I am indebted to *The Complete Directory to Prime Time Network TV Shows* (1981) for the information that when a proposed us series called *B.A.D. Cats* crashed in 1980, Everett Chambers, its executive producer, said, 'We bought $40,000 worth of cars to smash up, and we never got a chance to smash them up. I think that's kind of immoral, $40,000 worth of cars to smash up when people are starving in India.'

The nearest expression in *Casson/Grenfell* is, 'Think of all the poor starving children who'd be grateful for that nice plain bread and butter.'

a thousand a year or a handsome husband Said when offering the last portion of food, last sandwich or last cake on a plate. Current in the 1950s, this saying now seems to promise rather slight remuneration for accepting the offer.

Iona Opie and Moira Tatem in *A Dictionary of Superstitions* (1992) find various benefits linked to taking the last piece of food on a plate. Their earliest is a 'Lancashire legend' recalled in 1873. From 1923, in Kent: 'The person who, uninvited, takes the last slice of bread and butter from the plate will die unmarried. But the person who takes the last slice upon invitation will have a handsome spouse and an income of thousands amounting to the number of people at the table.'

Sylvia Dowling, Lancashire (1998), wrote that in the 1950s it usually attracted the smart reply: 'I'll take the thousand a year and then I'll have my choice of handsome husbands.'

See also DON'T SAY 'NO' ... (page 176).

Chapter 12

AS LONG AS YOU'VE GOT YOUR HEALTH

On matters of health, clichéd phrases resound – and none more so than **"as long as you've got your health, that's the main thing"**, *as uttered in BBC TV,* Hancock, *'The Blood Donor' (23 June 1961). Some kind soul has now drawn my attention to this from Emerson's* Nature *(1836/49): 'How does Nature deify us with a few and cheap elements! Give me health and a day, and I will make the pomp of emperors ridiculous. The dawn is my Assyria; the sun-set and moon-rise my Paphos, and unimaginable realms of faerie; broad noon shall be my England of the senses and the understanding; the night shall be my Germany of mystic philosophy and dreams.' The corollary,* **if you haven't got your health, you haven't got anything,** *was current by the 1880s, at least.*

as right as rain Completely well and healthy – but also 'very right, proper, correct, in order'. A correspondent asked (2006), 'Considering that aside from its practical use to farmers and the like, all connotations of rain are negative, so how did this expression come about?' One explanation is, indeed, connected to this 'practical use', in that rain brings growth and is thus a good thing. Another theory is that the expression is a pun on the meaning of the word 'right', which is 'straight' and rain is sometimes said to be 'coming straight down'. I am not persuaded by this. The *OED2*'s earliest citation is from 1909, though *Apperson* finds the earlier '"Tes so right as rain, zir" zes I', from W. Raymond, *Love and the Quiet Life* (1894).

the best doctors in the world are Doctor Diet, Doctor Quiet and Doctor Merryman This nannyish sentiment goes back to Jonathan Swift, who included it among the clichés gently mocked in *Polite Conversation* (1738). Nay, even further: *Apperson* has a citation from 1558 and the idea may be found in a poem by Lidgate (1449).

Theatre people have a similar expression that reflects rather the curative powers of getting on with the job – 'Doctor Greasepaint/Doctor Theatre will cure me'. Both versions were quoted in obituaries for the actress Irene Handl in November 1987 as being favourite phrases of hers. They not only suggest that acting is a cure for ailments, but also imply that actors *have* to be well most of the time to perform their function. The actor Bernard Bresslaw told me in 1991 that his preference was for 'Doctor Footlights will cure me'.

The creation of an imaginary doctor's name can also be found in the nickname 'Doctor Brighton' for the healthy seaside resort.

Breathe deeply. Every lungful is worth a guinea in the bank of good health 'I have known this phrase for years but I don't have the remotest idea where it originated. To use the phrase, I would adopt a quite pompous tone when out walking with my step-children along a shoreline' – Tony Eivers, Flint (2002).

Mike Morgan-Finch was puzzled by the American armed forces' idiom **'to buy it/buy the farm/buy the ranch'** meaning 'to die/be killed'. How had it arisen? Robert L. Chapman in his *Dictionary of American Slang* (1987) suggests that it began with the earlier USAF term 'to buy a farm', meaning 'to crash' – 'probably from the expressed desire of wartime pilots to stop flying, buy a farm, and live peacefully'. I went with this and put it on the radio show. Then the floodgates of what I think of as 'popular folklore origins' opened: 'My understanding is that the saying originated in the earliest days of flying in the USA. The early aviators used farmland to land and take off. It was apparently an accepted convention that crops damaged by aircraft landing or taking off had to be paid for by the pilot. From this derived the phrase "buying the farm" or "he bought the farm", meaning the crash was so serious that they might as well buy the farm ... Tom Wolfe used this explanation in *The Right Stuff*' – D.D., Oxford. 'I have it on good authority from a friend of mine from Mississippi that the expression "bought the farm" goes back to the American Civil War or earlier. Apparently, unlike the British Army, who have difficulty obtaining life insurance, American soldiers who went into combat were given life insurance by the government. They were mostly from subsistence farms, so signing up was a good way out of their misery. If they were killed in combat, the money was sent to their families' – Nic Jamin. 'In the Second World War, GI insurance for death in action was $10,000 and said to be the cost of a mid-America (e.g. Iowa) farm' – Roberto Hoyle, Spain. 'The term refers not to WW2 fliers but to the fact that American farmers took out life insurance which would cover their mortgages – so when the farmer died, the farm loan was paid off. Thus, by dying, "he bought the farm"' – Julia Vitale, North Carolina. So, plenty of theories to choose from here.

'I was an asthmatic and my mother used to say to me during an attack when coughing and wheezing, **"Choke up, chicken, if it's only a bucketful it'll ease you"** – T.W. Tincombe, Norfolk (1996). 'My mother's family is from the West Midlands and it is customary when someone coughs to say (like "Bless you!", when someone sneezes), "Choke up, chicken; your mother was a duck!"' – Anon (2000). 'When my wife was a girl, if something "went down the wrong way" and made her cough, her father would say, "Choke up, chicken – it might be a watch"' – Ian Forsyth, Durham (2006).

Apperson has various 'choke up' phrases, from 1605 onwards. Swift's *Polite Conversation* (1738) has: 'Choke, chicken; there's more a-hatching.' See also COUGH IT UP (below).

a cold takes three days to come, is here three days, and takes three days to go From the folklore of health – no citations yet, just hearsay. Another version: 'A cold takes three days coming, three days at its worse, and three days to go away.'

cough it up – it might be a gold watch 'Said to someone having a coughing fit' – *Wickenden.* 'The father of an old girlfriend of mine always used to say, "Cough it up, it might be a gold watch", but followed it up, in his broad Dawley [Shropshire] accent, with "as big as an owd banjo!"' – Rod Anderson (2006). *Partridge/Catch Phrases* has '... could be a gold watch', from the early 20th century, as well as '... (even) if it's only a bucketful, it will ease you'. 'A saying from my maternal grandfather who died in the early 1960s: "Cough it up, it might be a piano'" – Ann Bamford, Cumbria (2006). Compare CHOKE UP CHICKEN (page 190).

a creaking gate hangs longest Commonly said of a (complaining) person in poor health who outlives an apparently healthier person. *Apperson* finds 'a creaking gate (or door) hangs long' by 1776. Other variants are: 'A creaking cart goes long on the wheels' (quoted as a common proverb in 1900) and 'Creaking carts go a long way.'

Mick Hawes of Eydon, Northamptonshire (2001), recounts the origin of one of his family's sayings: 'This was often said when referring to some friend, relative or vague acquaintance who had died some time before. The origin was supposed to be a lady in the small town who had nursed her father through his final illness. In the street, she would be asked, "How is your father today?" Sometimes the answer would be, "Oh, he is a little better today, thank you (for asking)." Another time it might be, "He's not quite so well today, thank you." Of course the routine continued until one day when someone who had not seen the lady for some time asked the familiar question. The answer was, **"He's dead now, thank you."**'

'After 'flu, for instance, upon inquiry as to how I am feeling, I find myself saying, "Better, thank you, but **I don't feel like knocking doors out of windows**" – an expression from my Durham/Northumberland roots, perhaps?' – J. Allum, Suffolk (1998).

'Whenever a member of the family has a minor physical accident (bump, bruise, cut finger, bee sting), my father says, "**Don't worry – you'll die before it kills you**." This also gets applied to food that his granddaughters think "tastes a bit funny"' – Ivor Hunt, Leeds (2002).

every cripple has his own way of walking 'A rather eccentric uncle lived with us for a while and if anyone queried his manner of doing anything, he always answered in this fashion' – Mrs Valentine Culmer, Hampshire (1996).

fit as a butcher's dog 'I found myself using this expression recently to express an opinion on someone's state of health' – Basil Frost (2002). *Partridge/Slang* has this, dating it '20th century'.

'When we children used to complain about feeling ill – wanting a day off school – my mother would say, "**Go and lie in the graveyard until God calls you!**"' – Patsy Howson, Herefordshire (1995).

'My grandmother, who was always full of arcane sayings, had a particular saying she used when children were ill. If they coughed or complained of a pain anywhere, she'd always coo this question indulgently, "**Have you got oopasooticks in your pretty cardigan?**"' – Jenny Webb (2002).

Curiously enough, *Partridge/Slang* has an entry for this under 'oopizootics, the', meaning 'an undiagnosed complaint' as remembered from about 1900. Then he quotes the chorus of a popular song from 1890:

> Father's got 'em, father's got 'em,
> He's got the ooperzootics on the brain,
> He's running round the houses,
> Without his shirt and trousis,
> Father's got 'em coming on again.

Plenty of variety in the spelling of the word.

On *Quote ... Unquote* (23 September 1994), the writer Antony Jay recalled that when his mother was about five she was told by a mischievous elder cousin that the cure for warts was to stand outside church on a Sunday and say, as the vicar came out, '**I wish me warts were up your bum!**' It is not known how effective this is as a remedy.

'My grandfather, a Lancashire coalminer, had a number of sayings that stick in my memory. Whenever I used to ask him how he was, he would reply, "I'll tell you what it is, lad, **I'll be glad when I've had enough**"' – Phil Lister, Ulverston, Cumbria (2003).

'My mother, who died recently aged 102, used to say (among *much* else), "**If you've got the health and strength to grumble, you're all right**"' – Miss Anna Zaharova, London E11 (1996).

in case I peg out in the night ... (and **in case I should 'appen summat**) 'Phrases for covering eventualities and said at the end of the working day' – Margaret Cooper, Melton Mowbray (2000).

it won't hurt – where there's no sense, there's no feeling 'Of a bump on the head' – Stella Richardson, Essex (1998).

'The phrase which my father (1892–1988) always quoted if he saw someone scratching at a spot or scab was, "Remember the words that our brave Nelson said, '**It'll never get well if you pick it**'" – said in a sort of sing-song rhythmic fashion as though they were words from a song or poem' – Douglas Linnington, Surrey (1998). This is included as a nannyism in *Casson/Grenfell*.

'My husband's mother used to say, "**It's not the cough that carries you off . . .**" and add, "**It's the coffin they carry you off in!**"' – Mrs M. Jones, West Midlands (1995). 'In my boyhood, my elderly uncle Ed from Essex, with whom I lived for several years just after the war, had a stock comment, "It wasn't the cough that carried him off, it was the coffin they carried him off in"' – Robert Priddy, Nesoddtangen, Norway (1998). 'Used whenever someone has a coughing fit' – Marian Horner, Cambridgeshire (1998). Iona and Peter Opie include this in *The Lore and Language of Schoolchildren* (1959) as a type of ghoulish catchphrase enjoyed by ten-year-olds.

But where does it come from? When I heard Billy Cotton's recording of Alan Breeze singing 'It Ain't the Cough' (written by 'Mann', about 1956), I made the assumption that this was based on some earlier song, but that it might lead us to the original. In time, it did. I obtained the music of a comic song called 'The Cough-Drop Shop' written by Leslie Sarony in 1932. It ends:

> When you get to the cough-drop shop,
> Remember when you're coughing,
> It's not the cough that carries you off,
> It's the coffin they carry you off in!

William Crowe, meanwhile, recalled very definitely hearing the last line in 1927, so perhaps both songs are borrowing from something even earlier.

'Eavesdroppings on the bus, late 1940s, that lingered: one woman telling another how much she had enjoyed seeing the film "The Force It Sayga"; and another, on her medical history, in a loud voice, "**It's not the womb, ducks – it's me chuubs.**" Several other sayings, as is probably so in many families, are private and perhaps rather cruel jokes against members of the family for some lapse in manners, taste or unselfishness' – Paul Beale (1994).

'I remember my mother (a Cockney woman) always quoted, "**(No. 9) Medicine and Duty**" whenever the number 9 was mentioned. As my house number is 9, I often think of this but have no idea what the expression meant' – Mrs H. Calver, Halesworth, Suffolk (2003).

I replied, 'I think your mother brought together two phrases from around the First World War. "No. 9" or "No. 9 King" was used to describe a medical officer in the army and was named after "No. 9", the standard purgative pill, given to all and sundry. Also "Number Nines" was a name given to prunes.

'As a result, "the doctor" became the cry when "No. 9" came up in the game of House (lotto). As for "Medicine and Duty", this was the standard medical prescription for treatment of a minor illness (in the army). It was also known as "Doctors Orders".'

Most of this information can be found in *Partridge/Slang*.

my dogs are barking Meaning 'I have sore feet'. John Moorley of Chippenham asked me to explain the origin of this expression (2001), while pointing out that, in the 1970s, there was an annual 40-mile charity walk from Keswick to Barrow in Furness and that those completing the distance received a certificate of membership of 'The Order of Barking Dogs'.

Partridge/Slang suggests that the expression was adopted from the US in the 1930s and that 'dogs that bite' became a British elaboration for 'sore feet' in the following decade. The explanation probably lies in Cockney rhyming slang, where 'dogs' is sometimes equated to 'feet' via 'dog's meat' rather than the more usual 'plates of meat'. In this way, the phrases 'barking dogs' or 'dogs that bite' become more understandable.

'One of the technicians at work, when asked how he was, always replied, "**Not so dusty, well-brushed**", though he never explained what it meant. I still use it after all these years when I'm asked how I am …' – Cyril S. Myers, Stokenchurch, Buckinghamshire (2002).

'My grandfather was William Drummond Paul, originally from the Black Isle but who worked in the cotton trade in Manchester. When someone was very ill and approaching death, he would refer to them as "**very ill in bed, on two chairs!**" Never, ever, heard this since, but a family saying' – Rosalind Furlong, Northumberland (2002).

'Said to a young wife ill in bed and feeling a bit sorry for herself: "**You'll last a man a lifetime with care**"' i.e. for sex and housework, presumably. Quoted in Richard Hoggart, *The Uses of Literacy* (1957).

Chapter 13

NO PLACE LIKE HOME

From the opera Clari, or, The Maid of Milan *(1823), written by the American actor and songwriter J.H. Payne (1791–1852), comes the song '***Home sweet home***'. And as if the title phrase were not sufficient, the song also contains that other great sentiment:*

> *'Mid pleasures and palaces though we may roam,*
> *Be it ever so humble,* **there's no place like home.**

This appears to build on the earlier proverb (1546), 'Home is home though it's never so homely.' An advertising slogan, quoted in 1982, was, 'Come to Jamaica, it's no place like home', which nicely plays upon the other, derogatory, view of home. In this chapter, we will also naturally include phrases about family life.

the cocks may crow but it's the hen that lays the egg An informal proverb uttered by Margaret Thatcher, when British Prime Minister, at a private dinner party in 1987 – according to Robert Skidelsky in *The Sunday Times*, Books (9 April 1989). On a London News Radio phone-in (December 1994), I was told, 'The cock does all the crowing but the hen lays all the eggs.' 'My grandmother's all-embracing put down of males: "He's a clever old cock, but he can't lay eggs"' – Margaret Rawles, Suffolk (2000). *Apperson* finds the obvious original, 'The cock crows but the hen goes', in use by 1659.

A most tantalizing query came from Joy Troughton (2002): 'Approaching home after a long family walk over Hampstead Heath, my father – long since dead – would say, "**Home at last, all dangers past, we hail the native village!**" Doesn't this sound familiar?' But it can't be because, as Pat Guy found, through more diligent googling than I was capable of, it comes from a completely unknown musical fairy tale in one act called *Creatures of Impulse*. The words are by W.S. Gilbert and the music (now lost) is by Alberto Randegger. It was first performed at the Court Theatre in London in 1871 and has barely been revived since. Amazingly the full libretto is available on the internet and here is Sergeant Klooque's song from fairly early on in the proceedings:

> At home at last all danger past
> I hail my native village.
> Farewell awhile to warlike style
> To battle and to pillage.
> Although no doubt in battle's rout
> My life, I'd rather spend it,
> When battles cease, a state of peace
> Has much to recommend it.
> No parade and no drill,
> I can do as I will.

I can eat, I can drink all the day.
I can sing, I can dance
With the daughters of France,
While her sons are at work, far away!

home, James, and don't spare the horses ... 'A phrase often used for many years in my family' – Jane Williamson, Angus (1998). This is indeed a catchphrase used jocularly, as if talking to a driver, telling someone to proceed or get a move on. It is from the title of a song (1934) by the American songwriter Fred Hillebrand, recorded by Elsie Carlisle in that year and by Hillebrand himself in 1935. The component 'Home, James!' had existed long before – in the works of Thackeray, for example.

it's all in the family A saying with the implication that there's no need to be over-punctilious or stand on ceremony, or fuss too much about obligations, because nobody outside the family is affected and those who are in the family will understand. For example, 'It's okay for me to borrow money or clothing from my sister without asking her first ... because it's all in the family.' Compare: 'We are all friends here!'

All in the Family was the title of the American TV version (1971–83) of the BBC's sitcom *Till Death Us Do Part*. The respective main characters were Archie Bunker and Alf Garnett, racists and bigots both. The phrase had a double meaning as the show's title: that Archie's rants would be mortifying if overheard by anyone outside of the family and that such wildly different types of people find themselves related to each other. There is not a trace of the phrase in the *OED2*. However, there is an 1874 citation 'all *outside* the family, tribe or nation were usually held as enemies', which may hint at the possible existence of an opposite construction.

The phrase occurs in Chap. 25 of James Fenimore Cooper, *The Pioneers* (1823): 'David says, in the Psalms – no, it was Solomon, but it was all in the family – Solomon said, there was a time for all things; and, in my humble opinion, a fishing party is not the moment for discussing important subjects.' Then there is Herman Melville, *Moby Dick*, Chap. 21 (1851) in which Elijah is trying to warn Ishmael and Queequeg against the *Pequod* and its captain: '"Morning to ye! morning to ye!" he rejoined, again moving off. "Oh! I was going to warn ye against – but never mind, never mind – it's all one, all in the family too; – sharp frost this morning, ain't it?"'

From Robert Louis Stevenson, *Catriona*, Chap. 9 (1893): 'It was old Lovat that managed the Lady Grange affair; if young Lovat is to handle yours, it'll be all in the family.' From Bret Harte, *A Ward of Colonel Starbottle's* (1903): '"Don't mind us, Colonel," said Judge Beeswinger, "it's all in the family here, you know! And – now I look at the girl – hang it all! she does favor you, old man. Ha! ha!"' From Jack London, *The Sea-Wolf*, Chap. 32 (1904): 'All hands went over the side, and there I was, marooned on my own vessel. It was Death's turn, and it's all in the family anyway.' All these citations – even the Stevenson – confirm a likely American origin for the phrase. It is hardly known elsewhere.

The expression '**keep it in the family**' means that outsiders are not allowed to share in anything that belongs to a family. For example, by employing relatives to do a job or task, it 'keeps it in the family'. Often the 'family' is not literal but may simply be some group or organization that is protective of its members. *Keep It in the Family* was the title of a British TV sitcom written by Brian Cooke in 1980–3. (This was later remade in the US as *Too Close for Comfort*). It is hard to say when the saying originated, but it is probably quite old. From this translation of Émile Zola's novel *Thérèse Raquin* (1867), it would appear there is an exact French equivalent: 'Madame Raquin, who would have wept to see a stranger kiss her son's widow, felt no objection to the idea of handing her over to the embraces of his former friend. She thought it was keeping it in the family, as the saying goes [*Elle pensait, comme on dit, que cela ne sortait pas de la famille*].'

let's go so that we can come home 'One of my aunts – a somewhat lugubrious woman with a strong sense of duty – would always say this when setting off on a visit from which there was little expectation of pleasure. In childhood I thought it slightly absurd. Fifty or so years on, I find myself saying exactly the same thing!' – Guinevere Ventress, Linton, Cambridgeshire (1995).

like mother used to make i.e. like home cooking and very acceptable. This expression seems to have acquired figurative quotation marks around it by the early years of the 20th century. It is of American origin and was soon used by advertisers as a form of slogan (compare the US pop song of the Second World War, 'Ma, I Miss Your Apple Pie').

'The kind mother used to make' was used as a slogan by New England Mincemeat around 1900. The American writer Vance Packard in *The Hidden Persuaders* (1957) records an example of the phrase's effectiveness when slightly altered: 'When the Mogen David wine people were seeking some way to add magic to their wine's sales appeal, they turned to motivation research via their agency. Psychiatrists and other probers listening to people talk at random about wine found that many related it to old family-centred or festive occasions. The campaign tied home and mother into the selling themes. One line was: "the good old days – the home sweet home wine – the wine that grandma used to make." As a result of these carefully "motivated" slogans, the sales of Mogen David doubled within a year.'

One of numerous advertising lines playing on assumptions about the goodness of home produce and the good old days was the advertisement

that proclaimed: 'Buck Wheat Cakes/Like mother used to bake –
$1.25/Like mother thought she made – $2.25.'

'When our family had all been out somewhere and we returned home,
my father always walked into the living room and said, "**No one's in
but the fire and it's out.**" He still does it now' – Eleanor Sloan (2002).

ours is a nice 'ouse ours is An ironic and possibly Cockney description
that *Partridge/Catch Phrases* dates from 1925 – the sort of argument a
respectable matron might advance to discourage any behaviour in her
home of which she might disapprove.

In fact, 'Ours Is a Nice House Ours Is' was the title of a song written
by Herbert Rule and Fred Holt (1921) and sung notably by Alfred Lester.
The spoken phrase was also popularized by the comedian Cyril Fletcher
(1913–2005) in radio shows from the 1930s onwards.

you treat this house like a hotel What parents inevitably end up saying
as their offspring grow up and linger in the nest. I know mine said it to
me, as I recorded in my book *The Joy of Clichés* (1984). Confirmed by
Mark Billingham, comedian and crime novelist, on *Quote ... Unquote*
(23 October 2006).

Chapter 14

TOGETHER LIKE A HORSE
AND CARRIAGE

Love, marriage, couples, courting, romance … all amorous human
life is here:

as He makes them, so He matches them Said of any rather odd-looking married couple. Doris Humphrey, Lincolnshire, wrote (1995), 'I had an aunt who had an apt and witty saying for every eventuality – sometimes rather sharp and not very kind, but always apt' – and this was one of them.

bread and butter! Phrase uttered when two people – who are a couple – walk along, come to an obstacle and separate to go round it. Mostly American usage, though a Russian origin has been suggested. Marian Bock remembered (2002) saying it in the 1960s: 'Approaching we would say, "Bread and butter" and rejoining hands on the other side of the obstacle we would say, "All good wishes come true." I was grown before I realized that my sisters were in the habit of *making* a wish in the interim.'

There is obviously a superstition involved, but why say 'bread and butter' (or 'salt and pepper', another version)? Is it because these are things that *belong together*? Apparently, the expression occurs in a number of Hollywood films of the 1930s/40s and also in *Hans Christian Andersen* (US 1952). One explanation is that, if you are walking with a friend and you each walk on a different side of a telephone pole or a street-sign pole, you will soon quarrel. To stave off the consequences, you have to say 'Bread and butter' or 'Salt and pepper.'

'My parents, both born in Victoria's reign, were engaged for seven years before my father could afford to marry. It was acceptable for an engaged couple to have evenings out together, but my mother's father, a prosperous tailor, objected to long farewells on the doorstep. If he thought the goodbyes had gone on too long, he would call out, "**Chalk your bobbins!**" Can you explain this admonition?' – Kathleen I. Barratt, Newcastle upon Tyne (2002). Well, *Partridge/Slang* has 'chalk your pull', meaning, 'hold on, steady on', as also '(that's the) end of the bobbin' for 'that's the end of it' (i.e. all the thread is wound off the bobbin), but the link, if any, escapes me.

cheek by jowl Meaning 'close together, side by side, in the closest intimacy' – because one's cheeks are indeed next to one's jowls. It is a quotation from Shakespeare's *A Midsummer Night's Dream* (III.ii): 'Follow? Nay, I'll go with thee, cheek by jowl' – but the phrase predates Shakespeare and was originally 'cheek by cheek'. Now also the name of a British theatre company – Cheek By Jowl – and chosen, as they explained, because it emphasizes the closeness of actors and audience that they aim for.

come up and see my etchings This nudging invitation from a man to a woman, as though he were an artist plotting to seduce her, was probably established by the 1920s, at least. A bit puzzling why he should choose 'etchings' rather than anything else, but there we are. The earliest citation to hand is by Dorothy Parker from *The New Yorker* (25 July 1931): 'Come on down to my apartment – I want to show you some remarkably fine etchings I just bought.' There is also a later James Thurber cartoon of a man and a woman in a hotel lobby, to which the caption is: 'You wait here and I'll bring the etchings down.'

Compare the similar invitation to have sex contained in '**Come and have a look at my photograph album/stamp collection.**' It apparently passed by Eric Partridge and Paul Beale completely, but Jaap Engelsmaan in Amsterdam spotted this in Somerset Maugham's *Cakes and Ale*, Chap. 26 (1930), Rosie speaking:

> 'When we'd finished our supper Harry said: "Well, what about it?"
> '"What about what?" I said.

'There wasn't any dancing in those days and there was nowhere to go.
'"What about coming round to my flat and having a look at my
    photograph album?" said Harry.
'"I don't mind if I do," I said.
'He had a little bit of a flat in the Charing Cross Road, just two
    rooms and a bath and a kitchenette, and we drove round there,
    and I stayed the night.'

It has also been noted that in performing '(Have Some) Madeira,
M'Dear' in *At the Drop of a Hat* (early 1960s), Michael Flanders sang,
'He had slyly inveigled her up to his flat/To view his collection of
stamps' – sometimes adding, 'All unperforated – ha ha ha!'

'When I was a young girl going to parties, my mother always gave the
order, "In at ten o'clock, my girl." Should I be only a couple of minutes
late, she would say, "If you keep this late homecoming up, **you'll be
coming home with a belly full**." Of course, I took no notice at the
time. It was not until I was much older and well married that I realized
what she was meaning and it really shocked me to think she thought
such thoughts!' – Patricia Sheils, Old Colwyn, Clwyd (2003).

Trevor Kirk, K.A. Macleod Lewison and Sydney Treadgold were just
some of those who recalled versions of the joke '**Getting married and
not pregnant – that's posh!**' Kenneth Pearson dates this one to 1956:
'I hear your Myfanwy's getting married, Mrs Jones.' 'Yes, she is, Mrs
Evans.' 'Oh, I didn't know she was pregnant.' 'She isn't pregnant!'
'Oh, getting married and not pregnant – there's posh for you!'
    The characters and setting are invariably Welsh. So, just a traditional
Welsh tale, methinks. Marian Bock found an elaborate telling of it in
a 1999 issue of Merseyside Mountaineering Club's *Journal*. When

contacted, Fred Smith, who wrote it up, dated the anecdote to 'the late 1940s'.

An appearance was also suggested in Bryan Forbes's screenplay for *Only Two Can Play* (1962) – where many a cliché of Welsh life is given an airing – but was not found in it.

a good woman will draw a man further than gunpowder would blow him 'My father-in-law used to say this' – Violet Cowley, Buckinghamshire (1995).

Compare: 'Crumpet can pull you further than gunpowder can blow you' – a father's advice from a London News Radio phone-in (December 1994).

I'd rather have a good meal any day 'A debunking comment on a woman whose physical attractions are all too noticeable' – quoted in Richard Hoggart, *The Uses of Literacy* (1957). One might compare the much-repeated observation on sex by the singer Boy George: 'I'd rather have a cup of tea than go to bed with someone – any day', a remark variously expressed since about 1983.

According to Tennyson's 'Locksley Hall' (1842), '**In the Spring a young man's fancy/**Lightly turns to thoughts of love', but in popular use, 'The variation I have felt even more relevant is: "In the Spring a young man's fancy lightly turns to thoughts of what he's been thinking about all Winter"' – Owen Friend, Torrington, North Devon (1996). In fact, this revision occurs in a couple of films: Cary Grant says it in *The Awful Truth* (US 1937) and Zachary Scott reprises the line in *Mildred Pierce* (US 1945).

it's nourishment I want, not punishment 'Said by a Lancastrian woman in her eighties, when asked why she had not remarried' – according to the historian Michael Wood on *Quote… Unquote* (13 July 1985). Compare KEEP YOUR HAND ON YOUR HA'PENNY (page 116).

An informal proverb (or, possibly, just a once-only utterance) is to be found in Arnold Bennett, *The Journals* (1971): 'Thursday, 10 August [1899] – I have just remembered a saying of Mrs Drummer, our new housekeeper at Witley. She said to me: "There's a lot of old maids in the village, sir, as wants men. There was three of 'em after a curate as we had here, a very nice young gentleman he was, sir. No matter how often the church was opened those women would be there, sir, even if it was five times a day. **It's a sign of a hard winter, sir, when the hay begins to run after the horse**.'

Compare these similar proverbs from John Ray's collection (1678): 'It's time to set when the oven comes to the dough' and 'It's time to yoke when the cart comes to the caples [horses].'

'During World War 2, my cousin acquired a soldier pen friend who always ended his letters, to our great delight, "**Keep hopping and smilling**" [presumably he intended to put 'keep hoping and smiling']. Sad to say, no romance blossomed between them as she felt his spelling was such a passion-killer. However, his cheerful advice has become a real family motto and when we're feeling a bit sorry for ourselves, we have only to remember those wise words and we're "hopping and smilling" all over the place' – Jean Mallinson, Harwich (1999).

she married straight out of the schoolroom Meaning, 'She married at
a very young age, as though straight after school' – and perhaps with the
implication that she had to. 'Louisa, of course, was never any trouble,
she had a nicer character and then she married straight out of the
schoolroom' – Nancy Mitford, *Love in a Cold Climate*, Chap. 8 (1949).

'[I] was mildly excited by their purple blazers, shirts and ties, grey
flannel skirts and black woollen stockings and would sometimes murmur
with wistful lasciviousness a phrase I'd heard used by great aunts when
I was a small boy – "She married straight out of the school room"'
– George Melly, *Rum, Bum and Concertina*, Chap. 2 (1977).

my old Dutch My wife.

> We've been together now for forty years ...
> And it don't seem a day too much ...

is the chorus of the song 'My Old Dutch' written by Albert Chevalier
and his brother Auguste (pen-name Charles Ingle) and published in 1911.

However, in the Museum of London's substantial music-hall section,
there are Albert Chevalier's scribbled notes for the song dating back to
1892, in which year it was first performed at the Alhambra, Brighton.

It goes on:

> There ain't a lady livin' in the land
> As I'd 'swop' for my dear old Dutch.

It was his most successful song. He died in 1923.

But why 'Dutch'? It is thought this has to do with the resemblance of
the wife's face to an old Dutch clock – and nothing to do with the
rhyming slang, 'Duchess of Fife' – 'wife'.

never chase girls or buses – there will (always) be another one coming along soon *Partridge/Catch Phrases* dates this from the 1920s and derives it from the early US version with 'streetcars' instead of 'buses'. Slightly later in the UK.

The earliest citation so far found is: 'Once he was heard to say: "No need to fuss over any girl; let the girls fuss after me. Are they not like London 'buses: one goes, another comes"' – George Huddleston, *The White Fakir: A Tale of the Mystical East* (1932).

Compare this allusion to the saying by Derick Heathcoat-Amory when British Chancellor of the Exchequer (1958–60): 'There are three things not worth running for – a bus, a woman or a new economic panacea; if you wait a bit another one will come along.'

Talking of London buses, there is also, of course, the saying that '**you don't see any for ages and then three come along at once**'. 'Prefab apartment buildings are a bit like London buses: you don't see any for a couple of decades and then three come along at once' – *Icon* Magazine (June 2003).

one wedding begets/breeds/brings on another A proverbial superstition known since 1634. 'I am glad you are no enemy to matrimony however. Did you ever hear the old song, "Going to one wedding brings on another?"' – Jane Austen, *Northanger Abbey*, Chap. 15 (1818). Compare: **one funeral makes many**, a proverb known since 1894.

the partner of one's joys and sorrows A term for one's spouse (usually) and as such a more or less direct quotation from Charles Dickens, *David Copperfield*, Chap. 42 (1849–50). In a letter to David, Mrs Micawber refers somewhat archly to herself, first as 'the bosom of affection – I allude to his wife' and then to 'the partner of his joys and sorrows – I again allude to his wife'.

Dickens may, however, have been using an already existing, if looser, formula. Earlier, Sir Walter Scott, in *The Talisman,* Chap. 6 (1825) has: 'The Almighty, who gave the dog to be companion of our pleasures and our toils …' and in Motteux's 1703 translation of *Don Quixote,* Sancho Panza refers to his horse Dapple as 'my faithful companion, my friend, and fellow-sharer in my toils and miseries'.

A later use: in P.G. Wodehouse, *Ring for Jeeves,* Chap. 9 (1953), Rory refers to Monica (to whom he is indeed married) as 'my old partner of joys and sorrows'.

a penny bun costs twopence when you have a woman with you 'This was my father-in-law's advice to my husband when we started courting' – Mrs Rita M. Kirton, West Yorkshire (1995).

Peter, Peter, pumpkin eater *The Pumpkin Eater* is the title of a novel by Penelope Mortimer. It was published in 1962 and describes the breakdown of a woman with many children and the disintegration of her marriage to an impossible husband, though quite what all this has to do with eating pumpkins is not immediately obvious.

However, it is derived from a nursery rhyme – though what children would make of it, I don't know:

> Peter, Peter, pumpkin eater,
> Had a wife and couldn't keep her.
> He put her in a pumpkin shell
> And there he kept her very well.

This was known by 1825 but what does it mean? Susan Smith of Lichfield wrote (2005), 'Isn't it a pun on the word "keep"? In the first instance, Peter can't "keep" his wife (i.e. afford her). In the second, he puts her in the pumpkin shell, where he "keeps" (i.e. imprisons) her very well.'

At the same time, Margaret Campbell reminded us of another sad rhyme about a failed marriage:

> Eaper, weeper
> Chimbley Sweeper,
> Had a wife and
> Couldn't keep 'er.
>
> Had anuverr,
> Didn't love 'er,
> Up the chimbley
> 'E did shove 'er.'

'My great grandmother's saying – her son had an admirer who used to walk past the cottage where they lived. His brothers and sisters would tease him that "Mary was looking in" to see if she could see him. His mother would sarcastically remark from the armchair, "**She may look in, but she will never look out**." Consequently, he remained a bachelor all his life!' – Ann Dalton (2000).

a slice off a cut loaf is never missed In other words, it doesn't matter a woman having a bit on the side once she's taken the plunge and got married. In her autobiography *Billie Whitelaw: Who He?* (1995), the actress recounts how her mother drew her aside when she was about to get married for the first time and told her to remember this bit of advice. 'After forty years I'm still trying to work out what she meant.'

Well, I took it upon myself to tell her not so long ago ... One has to say that it was an extraordinary thing for a mother to say on such an occasion. But it is a very old saying indeed. *Apperson* has it as, 'It is safe taking a shive [= slice] of a cut loaf' and traces it back to Shakespeare, *Titus Andronicus* (II.i.87):

> What, man! more water glideth by the mill
> Than wots the miller of; and easy it is
> Of a cut loaf to steal a shive, we know.

Partridge/Slang has it that 'to take a slice' means 'to intrigue, particularly with a married woman'.

'"A slice off a cut cake is never missed" (on the easy sexual habits of some married women)' – quoted in Richard Hoggart, *The Uses of Literacy* (1957).

something old, something new, something borrowed, something blue This superstitious phrase listing the traditional components of a bride's wedding apparel does not seem to have been recorded before 1883, though some of the individual parts are certainly older. Blueness expressing trueness is mentioned by Ben Jonson in *Cynthia's Revels* (1601) and by Chaucer (in about 1390).

Walter Redfern, *Clichés and Coinages* (1989), simply calls the expression 'a motto for brides, stand-up comedians, and many writers'.

that's the worst of these cheap husbands 'My mother always made this joke whenever things went wrong' – Bee Lancaster, Essex (1995).

'I recall a particular saying of my Mother's which I have never heard voiced by anyone else. If ever she met up with a couple of rather unattractive appearance – i.e. husband and wife or newly engaged pair – she would invariably say with a resigned air – "Oh, well – **they'd spoil another pair**"' – Margaret Baker, Wolverhampton, West Midlands (1992).

'When people commented adversely about a married couple, my grandfather would say, "Leave 'em alone – they'd have spoilt two good couples"' – Graham Whitehead, Aughton, Lancashire (1997). 'An older lady when hearing that two people, both of unprepossessing appearance, were engaged to be married, was heard to say, "Well, they won't spoil two homes!"' – David Hine, Temple, Buckinghamshire (1998).

'My grandfather, a village blacksmith and farrier ... was much given to making comments on people generally, and the one he would make on ill-favoured couples, was, "Well, at least it's not spoiling two households"' – R. Craggs, Hampshire (1998).

Compare the illustrious remark that Samuel Butler made about Thomas and Jane Carlyle (in a letter to Miss E.M.A. Savage, on 21 November 1884): 'It was very good of God to let Carlyle and Mrs Carlyle marry one another and so make only two people miserable instead of four ...'

tinned salmon for tea 'This was sometimes felt to be an extravagance: "They're bringing t'salmon out for 'im now" was a phrase used to indicate that a suitor had been accepted by the parents' – Richard Hoggart, *The Uses of Literacy* (1957).

today's my daughter's wedding day ... 'My wife is unable to find the origin of this quote' – Ian Maillie, Bothwell, Lanarkshire (1999):

> A thousand pounds I'll give away
> To the man who weds my daughter.

> On second thoughts, I deem it best
> To keep my money in the old oak chest.

'I remember my dad quoting a different version of this' – Sue Wood (2002):

> Today it is my wedding day
> Ten thousand pounds I'll give away.
> On second thought, I think it best
> To put it back in the old oak chest.

'My father (who died over 30 years ago) used this saying. I have done my best to try and locate its origins but have failed miserably!

> Tomorrow is another day
> £1,000 I'll give away.

'But mutual friends of my father's say it went differently':

> Tomorrow's my daughter's wedding day
> £1,000 I'll give away.

– Mrs E.Y. Rawles, Chandler's Ford, Hampshire (2004).

The best answer I can give to these variations on the same puzzle is that the following has been found on a 'British Army Marching Chants' website: 'Before it is lost to posterity, I remember the following still in use in 1947. It was chanted rather than sung':

Chanter: Today's my daughter's wedding day. £10,000 I'll give away.
Chorus: Hooray! Hooray!
Chanter: On second thoughts I think it best
To keep it in the old oak chest.
Chorus: Boo! Miserable bastard etc etc.

Chapter 15

I'VE SEEN BETTER LEGS ON TABLES ...

The chapter heading here comes from a damning comment reported to me by Stella Richardson (1998). There are plenty more on physical characteristics – and here they are:

as ugly as sin Very ugly. From Sir Walter Scott, *Kenilworth*, Chap. 10 (1821): 'Though I am as ugly as sin, I would not have you think me an ass.' The 'as sin' construction can also be applied elsewhere, as in **guilty as sin**, etc. *Guilty As Sin* was the title of a film (US 1993). Perhaps the comparison is a euphemism for '… as the devil'. Compare AS MISERABLE AS (page 238).

'My mother, speaking of someone she didn't like, would say, **"I know he can't help his looks, but he could stop in"**' – Mrs Margaret Wilson, Kendal, Cumbria (1996).

Compare the story told by Abraham Lincoln: 'I feel like I once did when I met a woman riding on horseback in the wood. As I stopped to let her pass, she also stopped and looked at me intently, and said, "I do believe you are the ugliest man I ever saw." Said I, "Madam, you are probably right, but I can't help it." "No," said she, "you can't help it, but you might stay at home"' – quoted in *Abraham Lincoln by Some Men Who Knew Him*, ed. Paul M. Angle (1950).

a face like a bulldog chewing a wasp 'From my ex's family … about an angry or frowning person' – Ann Bamford, Cumbria (2006).

'My grandmother had a saying which always had our family wondering where on earth it had originated. My father recalls that it was only ever Nanna who used the phrase, never my Grandad. If ever she met or saw someone she didn't like, she would say, **"He's got a face like a Dutchman's arse – turned inside out and well whitewashed"**' – Linda Dillon, Sevenoaks (2001).

Compare: '"You have **a face like a farthing kite with a church**

painted on it" – said by my grandmother to me and my brothers whenever we had the sulks' – Isabel Pettifer, Faversham, Kent (2005). And:

'If you pulled a face, my mother would say, "**You've a face like a smacked bottom**"' – Gervase Phinn, former schools inspector turned best-selling storyteller (2006).

'My mother would describe a person with a miserable expression as "having **a face like a yard of pump water**"' – Robert Stokes, Surrey (1997). *Partridge/Slang* has this as 'plain as a yard of pump-water', meaning 'very plain', by 1890. *Apperson* has 'straight as a yard o' pump water' (often said of a tall, lanky girl) as from Cheshire in 1886. *Casson/Grenfell* has, rather, 'Your *hair* is as straight as a yard of pump water.'

that face would stop a clock Remembered by Stella Richardson, Essex (1998). *Partridge/Catch Phrases* gives a date of 1890 for this and rather suggests that it would be applied only to a female.

fat, fair and forty An alliterative phrase of some antiquity. 'Fat, fair and forty were all the toast of the young men' – John O'Keeffe, *The Irish Mimic* (or *Irish Minnie*), Act 2 Sc. 3 (1795); '"Fat, fair, and forty," said Mr Winterblossom; "that's all I know of her – a mercantile person"' – Walter Scott, *St Ronan's Well*, Chap. 7 (1823); '[A Frenchwoman] remembered an anecdote of George the Fourth [and one of his mistresses] which had led to a phrase, now passed into a proverb, always pleasantly recalled by beauties of a certain age. "Faat, farre, and forté"' – Fanny Trollope, *Hargrave* (1843).

'My mother, on seeing someone rather overladen with jewellery, would comment, "**She's got it all on in case of fire ...**"' – Hazel E. Simmons, London N20 (1998).

got up like a May horse – Stella Richardson, Essex (1998). A May horse was presumably a hobby horse of some sort. Thus, presumably, the implication is that the person so described is gaudily dressed or overdressed.

her suet dumplings are boiling over 'On a woman of ample proportions wearing a low-cut dress' – reported by relatives of Judith Mercalf, Newcastle, who said it (2000).

'When talking to someone who seemed particularly thick or who answered when not being directly addressed, my father would say, "**I am speaking to the butcher, not the block.**" Said, I may say, in a very good-natured way' – Celia Miller, Essex (1995).

'People will remember the rather silly, very small hats with veils that were all the rage in the late 1940s. They were made popular by Joan Crawford and other film stars. My mother saw my sister in one such hat and exclaimed, "Just look at that hat, it **looks like a tomtit on a round of beef**"' – Alan Spackman (2004).

This is quite well recorded. *Casson/Grenfell* has it, as does *Partridge/Slang*, which glosses it as a children's catchphrase 'shouted after someone wearing a cap, or a hat, too small; also used of anything small on anything large, e.g. of a lonely cottage on a hill.' Partridge, however, gives it as 'Tom Tit'.

looks like a sack of spuds tied up ugly 'Said of someone not dressed neatly' – Tony Malin, Blandford Forum (2003).

'According to my mother, a large mouth was "**like a parish oven**"' – Mrs Jean Wigget, Kent (1995).

like a streak of tap water dressed up 'Of a thin man' – Stella Richardson, Essex (1998). Compare FACE LIKE A (page 220–21).

more hair in his ears than he's got on his head A common enough observation. It occurs, for example, in the BBC radio show *Round the Horne* (2 May 1965).

Compare: 'I have very sparse hair. My four-year-old grandson, Ben, made this comment when standing behind my chair: "Gampy, why do you only have a moustache on the back of your head?"' – Paul Rubinstein, East Yorkshire (2002).

Compare also how Stella C. Fry of London NW3 (1997) overheard her four-year-old grandson, who was standing on his head, ask his grandfather, 'Grandpa, why does the hair from your head grow out of your nose?'

'My wife's Bedfordshire grandma used to say of someone, "**She had a mouth all mimped up like a duck's bottom**"' – Paul Thompson, Scone (2004). I'm not sure where 'mimped up' comes from – *OED2* has it by the 18th century – but it obviously means 'pursed' and ... well, one gets the picture.

mutton dressed as lamb Phrase used to describe something old got up to look like something younger – most often a woman wearing clothes that are ridiculously and noticeably too young for her. Since the late 19th century.

no oil painting Phrase for an unattractive woman (rarely of a man). Possibly dating from the 1930s – included, for example, in McConville & Shearlaw's *Slanguage* (1984).

In 2006, a correspondent who had been watching a TV adaptation of *Jane Eyre* wrote, 'The heroine is indicated as being "plain". Is this in fact the origin of the term "**Plain Jane**", meaning an unattractive, very ordinary female not likely to appeal to the desire of men and the envy of women?'

Well, while Jane Eyre, as narrator, makes no bones about her plainness – at one point she describes a 'Portrait of a Governess, disconnected, poor, and plain' – I doubt whether she gave rise to the phrase, of which there is no record anyway before 1912 (Charlotte Brontë's novel was published in 1847).

But, interestingly, when Compton Mackenzie used it in Chap. 2 of his novel *Carnival* (1912), he gave a fuller version: 'She sha'n't be a **Plain Jane and No Nonsense**, with her hair screwed back like a broom, but she shall be Jenny, sweet and handsome, with lips made for kissing and eyes that will sparkle and shine.' The capitalization of 'Plain Jane and No Nonsense' suggests an established phrase but also one conveying the idea that, although the female in question is plain-looking, she is reliable and capable.

silver threads among the gold What you call it when you find white or grey hairs among what you started out with ... It comes from Eben Rexford's song (about 1900) with the phrase as title:

> Darling, I am growing old,
> Silver threads among the gold
> Shine upon my brow today;
> Life is fading fast away.

skinny malinky long legs, big banana feet 'My grandmother used this saying to me and made me cringe; my mother said it to my daughter and made *her* cringe; and I now find myself saying it to my own grand-daughter to the same effect. Is this a quotation from anything? I have enormous feet and always felt this remark was directed at me personally. I would love to learn otherwise' – Karol Jury (2006).

The rhyme of which this is but the first line seems to have come out of Scotland, probably during the first half of the 20th century:

> Skinny malinkey long legs
> Big banana feet
> Went tae the pic-shurs
> Couldnae find a seat.
> When the pic-shur startit
> Skinny malinkey fartit.
> Skinny malinkey long legs
> Big banana feet!

'My Scottish mother's version was':

> Skinny ma linkie longlegs, big banana feet,
> Oh Mr. Thingameejig, you think you're awful neat.

– Janice Ure (2006).

'My mother's (Glasgow) version of the rhyme, on which I was brought up, was:

> Skinny-malinky longlegs, umbe-rella feet,
> Dip your nose in mustard and wipe it on your feet.

'I have always assumed "malinky" comes from the Russian diminutive for (I think) "small"' – John Campbell (2006).

'Growing up in 60s Dublin we learnt a different version:

> Skinney malinks malodion [pronounced *malogin*]
> Legs umbrella feet,
> Went to the pictures
> And couldn't get a seat.
> When the picture started
> Skinney malinks farted
> Skinney malinks malodion
> Legs umbrella feet.

'This was passed on to us by my Da, who learnt it in 1920s Kildare. Oh, by the way, a malodion (malogin) is a squeeze box' – Denis Begley (Jnr), Gloucester (2006).

In 1975, the Glasgow-born comedian Billy Connolly gave the title *Big Banana Feet* to a show at the London Palladium. However, 'skinny malink' may not be of Scottish origin. According to *Partridge/Slang*, it is a variation of the English 'skilamalink', originally meaning 'secret/ shady' but which as 'skinamalink' became a derisory term for anyone unusually skinny or undersized.

so thin, she looks like a matchstick with the wood shaved off
'On thinness' – *Wickenden*. In *The Lore and Language of Schoolchildren* (1959), Iona and Peter Opie record the similar expression for a skinny person: 'He's as fat as a matchstick with the wood shaved off.'

as though dragged through a hedge backwards Looking extremely dishevelled. Date of origin unknown. '"You look as if you'd been drawn through a quickset hedge backward," remarked the head gardener's wife one day when Laura was more than usually dishevelled' – Flora Thompson, *Lark Rise to Candleford*, Chap. 38 (1945).

'"You are a man of very wide literary cognisance. Have you ever encountered the expression, 'It was like being pulled through a hedge, backwards'?" – "Oh, yes, indeed ... very ... very racy"' – Henry Reed, BBC radio play *A Hedge Backwards* (29 February 1956).

Chapter 16

HAPPY AS A PIG WITH A SIDE POCKET

Tony Holroyd, Preston (2001), told me, 'My mother has a multitude of sayings but **"as happy as a pig with a side pocket"** *is my favourite, and possibly the most obscure.' Indeed. I think it may be a misquotation of 'as awkward as a pig with side pockets' (see page 236) but it gives one plenty of scope for speculation. Presumably, if the pig did have a side pocket it would be able to store yet more food in it for later consumption ... See also page 236 for more on the 'side pocket' front. Anyway, the theme now is contentment, happiness and — in one very popular phrase —* not *happiness.*

a good time was had by all When the poet Stevie Smith entitled
a collection of her poems *A Good Time Was Had By All* (1937), Eric
Partridge asked her where she had taken the phrase from. She replied:
from parish magazines, where reports of church picnics or social
evenings invariably end with the phrase.

'We have a mother known for her gems. She always insisted that so long
as my father had his pint, pipe and piano, he was **"happy as a skylight"'**
– Alison Rosenberg, London N10 (1995).

'An old lady friend of mine, now in her eighties, whenever she is happy,
which is often, comes out with the expression, **"I wouldn't call the
Queen my aunty."** She admits that she had amended this saying and
that when she was a little girl in Plymouth, Devon, they used to say, "I
wouldn't call the King my uncle" (presumably George V)' – J.A. Smith,
Chatham, Kent (2003).

'My father-in-law used to make a bizarre quotation if one was
presented with a good and usually generous helping of food. "If you
get outside that you won't call the king your uncle"' – Lucy Melrose
(2004).

This certainly seems to be an established saying – *Partridge/Catch
Phrases* has it by 1977 as an 'expression of contentment' in the form
'I wouldn't call the Queen my aunt'. I can't quite see the reason for
putting it like this ...

I'm chuffed to little apples Meaning 'I'm pleased' – reported by Alison
Emmett, London WC1 (1995), and several others. 'Chuffed' is famously
a Janus word, having two opposite meanings, either 'pleased' or

'displeased', according to context. *Partridge/Slang* does not have this precise example, but Paul Beale inserted 'chuffed to (little) naffy [NAAFI]-breaks' from the 1950s/60s.

not a happy bunny A popular comment on a person's miserable state. Remembered by some from the 1960s/70s, though the earliest citation found is only 1991. Possibly of American origin. 'After being led away in handcuffs for speaking out at a shareholders' meeting, Nigel Watts is not a happy bunny' – *The Sunday Times* (7 November 1993).

Maybe alluding to a children's story or to the 'Happy Bunny' character in Energizer battery advertisements whose battery lasted longer than its competitors?

Tony Percy, a Brit in the US, commented (2005), 'Over here, "**not a happy camper**" is much more in use.'

Compare an allusion from Terry Pratchett, *Equal Rites* (1987): 'There was a drawing of a creature on the front; it looked suspiciously like one of the things from the cold desert. It certainly didn't look like a happy kitten.'

'A family saying followed the visit of a local girl to Navy Days at Devonport. My mother asked her if she had enjoyed herself, and she said, "Oh, yes, it was lovely. **There was a sailor to lift you up and a sailor to lift you down.**" In our family, this came to express the maximum enjoyment' – Ruth West, Torpoint, Cornwall (2001).

snug as a bug in a rug Meaning 'well-fitting and/or extremely warm and comfortable'. It is often ascribed to Benjamin Franklin, the American writer and philosopher, who mentioned a type of epitaph in a

letter to Miss Georgiana Shipley (26 September 1772) on the death of
her pet squirrel, Skugg:

> Here Skugg lies snug
> As a bug in a rug.

But there are earlier uses. In an anonymous work, *Stratford Jubilee*
(commemorating David Garrick's Shakespeare festival in 1769), is:

> If she [a rich widow] has the mopus's [money]
> I'll have her, as snug as a bug in a rug.

Probably, however, it was an established expression even by that date, if
only because in 1706, Edward Ward in *The Wooden World Dissected* had
the similar 'He sits as snug as a Bee in a Box' and in Thomas Heywood's
play *A Woman Killed with Kindness* (1603) there is 'Let us sleep as snug
as pigs in pease-straw.'

Chapter 17

ALL GONG AND NO DINNER

I was introduced to the splendid descriptive phrase **'all gong and no dinner'** *– meaning, of a person, that he (it's usually a he) is 'all talk and no action' – by Anne Diamond, the TV presenter. On* Quote …Unquote *(20 July 1985), Anne said she had heard it in her father's family. Since then I have discovered that it is indeed what you might say of a loud-mouthed person who is somewhat short on achievement. I think it has been current since the mid-20th century at least.* Partridge/Slang *has a citation from BBC Radio's* The Archers *in 1981. Michael Grosvenor Myer, Haddenham, Cambridgeshire (1999), produced a Texan variant: 'All hat and no cattle.' 'So far, all we have had from the Government is "all gong and no dinner" – to use a phase that a constituent of mine used in a public meeting. In other words, the sound and the fury have been there but the delivery has been missing. The Government have been elected to deliver, and I hope that they will do that' – Welsh Grand Committee (Westminster) (3 July 2001). 'Diana is represented as a symbol of the fecundity of nature, but it needs to be fleshed out with character and incident before it can spring into operatic life. What we have here is the ritual but not the romance, the shell but not the meat – all gong and no dinner, as my grandmother used to say' –* The Daily Telegraph *(29 August 2006).*

    Now for some other personal characteristics, wonderfully caught in words.

all bitter and twisted Said about someone who is psychologically mixed-up and shows it. Sometimes made light of in the form 'all twitter and bisted'. Since the 1940s, at least.

all fur coat and no knickers Describing a certain type of woman, given to show but having no modesty; elegant on the outside but sleazy underneath. Encountered by me in a Welsh context (1988), it was also the title of play that toured the UK in the same year.

A variant (1993), said to come from Lancashire (or, at least, from the North), is: 'Red hat, no knickers'. 'Fur coats and no drawers' was quoted by Stella Richardson, Essex (1998).

A similar expression is **all kid gloves and no drawers**. This last was given as an example of colourful cockney bubble-pricking by the actor Kenneth Williams in his autobiography *Just Williams* (1985). He said it was used in his youth (1930s) to denote the meretricious.

Valerie Grosvenor Myer, Haddenham, Cambridgeshire, commented (1997), '"**Silk stockings and no knickers**" is another version, i.e. poverty concealed in an effort to keep up appearances.'

all mouth and trousers Describing a type of man who is 'all talk'. I don't think that the 'and trousers' suggests he is sexually active or successful, as the earlier term 'all prick and breeches' undoubtedly did. However, he may be boastful about his sexual exploits without any supporting evidence. Since the mid-20th century? McConville & Shearlaw's *Slanguage* (1984) describes it now as 'an insulting (non-sexual) catchphrase'.

From BBC radio's *Round the Horne* (15 May 1966): 'There he goes, his kilt swinging in the breeze – all mouth music and no trousers.'

Compare, from the BBC radio show *Hancock's Half Hour* (14 June 1955): 'All teeth and trousers', which I assume means the same thing.

all of a doodah In a state of dithering excitement. Known by 1915. From P.G. Wodehouse, *Jeeves and the Feudal Spirit*, Chap. 14 (1954): 'A glance was enough to show me that he [Uncle Tom] was all of a doodah.'

all of a tiswas Meaning 'confused, in a state'. Known by 1960, it might be from an elaboration of 'tizz' or 'tizzy' and there may be a hint of 'dizziness' trying to get in. But no one really knows. The acronym derived from 'Today Is Saturday, Wear A Smile' seems not to have anything to do with the meaning of the word and to have been imposed later. This was, however, the apparent reason for the title *Tiswas* being given to a children's TV show (UK 1974–82), famous for its buckets-of-water-throwing and general air of mayhem. Broadcast on Saturday mornings, its atmosphere was certainly noisy and confused.

all piss and wind Empty, vacuous – of a man prone to bombast and no achievement. Apparently derived from the earlier saying, LIKE THE BARBER'S CAT (page 33).

Describing a thin or abnormally slim person: 'He's **all skin and grief**' – John Ellwood, Kent (1995).

Anne Gallus not wearing a tie Meaning 'untidy' – specifically not wearing a tie – this was told to me on an LBC radio phone-in, London, in June 1990, but is otherwise untraced and unconfirmed. However, the novelist and short-story writer H.E. Bates, recalling his grandfather before the First World War in *The Vanished World* (1969), wrote, 'His sharpest rebuke ... was a mere "Drop it, boy," though very occasionally he might go so far as to refer to me as "that young gallus".'

These phrases are rather a puzzle. What we do know is that 'gallus' has been a pronunciation and spelling of 'gallows' since the 18th century and that 'gallows/gallus' has been used as an adverb meaning 'extremely, very' since about the same time. *Gallus* is the Latin for a 'fowl' or 'cock' and 'gallows/gallus' is also the name once given to 'suspenders for trousers', i.e. 'braces' in the US. But none of this is very helpful ...

'This is one of my mother's sayings which I have never heard anyone else use. She would say, "He/she is **as awkward as a pig with side pockets**" – Miss F.M. Smith, Hertfordshire (1995). *Apperson* finds '**as much need of it as a toad of a side pocket**', said 'of a person who desires anything for which he has no real occasion', by 1785, and '**as much use as a cow has for side pockets**', in *Cheshire Proverbs* (1917).

as camp as Chlöe 'My mother preferred in general the company of homosexuals ... her fondness for the theatre and, more particularly, the theatrical atmosphere added to her circle a number of visiting firewomen all as camp as Chlöe' – George Melly, *Rum, Bum and Concertina*, Chap. 1 (1977). This could well be Melly's own coinage, but it sounds so natural that it may have been in general use in the Liverpool of his childhood or in the Bohemian circles he moved in later on.

as clever as Kit Mullett 'As a child growing up in South London in the late 1940s, my parents referred to people with a penchant for grandiose but ultimately doomed plans as "as clever as Kit Mullett". This epithet was levelled at all sections of society from five-year-olds determined to tunnel to Australia through to world leaders carving up Europe. I never managed to discover the source' – Derek Maguire (2001).

I have been unable to trace who this gentleman was, nor indeed whether anyone else has used the phrase, though in 2002 there was an inquiry on the internet for the origin of '*daft* as Kit Mullet'.

as dim as a Toc H lamp Very dim (unintelligent). Dates from the First World War, during which a Christian social centre for British 'other ranks' was opened at Talbot House in Poperinghe, Belgium, and named after an officer who was killed – G.W.L. Talbot, son of a Bishop of Winchester. 'Toc H' was signalese for 'Talbot House'. The institute continued long after the war under its founder, the Revd P.B. ('Tubby') Clayton. A lamp was its symbol.

'When one was reluctant to do the shopping or washing up, my mother used to say, **"You're as lazy as Ludlum's dog who lay down to bark"**' – Joan Hartley, West Yorkshire (1998). *Partridge/Slang* has 'lazy as Ludlum's/(David) Laurence's/Lumley's dog ... meaning extremely lazy ... According to the [old] proverb, this admirable creature leant against a wall to bark' and compares the 19th-century 'lazy as Joe the marine who laid down his musket to fart' and 'lazy as the tinker who laid his budget to fart'. *Apperson* has 'lazy as *Ludlam's* dog, that leant his head against a wall to bark' from Ray's proverb collection (1670).

The comparable **lazy Larrence/Laurence/Lawrence** dates back to 1650, by some accounts. 'One of my father's sayings if we said we were too tired to do anything was "You've got Laurence"' – Mrs K.Y. Williams, Herefordshire (1998). The reference may be to the general 'heat around St Lawrence's day (10 August) or to the legend of the martyred St Lawrence being too lazy to move in the flames' – according to *Apperson* and *Partridge/Slang*.

I was keen to find some early uses of the expression **'as miserable as sin'**, which is curiously ignored by *OED2* and others. Joe Kralich found these instances, working backwards: 'We are as miserable as we are wicked' – C.S. Lewis, *Studies in Medieval and Renaissance Literature* (1966); 'To make yourself as miserable as you have made yourself sinful' – Harriet Beecher Stowe; 'He leads a life as miserable as the most miserable sinner could do' – Richard Savage, in *Dublin University Magazine* (1870); 'As miserable as a lost soul' – Nathaniel Hawthorne (1853). I think we'd better call these 'notes towards a solution', as none quite gives us what we are looking for.

as much use as a chocolate kettle Phil Read, Staffordshire (1986) added to our stock of colourful expressions with this overheard remark at a Port Vale football match. It was made after the team had let slip another opportunity to score. '"Chocolate *teapots*" seem more in vogue than kettles at the moment' – Veronica M. Brown, Wigston, Leicestershire (2002). 'A saying from my ex's family: "As much use as a chocolate fireguard"' – Ann Bamford, Cumbria (2006). And compare:

as much use as half a scissor 'Said about a useless person' – Reg Stainton, North Yorkshire (2000).

as queer as Dick's hatband Very odd. Numerous versions of this saying have been recorded but all indicate that something is not right with a person or thing. The *OED2* gives the phrase thus: 'as queer (tight, odd, etc.) as Dick's (or Nick's) hatband', and adds, 'Dick or Nick was probably some local character or half-wit, whose droll sayings were repeated.'

Partridge/Slang describes it as 'an intensive tag of chameleonic sense and problematic origin' and, dating it from the mid-18th to the early 19th century, finds a Cheshire phrase 'all my eye and Dick's hatband', and also a version that went, 'as queer as Dick's hatband, that went nine times round and wouldn't meet'.

In Grose's *Dictionary of the Vulgar Tongue* (1785) is the definition: 'I am as queer as Dick's hatband; that is, out of spirits, or don't know what ails me.' But who was Dick, if anybody? *Brewer* (1894) was confident that it knew the answer: Richard Cromwell (1626–1712), who succeeded Oliver, his father, as Lord Protector in 1658 and did not make a very good job of it. Hence, 'Dick's hatband' was his 'crown', as in the following expressions: *Dick's hatband was made of sand* ('his regal honours were a "rope of sand"'), *as queer as Dick's hatband* ('few things have been more ridiculous than the exaltation and abdication of Oliver's son') and *as tight as Dick's hatband* ('the crown was too tight for him to wear with safety').

Tony Brisby, Staffordshire, recalled (1992), 'A sentence used by my grandmother was, "He's as queer as Dick's hatband – it went round twice and then didn't meet." I have absolutely no idea what she meant.'

Marjorie M. Rawicz, Nottinghamshire, added (1993), 'As a young person in the Twenties, I remember my mother (Derbyshire with Yorkshire roots) saying, "You're as funny as Dick's hatband" when either my sister or I was being contrary and difficult. I heard no more of this expression until the late Sixties when a Miss Emily White (from Cheshire) told me that *her* mother finished the quote – "Funny as Dick's hatband – it went twice round and then would not tie".'

David Scott, Cumbria (1994), remembered his grandmother saying in the 1930s – if things didn't work out, 'That's like Dick's hatband – it went round twice and still didn't fit!' Dorothy Hoyle, Lincolnshire, added that, in her family, it was always 'as *black* as Dick's hatband' when something was very dirty. Mrs J.M.H. Wright, West Yorkshire, countered with: 'The correct version – "as *near* as Dick's hatband" – makes the saying self-explanatory, at least to a Yorkshire person. "Near" in Yorkshire speech as well as meaning "close to" also means "mean or stingy with money". Thus the person referred to is as "near" with money as Dick's hatband is "near" to Dick's head.' 'A botched-up job done with insufficent materials was "like Dick's hat-band that went half-way round and tucked"' – according to Flora Thompson, *Lark Rise*, Chap. 3 (1939).

Compare what Harry Richardson, Surrey, remembered his grandmother (1870–1956) saying, in answer to a child's curiosity, '"**You are as queer as a Norwegian fiddle**".... I saw the artefact many years later. It has two frets!'

as thick as two short planks Very thick (or stupid) indeed. *OED2*'s sole mention of the phrase dates only from 1987, though *Partridge/Slang* dates it from 1950. I had always thought that the length of the planks was irrelevant until David Elias commented (2004), 'From memories of my grandfather's carpenter's shop, long planks are flexible, even if quite thick, and may be springy. Short planks, however, seem stolid and inflexible, so I think the length of the plank is far from immaterial.'

a big girl's blouse Used about a man who is not as manly as he might be. A rather odd expression, possibly of Welsh origin, and suggesting what an effeminate football or rugby player might wear instead of a proper jersey. Could it have something to do with the wobbliness of the image conjured up? *Street Talk: The Language of Coronation Street* (1986) states that it 'describes an adult male who has a low pain threshold, a "sissy". When trying to remove a splinter someone might say, "Hold still, you big girl's blouse. It won't hurt."'

Confirming its mostly North Country use, the phrase has also been associated with the British comedienne Hylda Baker (1908–86) in the form 'you big girl's blouse', probably in the ITV situation comedy *Nearest and Dearest* (1968–73).

From *The Guardian* (20 December 1986) – about a nativity play:
'The house is utterly still (except where Balthazar is trying to screw the
spout of his frankincense pot into Melchior's ear, to even things up for
being called a big girl's blouse on the way in from the dressing room).'
From *The Herald* (Glasgow) (20 October 1994): 'His acid-tongued
father [Prince Philip] might be reinforced in his view of him as a big
girl's blouse, but Prince Charles is actually a big boy now. His children,
locked away in the posh equivalent of care, are not.' From *The Sunday
Times* (6 November 1994): 'Men, quite naturally, are equally unwilling
to accept paternity leave, because of the fear that this will mark them for
ever as a great big girl's blouse.'

he has none of his chairs at home Elizabeth Monkhouse recalled
(1997) that in her bit of Cheshire, 'He's got all his chairs at home' was
an expression used to mean, 'He's all there, alert.' Hence, a home
without furniture is empty, so 'no chairs at home' = empty-headed,
no longer at home, no longer 'there'. This was also reported from
Lancashire. Meanwhile, Joyce Hanley wrote, 'In Yorkshire, if someone
is a bit lacking in the head, we say that they haven't got all their
furniture at home.'

This information came to me when I was looking at the origin of
the phrase 'to lose one's marbles', meaning 'to lose one's faculties',
and was wondering whether it could have anything to do with the
French word *meubles* (furniture). *Apperson* finds the Lancashire use
by 1865.

'It was around 1940 and I was four or five years old. A carrier [i.e. man
with a horse and cart] came to the house to deliver some item – it may
have been a gramophone. He was given a cup of tea, which he partially
poured into his saucer, blew on it and sort of slurped it up, quite noisily.

My father glanced at my mother and remarked *sotto voce,* "**Chap or no chap.**" I have never heard this since' – Margaret Smith, Barnstable (2001). Indeed, what did this mean?

you couldn't knock the skin off a rice pudding 'Said to a weak person or to a big-headed one' – Stella Richardson, Essex (1998). In order to put them down, of course. *Partridge/Catch Phrases* dates it from the First World War. 'There seems to be some dispute as to what Mr Roy Hattersley actually said to Mr Michael Foot about the quality of Mr Foot's leadership [of the Labour Party]' – John Junor in *The Sunday Express* (24 July 1983). This did not restrain *The Observer,* which printed this exchange in its edition of 31 July: '"I'd have the skin off your back" – Mr Michael Foot to Roy Hattersley. "You could not knock the skin off a rice pudding" – Mr Roy Hattersley to Michael Foot.'

you couldn't punch a hole in a wet *Echo* 'Said to a weak person – in Liverpool' – Stella Richardson, Essex (1998). The *Liverpool Echo* is one of the city's newspapers. A local version of the more common 'couldn't punch your way out of a paper bag' which *Partridge/Catch Phrases* has as one of the variants of the previous phrase.

cowardy, cowardy custard! This is one child's taunt to another who is holding back from some activity or who runs away. First recorded in 1836. The original rhyme was, 'Cowardy, cowardy custard/Can't eat bread and mustard.' 'Costard' was an old comptemptuous name for a 'head', which may be relevant. Cowardice is often associated with the colour yellow, of course. 'Then [the two tamer children] would make a dash on their long stalky legs for their own garden gate, followed by stones and cries of "Long-shanks! Cowardy, cowardy custards!"' – Flora Thompson, *Lark Rise*, Chap. 2 (1939).

A revue devoted to the songs of Noël Coward was presented in London with the title *Cowardy Custard* in 1972, with no reflection on his moral standing.

daft as a brush Meaning 'stupid', this expression was adapted from the northern English '**soft as a brush**' by the comedian Ken Platt (1921–98), who told me in 1979, 'I started saying "daft as a brush" when I was doing shows in the army in the 1940s. People used to write and tell me I'd got it wrong!' *Partridge/Slang* suggests that 'daft …' was in use before this, however, and Paul Beale reports the full version – 'daft as a brush without bristles' – from the 1920s.

'If my mother thought someone was "street-wise", as we say today, she would comment, "**He didn't come up on the down train**"' – W.A. Vigs, Staffordshire (1996). 'My mother when being teased would say, "Do you think I came up in a down train?" and "I didn't come over with a foot in each funnel"' – Keith Nixon, Biggin Hill, Kent (2000).

The phrase 'up train' to describe a train going up to town (as opposed to the 'down train' coming down from town) was in use by 1841 and followed on from the earlier 'up coach' and 'down coach'.

doesn't know whether to shit or light a fire 'My grandfather always says this of people who can't make up their minds. Apparently this refers to soldiers who, at the end of a long day's march, can't decide whether to warm up first, or …' – Suzanne King, Glasgow (2000). Surprisingly, Eric Partridge (with his army background) does not appear to have known this expression. However, he does include (to describe ignorance rather than indecision): 'He doesn't know whether to shit or go blind/whether he wants a shit or a haircut/whether to scratch his watch or wind his ass', some of which are American in origin. In 2001, I was told this version by a W.I. member in Spalding, who had best remain anonymous: 'I don't know if I want a shit, shave or shampoo'.

'In Norfolk, of a person considered a bit simple, it was said, "He/she **don't go no further than Thursday**"' – Mrs Monica Nash, Nottinghamshire (1995).

don't some mothers have 'em? Comment about a stupid person. The British comedian Jimmy Clitheroe (1916–73) was a person of restricted growth and with a high-pitched voice who played the part of a naughty schoolboy until the day he died. The BBC radio comedy programme *The Clitheroe Kid*, which ran from 1957–72, popularized an old Lancashire – and possibly general North Country – saying, 'Don't some mothers have 'em?'

In the form 'Some mothers do 'ave 'em', the phrase was used in the very first edition of TV's *Coronation Street* (9 December 1960) and later as the title of a series on BBC TV (1974–9), in which Michael Crawford played an accident-prone character, Frank Spencer.

to have enough yap for another set of teeth 'To have too much to say for oneself'. A possibly Cornish saying submitted by Tim Thomson (2001). Alternatively, **to have too much of what the cat licks his arse with.**

the ever-open door Slogan phrase describing Dr Barnado's Homes, the orphaned children's charity in the UK, and well-known by the 1910s. Although not used now, it was inscribed on Barnardo's collecting boxes (in the shape of a house) into the 1950s. There appears to have been a play with the title *The Ever-Open Door* in 1913 and *Punch* had a political cartoon with the phrase as caption (26 November 1913).

However, I recall it being applied to the insatiable mouth, representing the appetite of an un-orphaned youth (me), in the 1950s. Pat Tomalin, Gussage All Saints, Dorset (2000), recalled her grandmother using it to describe her son (born 1900). And note this, from Alexander Pope's translation of the *Iliad*, VI.14 (1715–20): 'He held his seat; a friend to human race/Fast by the road, his ever-open door/Obliged the wealthy and relieved the poor.'

everything's done in my own little way/My own little tea-set, my own little tray Barbara Wild of Rye, East Sussex, asked (1993) about this couplet – 'which has rung round our house for years. Edward Lear perhaps? It is completely evocative of a certain type of person – our type, I fear.' It remains untraced.

'My mother, who was born in Lincolnshire, was wont to say of a person she considered too inquisitive, "He always **wants to know the far end of the fart and where the stink goes**"' – W.G. Wayman, Hertfordshire (1993). 'My grandmother said of an inquisitive woman of her acquaintance, "She wanted to know the far end of a goose's trump, how many ounces it weighed, and which way the stink blew"' – Anne Marie Hawkins, South Glamorgan (1994). 'One of my mother's sayings: "She is so nosey she wants to know the far end of a fart and which way it blows"' – Margaret Jones, Newcastle upon Tyne (2002).

you're as gormless as a haporth of cheese in a washing mug 'Said by my mother' – Stella Richardson, Essex (1998).

'Here is one from my father – and occasionally still heard in Belfast today, **"He's a great man with a hanky ball but the bounce beats him on a wet day"**, usually shortened to "He's a great man with a hanky ball." It refers to the fact that apprentices in the mills and shipyard of Belfast used to construct a ball by wrapping some newspaper in a handkerchief in order to play football in their lunch break. Of course, a "hanky ball" had absolutely no bounce, no matter what the weather conditions. Therefore, "a great man with a hanky ball" is one of those people (we all know at least one) who is always the first to volunteer for a given task but always has a reason why it could not be completed as arranged' – Ian White, Bolton, Lancashire (2004).

if it's not there, you can't put it there Of the intelligence needed to pass a scholarship examination – a popular saying quoted in Richard Hoggart, *The Uses of Literacy* (1957).

In October 2000, Fred Reece asked about an expression used by the father of a friend of his: **'If your brains were gunpowder, you wouldn't have enough to blow your hat off!'** Jon Richfield spotted this as the caption to a cartoon in an edition of *Punch* dating from 1923: *Exasperated Bos'n*: 'If yer brains was dynamite they wouldn't blow yer blinking 'at off!' Jon commented, 'This is not likely to be the origin, but is quite possibly the first time in respectable print, having been coined long before by an inventive, unsung matelot.'

On the other hand, Ian Forsyth said, 'I have heard this before, as a traditional insult in country places. I would suggest that it goes back a long way, to the days when sporting guns were charged with loose powder and shot, and people were familiar with the loud bang made by a very small amount of gunpowder.'

'My mother (1896–1992) used to greet any statement which she thought preposterous by saying derisively, "**In a pig's eye.**" I have never heard anyone else say this' – Chris Anderson (2003). But they do. *Partridge/ Slang* seems to think this is North American in origin, from the mid-20th century and euphemistic of 'in a pig's arse/arse-hole'.

in and out – like a dog at a fair [also **up and down ...**] Irritating – as said, for example, to a child running in and out of the house. The mother of Max Stafford-Clark, the theatre director, came from Nottinghamshire and 'kept a very clean house', as he put it on *Quote ... Unquote* (18 May 1993): 'We used to have to take our shoes off when we came in the door, if she'd done the cleaning that day. If we'd been in and out of the back door more than twice in a morning, she would say, "Either in or out – you're like a dog at a fair." Max wondered if this was a local expression.

Well, his mother was not alone in using it and, in fact, it also happens to be a *quotation* from R.H. Barham's poem 'The Jackdaw of Rheims', published with *The Ingoldsby Legends* in 1840. The eponymous bird busies itself on the Cardinal's table:

> In and out
> Through the motley rout,
> That little jackdaw kept hopping about:
> Here and there,
> Like a dog at a fair,

> Over comfits and cates [dainties],
> And dishes and plates ...

Barham seems, however, to have been using an already-established expression. *Apperson* finds 'As sprites in the haire, Or dogges in the ffayre' by 1520. In 1893, G.L. Gower's *Glossary of Surrey Words* had the version 'They didn't keep nothing reg'lar, it was all over the place like a dog at a fair.'

'My mother used to say, "In and out like a French Prime Minister" – referring, I believe, to the shortness of pre-de Gaulle governments and not to the French President who died in his mistress's bed' – Veronica M. Brown, Wigston, Leicestershire (2002).

'When confronted by any complicated form to be filled in, my mother would remark that the inquirer wanted to know "**the ins and outs of a Merryman's backside**". This rather unrefined expression became general in the family' – Rose Shipton, Gloucestershire (1994).

'Merryman' here has the sense of a jester or buffoon, defined by Francis Grose's *Dictionary of the Vulgar Tongue* (1785) as 'Merry Andrew, or Mr. Merryman, the jack pudding, jester, or zany of a mountebank, usually dressed in a party coloured coat.' Compare:

'As my long-departed Mum used to declare when talking about someone unduly inquisitive, "**She wants to know the ins and outs of a nag's arse**." The expression has not been lost with her passing!' – Eric Silvester, Wiltshire (1995). 'My grandmother (born around 1890) met any child's inquisitive questions with "You want to know the ins and outs of Mag's behind"' – David Coles, London N21 (1998). 'Mag's' would seem to be a softer substitution for 'nag's'.

Or possibly 'magpie's': 'My paternal grandmother, born in 1881, when presented with a seven- or eight-year-old who was asking far too many questions, would suddenly erupt with this saying: "Goodness, boy – you would want to know the ins and outs of a *magpie's* bottom". This truly astounded me as Gran was never known to utter an oath of any kind' – Alan Jordan, Balham (2001). 'If we persisted in asking, "'Why?', my Derbyshire grandmother would say, "You want to know top and bottom of t'Meg's arse and how far it is tut [to it]"' – Jim Martin (2001).

And a cleaned-up version: "My mother, Lilian Rose Rees, born 1901, would say in exasperation at a constantly questioning son, "You want to know the ins and outs of a cat's behind"' – George Rees, Swansea (2001).

it is better to be born lucky than rich Another of the comforting phrases used by the theatre director Sir Peter Hall's mother and quoted in his memoir *Making an Exhibition of Myself* (1993).

Nimmo Clarke of Northallerton (2000) commented on the expression, '**It's a good job that we are all different**': 'A Scottish friend of mine told me that his aunt had an addendum to this, which was, " **...** **otherwise they wouldn't sell many mixed biscuits.**"' A universal truth, surely?

'I went with a group of friends, including one Roddy, to see the film *Monty Python and the Holy Grail*. We greatly enjoyed it, except Roddy, who fell asleep. On the way out, we asked Roddy, "What did you think of it?", to which Roddy (not well-endowed in the top storey) answered, "**It's not my period of history.**" We have cherished this ever since and use it for any occasion when ignorant or bewildered' – Mrs J.D. Marston, Barney, Norfolk (2001).

"He's a Joe Thick!"' – Geoff Wilde of Great Crosby, Lancashire (2004) reported that his father would say this to describe 'any person who always came up smelling of roses from a position of obvious disadvantage'.

to know one's onions To be knowledgeable in a subject area, to know what you are about. This does not appear to have existed before the 20th century. Quite how the onions fit in to this, I don't know, but I have always thought the theory far-fetched that it had anything to do with the lexicographer C.T. Onions (1873–1965). The phrase was in use by the early 1920s, by which time Onions was working on the *Shorter Oxford Dictionary*, not published until the 1930s, and thus was not yet exactly a household name. Perhaps there is a connection with the expression 'off his onion' for 'off his head', where the onion may represent the mind.

the left hand doesn't know what the right hand is doing A popular description of chaotic uncoordinated activity. Date of origin unknown but probably not before the 20th century.

the lights, the lemonade! Sean O'Connor asked (1999) about a verse his mother used on 'weedy cousins and the like':

> Nine – ten – eleven-thirty –
> And still the music played.
> O heavens, the mushroom-sandwiches,
> The lights, the lemonade!

Jane Gregory spotted that this was from A.P. Herbert's poem, 'Don't Tell My Mother I'm Living in Sin; Or, See What It Done to Me'. This was probably first published in *Punch* and was collected in *Laughing Ann* (1925).

like a cat on hot bricks The common English expression meaning 'ill-at-ease, jumpy'. John Ray in his *Collection of English Proverbs* (1670–8) has: 'to go like a cat upon a hot bake stone'. Another English proverbial expression (known by 1903) is 'nervous as cats'.

What I take to be a mostly American derivative of this, 'as nervous as a cat on a hot tin roof', gives us the title of the play *Cat on a Hot Tin Roof* (1955; film US 1958) by Tennessee Williams. Here, the 'cat' is Maggie, Brick's wife, 'whose frayed vivacity', wrote the critic Kenneth Tynan, 'derives from the fact that she is sexually ignored by her husband'.

'My mother (who is Scottish) has a habit of describing a person in this way: "**she is like a Christmas card – she's aye greetin**" – "Aye greetin'" means, here, "always crying" – Doug Stokoe (2001).

Indeed, I might mention that 'greetin'fu' is Scots for 'drunk', where the original phrase actually means 'crying-drunk'.

you are like a cow with a musket 'When one was being awkward in some task' – Miss O.E. Burns, Stourbridge, Gloucestershire (1995). 'As awkward as a cow with a musket' – Andrew Craton, Hampshire (1999). Cherry Norman of Tadworth, Surrey (2001), reports 'I feel as useless as a cow with a musket' as a response from an elderly person to the enquiry, 'How are you?'

'I'm 70 years old and was brought up by a grandmother who in turn was brought up by a mother who took in washing at the back of Leicester Square. When I came home crying because I'd fallen over and hurt myself, my grandmother always said, "**You're like a Drury Lane fairy – always in trouble**." She would never tell me what a Drury Lane fairy was...' – Violet Mills, West Sussex (1994).

Understandably. J. Redding Ware's *Passing English of the Victorian Era* (1909) defines a 'fairy' as 'a debauched, hideous old woman, especially when drunk'. Francis Grose's *Dictionary of the Vulgar Tongue* (1785) has 'Drury Lane vestal' = 'harlot'.

Compare: 'My family always said, "You sound just like a Drury Lane dressmaker" to anyone complaining of various aches and pains, usually trivialities. Sometimes combined with the maladies there would be a moan about their general life' – Mrs B. Parker, Bedfordshire (2000).

like a fart in a colander Indecisive, dithering, all over the place, rushing around. *Partridge/Catch Phrases* suggests an origin sometime in the 1920s. The phrase is also used when describing someone particularly evasive or slippery. I was first introduced to this wonderful expression by Roy Hudd on *Quote... Unquote* (24 May 1994). Although I found it hugely amusing, I did not quite understand the mechanics of it until Mrs J. Harrison in Powys wrote that, as she knew it, the phrase was used to describe someone who was *indecisive* and that the complete version was 'He's like a fart in a colander – can't make up his mind which hole to come out of!'

A slightly different version of the same idea: 'My own grandmother used a wealth of descriptive and colourful expressions. One frequently addressed to me was, "Can't you just sit still, child, fidgetting about like a parched pea in a colander!"' – Mrs Stella Mummery, London SW14 (1995).

you're like a wooden man made of smoke 'As a young child in the 1950s, I can remember my grandfather saying this when either my brother or myself was not being very successful in our attempts to do something' – Judith Hughes, Preston, Lancashire (1994).

'My mother came from a small village in Lancashire and her sayings really have to be heard in her accent. Speaking of someone who thought themselves a cut above everyone else, she would say, 'He/she is **like an angel with pit clogs on**' – Margaret Rowden, Somerset (1998).

you look like you've lost a shilling and found a tanner 'My late father used this saying if he saw an old friend who looked a bit down in the mouth' – Arthur W. Jillions, Essex (1995). 'You look as though you've lost a bob and found a tanner' – father of E.N. Rouse, Worcestershire (2000).

A 'bob' or shilling was worth twice a 'tanner' or sixpence, hence the disappointment. This probably derived from earlier sayings around the name of **John Toy** – as in *Cornish Proverbs* (1864). For example, C.H. Spurgeon, *Ploughman's Pictures* (1880) has: 'The luck that comes to them is like Johnny Toy's, who lost a shilling and found a two-penny loaf.'

they look like they had been drinking vinegar off a fork 'My grandmother (who looked like a cross between Golda Meir and Peter Ustinov) used to say this of people with particularly sour faces' – Helen Christmas, Cardiff (2000). *Partridge/Slang* has the same expression from the mid-19th century. Compare: TO HAVE VINEGAR ON A FORK (page 268).

'My great uncle was a teacher who had a quote for every occasion, be it from Shakespeare, Dickens or the Bible. He amused us for hours with his poems recalled from who knows where about Jimmy and his liver pills, or Ben Battle laying down his arms and someone and Bartholomew going down to the woods. Most of his sources I have now found but one eludes me and all the family. That elusive character is "**Mr Brooks of Sheffield**". He seemed to crop up when a culprit for a minor or funny misdemeanour had happened. The question would be asked, "Who did that?" to which, after a suitable silence, he would reply, "Mr Brooks of Sheffield." Is the infamous Mr Brooks a literary character? Was he a politician? Who was he and where, other than Sheffield, does he come from?' – Charles L. Sanders, Stockport, Cheshire (2006).

For the answer to this, see Charles Dickens, *David Copperfield,* Chap. 2 (1850). The *Dickens Index* comments: 'Name used by Murdstone for referring to David without David realizing he is being talked about. Mrs Copperfield suggests he may be "a manufacturer in the knife and fork way", but Dickens did not know that by coincidence, this was so until he heard from the delighted firm of cutlery makers, Brookes of Sheffield.'

Sheffield, of course, has been the centre of the English cutlery trade for centuries. Was there also an implication that David was 'sharp'?

Norman Beaumont of Ropley, Hampshire (1993), wrote, 'I was born in 1941. If I had the grizzles as a toddler, I used to be told, "**You are a moaning Minnie.**"' Indeed, like so many alliterative phrases this has had considerable staying power. Anyone who complains is a 'moaner' and a 'minnie' can mean a lost lamb that finds itself an adoptive mother. But the original 'Moaning Minnie' was something quite different.

In the First World War, a 'Minnie' was the slang name for a German *minenwerfer*, a trench mortar or the shell that came from it, making a distinctive moaning noise. In the Second World War, the name was also used for air-raid sirens which made that sort of sound. Subsequently the term was applied to people rather than things. *OED2*'s earliest citation in this sense is 1972. On 11 September 1985, Margaret Thatcher paid a visit to Tyneside and was reported as accusing those who complained about the effects of unemployment of being 'Moaning Minnies'. In the ensuing uproar, a Downing Street spokesman had to point out that it was on the reporters attempting to question her, rather than the unemployed, that Mrs Thatcher had bestowed the title.

Another example, from *The Observer* (20 May 1989): 'Broadcasters are right to complain about the restrictions placed on them for the broadcasting of the House of Commons ... But the Moaning Minnies have only themselves to blame.'

'When I was a lethargic teenager just hanging around doing nothing, my mother would admonish me by saying, "**Don't just stand there like a stuffed mourkin**"' – W.A. Vigs, Staffordshire (1996). 'Mourkin' is a Warwickshire word for a scarecrow, also spelt 'maukin'.

he never likes to get up before the streets are aired Said by the mother of Richard Knowles, London SW12 (1998) about him, a late riser.

he will never make old bones i.e. he won't live long, certainly not to a ripe old age. Known by the second half of the 19th century and still quite often encountered. '"You will be a wonderful old gentleman, Davey," said Linda. "Oh, me? I fear I shall never make old bones," replied Davey, in accents of the greatest satisfaction' – Nancy Mitford, *The Pursuit of Love*, Chap. 21 (1949).

'If you explained things in too much detail or she thought you were talking down to her, my aunt would say, **"I'm not so green as I'm cabbage looking"**' – Mrs J. Payne, North Yorkshire (1995). The implication here is that the person is not green in the sense of innocent or naive, but just looks like a cabbage. 'My Grandma, who lived almost all her life in the West Riding of Yorkshire, had a different version when anyone, usually me, tried to beat her at something with a trick. It was, "I'm not as *daft* as I'm cabbage looking"' – Norman Woollons, East Yorkshire (2000). '"I may be cabbage-looking but I'm not green" – better sense?' – Stella Richardson, Essex (1998).

The expression appears to have been around since the late 19th century. How about this from James Joyce, *Ulysses* (1922): 'Gob, he's not as green as he's cabbagelooking'? Indeed, I wouldn't be surprised if it was originally an Irish expression.

'I only heard this once, but it gives me huge pleasure! After many years in England, my English father died and my Scots Mama returned to Dundee, her original home town, and caught up with lots of wayback friends. On one of these occasions, a friend said something pretty snide, and when I commented later, my Mum said, **"Oh, she was always like that – had a boat of her own at the Flood!"**' – Liz Smelt, Hurstpierpoint, West Sussex (1994).

one of those six who came over in seven boats 'Anyone a bit too clever was so described by my mother' – Ethel S. Dowey, Scarborough (1995).

'You may be interested to hear my mother's rather obscure definition of meanness. After years of Sunday tea with a rather penny-pinching aunt of mine – who was less than generous with the butter on the bread – my mother always referred to anyone on the mean side as **"another one of those who puts it on and scrapes it off"**' – Betty Abbott, Redruth, Cornwall (1996).

Paul Pry 'Another saying would pop out if I had asked my grandmother what she was doing (especially in the kitchen) … Needless to say, the message was received and understood' – Alan Bennett, Shefford, Bedfordshire (2001).

Indeed, 'Paul Pry' has long been a name applied to one who pries furtively, a Nosey Parker, a Peeping Tom and any inquisitive person. It originated in an American song (1820) and was also the title of a comedy (1825) by John Poole and of a book (1845) by Thomas Hood.

As a result of the play title, several public houses have been called 'The Paul Pry' and their signs show him listening at doors marked 'Private' etc. 'The straitest champion of marital fidelity would, surely, not defend such monstrous Paul Prying' – *The Times* (4 March 1960).

they're getting peas above sticks 'On people bettering themselves' – Stella Richardson, Essex (1998). Doris Humphrey, Grantham, Lincolnshire (1995) remembered this saying of her aunt's: 'Of anyone she knew who had got above themselves, she would say, "The peas have grown above the sticks."'

'After my late father's retirement and living in the family home in Friern Barnet, North London, his old friends living next door moved away and were replaced by strangers. After a while, I asked him, "What are your new neighbours like?" He thought for a while, and then said –

"Well, **they're the kind of people who leave their pegs on the line.**" (Which tells you more about my father than his neighbours!)' – Clive Dellino (2006).

pissing in someone's soup Don't read this if you are having your tea … I first encountered the expression, 'It's a bit like pissing in your soup', when in my first job with Granada Television, Manchester, in 1967. The producer of the local magazine programme (upon which I was working as a researcher/performer) had chosen to devote an entire edition to publicizing a book that he himself had written. Noel Picarda, the lawyer and wit who happened to be passing through the studios, made this comment to me about the producer's behaviour. I am not sure, however, that Noel was using the phrase in the normal way. All he meant to say was that the producer was doing something reprehensible.

In the years since, I have occasionally attempted to use the expression myself but I have never actually encountered it in any reference book. Eric Partridge gets quite close with 'to piss in someone's chips' (i.e. wood-chips or potato chips), which he dates from the 1920s. Either way, the meaning is presumably that the pisser spoils or degrades something by his action.

Not so long ago, I was intrigued to hear from Mike Dickinson that he had first encountered the expression in Robert Townsend's *Up the Organization* (1970): 'I don't know what *you* call it, but we Polacks call that "pissing in the soup"' [referring to a proposal within AVIS to set up a discount car-hire business].

Ian Forsyth sought to clarify the matter thus: 'As you say, "pissing in the soup" is about spoiling or degrading something like salting the well. But it carries the additional force of a malicious action carried out *without the victim's knowledge* – the rumoured revenge of restaurant staff against rude customers.' Ian went on, 'I remember many years ago reading a report of the prosecution of the owner of a fish and chip shop who had been spotted in the backyard pissing on the (uncooked) chips. He maintained that it improved the flavour and was not a health hazard because of the subsequent deep-frying.'

This reminded me of the passage from *Down and Out in Paris and London* (1933) in which George Orwell describes meeting a Hungarian Communist waiter when he, Orwell, was working as a dish-washer in a Paris restaurant: 'He told me, as a matter of pride, that he had sometimes wrung a dirty dishcloth into a customer's soup before taking it in.' Apparently, he did this to get his own back on members of the bourgeoisie.

Then I spotted this splendid use in Alan Bennett's TV play *An Englishman Abroad* (1979). The actress Coral Browne (playing herself) meets Guy Burgess, the British spy who defected to Moscow, and says, 'Outside Shakespeare, the word "treason" means nothing to me. Only, you pissed in our soup. And we drank it.'

plus fours and no breakfast 'My aunts tell me that this was a remark always attributed to the nouveau riche, who wore all they had on their backs. Everything for show and no stability' – Mrs D.E. Thorn, Lincolnshire (1998). 'Speaks rather fancy; truculent; plausible; a bit of a shower-off; plus-fours and no breakfast, you know … a gabbing, ambitious, mock-tough, pretentious young man' – Dylan Thomas characterizing himself in a broadcast 'Return Journey' (1947). I suppose the implication is that the 'shower-off' is someone of limited means who spends what he has on flashy clothes and therefore can't afford any breakfast.

Then the variations: '"Plus fours and kippers for breakfast" had to do with genteel poverty in upper-class Jesmond' – from an 89-year-old in Newcastle upon Tyne (1998). 'Fur coats and no breakfast' – Stella Richardson, Essex (1998). '"All crepe sole and bay windows", said in an exaggerated posh voice (with an "h" in "whindows")' – Dave Hopkins, Kent (1998).

Paul Beale commented, '"Plus fours and no breakfast" seems to equate to "(all) bay-windows and no breakfast" = sacrificing everything for the sake of an appearance of social superiority. I heard "bay windows" soon after we came to live in Leicestershire 25 years ago.' Beale also rounded up 'kippers and curtains', 'brown boots and no breakfast' and 'empty bellies and brass doorknobs'. See also ALL CURTAINS ... (page 122); ALL FUR COAT ... (page 234).

Coming from the same direction: 'My mother used to use this saying, when describing someone with expensive tastes, but not a lot of money, as having "champagne tastes and ginger beer pockets"' – Rosemary Harvey, Bristol (2003).

a pound a word 'My late father would say this when describing someone not given to voluble utterances' – Roger D. Purvis, Stockton-on-Tees (1999). How original was this?

'When someone was rude to my father, he would put them down with, **"Tell me, do you have to practise at being rude ... or does it come naturally?"**' – Sheila Jacques, Halstead, Essex (2003).

like putting a poultice on a wooden leg 'When trying to persuade or encourage someone who did not respond' – Flora Thompson, *Lark Rise*, Chap. 3 (1939).

'My mother – born and bred a Lancastrian, but all Welsh forebears – was a belter at her little sayings' wrote Miss L. Williams of Tyldesley,

Manchester (1994). 'On hearing a friend criticized, she once said, "Not Doris, her's **as quiet as a bit o' bread.**"'

you could ride to York on that lip 'To a sulking person' – Stella Richardson, Essex (1998). Because the drooping lip looked like a saddle? *Casson/Grenfell* has the nannyism 'I could ride to London on that lip.' Compare YOU COULD RIDE BARE-ARSED TO LONDON (page 167)

rogues, thieves, mountebanks and banjo-players 'For many years, my late father was in the habit of dismissing any people that he took to be questionable by including them in the group of miscreants here given. I was never able to discover from whence this phrase came, but I must admit that I use it myself whenever possible' – Roger Lovell (2005). Still looking ...

'My wife had an unusual expression, which she would use when we might be discussing peculiarities of a certain family, such as the way they all walk in the same manner, or talk in a similar way. She would say, "**It runs in the family like wooden legs**"' – Neil G. Clark, South Yorkshire (1996).

Apperson finds this in Bridge, *Cheshire Proverbs* (1917): '*It runs in the blood like wooden legs.* I heard this saying from the mouth of an Ulsterman, in Surrey, in the sixties of the last century.'

'This was a saying of my late mother and I assume it originated in Dublin, her birthplace, although I never heard anyone else use it.

It is a response to that dreadful habit of name-dropping: "Ah, yes ... **his mother used to wash for us but we sacked her for eating the soap**"' – Paul Dann, Surrey (1995).

'When someone asked my grandmother if she knew some famous person or other, she would always say, "Yes, his/her mother used to do our washing." I can remember this from the early 1950s' – Patrick Martin, Winchester (2002).

Compare: 'To put down the arrogant: "Well, he used to chew bread for our ducks but one day I caught him swallowing some so we gave him the sack!"' – Lorna Hanks, Hampshire (1995).

'My father hated name-dropping and if some pompous person started some lengthy anecdote during which he/she namedropped with gusto, he would interrupt with: "Ah, yes! He/she used to cut chaff for our ducks." It was a guaranteed conversation stopper' – Diana Negus, Leicestershire (1996).

he/she says anything but his/her prayers A dismissive phrase for when the opinion of another is adduced. *Apperson* finds 'He says anything but his prayers and then he whistles' in 1732; six years later, Swift has this in *Polite Conversation:* 'Miss will say any Thing but her Prayers, and those she whistles'.

'I am an octogenarian, so my memory goes back a long way, although not always accurately,' wrote Jack Brookes (2003). 'I once heard said, **"Servants talk about people but people talk about things!"**'

Not sure about this, though Penelope Lively entitled a short story, 'Servants Talk About People: Gentlefolk Discuss Things', first published in *Nothing Missing, But the Samovar* (1978). Then I came across this in John Keatley's privately published *Commonplace Reflections* (2002):

> Third class minds talk about people,
> Second class minds talk about things,
> First class minds talk about ideas.

It is credited, without any supporting information, to Cressida, daughter of the late Labour Party leader, Hugh Gaitskell.

'For upwards of fifty years, among members of my family, the use of the phrase **"She did offer me a cup of tea"** has indicated disapproval of someone. My mother overheard it from a lady who was describing an acrimonious exchange she had recently had with a mutual friend. She finished her recital with the words: "The old sod did offer me a cup of tea, but I couldn't enjoy it!"' – Mrs D.J. Feehan, Oswestry, Shropshire (1994).

sing before your breakfast, cry before your tea 'To anyone who has the temerity to be cheerful in the morning' – Stella Richardson, Essex (1998).

Apperson has a version of the more usual 'Sing before breakfast, cry before night' dating from 1530.

'Of a person sparing with food, my mother would say, **"She'd skin a lop [flea] for its tallow"**' – Mrs J. Payne, North Yorkshire (1995).

Compare: 'My dear mother used a similar expression and as a young child in the 30s I was never quite sure what it meant – "She is *that* mean she would skin a flea for its hide and tallow"' – Rhena Stitt, Belfast (1996).

'My mother had a stock of the most original expressions from her dour Scottish upbringing. She would describe a Scrooge-like person as being "so mean he'd skin a gnat for its hide"' – Travers Billington, Devon (1996).

'My grandmother's definition of false economy: "Someone would skin a gnat to save a farthing, and spoil a sixpenny knife to do it"' – B. Rouse, Evesham, Worcestershire (1995).

he is so mean he can peel an orange in his pocket For some reason, I have a note of this expression as having being said by a 'Welsh woman in the 1920s/30s'.

she's so mean she wouldn't give you a fright if she were a ghost 'One of my mother's sayings (she was born in 1895) that I have not heard anywhere else' – Margaret Jones, Newcastle upon Tyne (2002).

she's so mean she wouldn't give you the dirt from under her finger nails 'Said by my mother' – Mrs Edna A. Smith, Isle of Wight (1995).

Compare, from *Casson/Grenfell*: 'Look at your dirty finger-nails. Are we in mourning for the cat?'

she's so miserable that every time she laughs a donkey dies 'My late father, John Berriman, used to say this of one particularly gloomy woman who lived in the next village to us in North Yorkshire' – Mrs Margaret Opie-Smith, London SE1 (1995).

somebody got out of bed the wrong side today i.e. 'you are in a temper'. A nannyism, as in *Casson/Grenfell*. Why this should have anything to do with the way you get out of bed is not clear. It is a more or less traditional saying: *Marvellous Love-Story* (1801) has: 'You have got up on the wrong side, this morning, George'; and Henry Kingsley, *Silcote of Silcotes* (1867) has: 'Miss had got out of bed the wrong side.'

'In the 1920s we had a neighbour who I thought must be the most patriotic man around. He flew the flag on every occasion and displayed photographs of the Royal Family. I asked my Dad, who had been with the fusiliers from 1912–18 (when he was invalided out with severe wounds), if Mr X had been in his regiment. He said, "No, **he was in the Stand-Back Fusiliers**." I now realize it was a way of describing someone who, while fit for service, avoided it' – Bill Lovett, Essex (1997).

Partridge/Slang notes 'the Skin-Back Fusiliers' as 'a satirical attribution of a Serviceman's affiliation to an imaginary regiment or unit: ww2'.

they'd steal the pennies off a dead man's eyes 'Of the dishonest' – Stella Richardson, Essex (1998). Or **'they'd steal the eyes out of your head and come back for the sockets'**. Compare: **'like taking money from blind beggars'**, meaning 'achieving something effortlessly, by taking advantage'; and 'as easy as taking/stealing pennies from a blind man' or 'sweets/candy/money from a child.' 'Like taking candy from a baby' occurs in a Fats Waller song, *The Meanest Thing You Ever Did Was Kiss Me*, recorded in 1936, and in the film *Mr Smith Goes to Washington* (us 1939).

I first heard 'like taking money from blind beggars' in about 1962, said by my English teacher who had just given a talk to a (wildly impressed) Women's Institute, or some such. But it is an old idea. Charles Dickens in *Nicholas Nickleby*, Chap. 59 (1838–9) has Newman Noggs say, 'If

I would sell my soul for drink, why wasn't I a thief, swindler, house-breaker, area sneak, robber of pence out of the trays of blind men's dogs ...'

'Of a garrulous woman, I heard it said, "Oh, you know her, **she'd talk a glass eye to death**"' – Mrs Winifred A. Shaw, Stalybridge, Cheshire (1995).

'My grandfather, who didn't suffer fools gladly, used to say of a female relative who he considered lacked common sense, and talked a lot of rot, "**She talks as her belly guides her**." Two generations later it is still trotted out when someone is heard to make a stupid remark' – Mary Carver, Findon, West Sussex (1996).

'When I was younger, my mother used to say of certain people that they "**told more lies than Tom Pepper**". I have never found a reference for this insult' – Peter Dawson (1999).

Partridge/Slang has a citation for this nautical name for a liar, dating from 1818. Tom Pepper was, apparently, 'the sailor who was kicked out of Hell for lying'. *Apperson* has from *Dialect of Leeds* (1862): 'A noted propagator of untruths is "as big a liar as Tom Pepper".'

'When I was a small boy and when I got into a tantrum, as small boys (and girls) occasionally do, my Grandma could always calm the situation and make me laugh. She said, "**Temper like an 'orse, shit and stamp in it.**" Of course, as a small boy, this left me in fits of laughter. To which

I replied, "Shit in yer 'at and punch it'" – J.J. Furneaux, Warminster, Wiltshire (1995).

them as 'adn't teeth gnashed their gooms! 'A quotation or what?' – Mrs Wendy Eastaway, Co. Cork (1995). Obviously an allusion to the biblical 'But the children of the kingdom shall be cast out into outer darkness: there shall be weeping and gnashing of teeth' – Matthew 8:12.

Jennifer Paterson, the chef (1928–99), recalled her grandfather saying, also regarding teeth, 'Let 'em gnash 'em as have 'em' – on *Quote . . . Unquote* (2 May 1995)

'My mum always used to say of talkative women, "**She's got a tongue like an attorney**" – and for years I thought attorney was an animal . . .' – Mary J. Price (2001).

one o' them as is either up on the roof or down the well 'Of a temperamental person' – Flora Thompson, *Lark Rise*, Chap. 3 (1939).

Geoff Wilde of Great Crosby, Lancashire, reported (2004) that his late father used to say, 'With regard to a female (usually my mother) who had temporarily disappeared, thus delaying departure, eating etc., "**She's upstairs changing her mind.**"' My own father, who also lived in that place, was equally fond of saying it about my mother.

to have vinegar on a fork 'To be sharp or scary' – *Wickenden*. Compare: 'Negotiating with [the Irish politician Eamon] de Valera ... is like trying to pick up mercury with a fork' – David Lloyd George (1st Earl Lloyd George of Dwyfor), British Liberal Prime Minister (1863-1945). Quoted in M.J. MacManus, *Eamon de Valera* (1944). To which de Valera is said to have replied, 'Why doesn't he use a spoon?' – according to Bernard Baruch, *The Public Years* (1960).

'My mother used to say, if anyone was fooling about or doing something silly, **"She ain't so well since she fell off the organ"**, and it was years before I realized that this must refer to the little monkeys which the old-time organ-grinders kept and used to collect money from passers-by' – Mrs P.E. Stevens, Bexleyheath, Kent (2003). I hope she's right.

where the ladies scrubbed their front steps in their fur coats 'Of Duffield, a posh area of Derby in the 1930s/40s' – Joy Beecham, Boston, Lincolnshire (2000).

you give them a book and they chew on the covers 'My wife (who is American) introduced me to this saying. It is used to describe a person who acts stupidly, not making the most of their potential' – Simon Rickman (2004).

As sometimes happens, I received an identical query within a short while of being first presented with a completely baffling saying to investigate. In 2002, Sarah King wrote that whenever her grandmother (a Yorkshirewoman from Wakefield) wanted to say, 'You are as bad as each other', she would remark, '**You're Marry to Bonny**.' 'This is how it sounded; she didn't know how the two words were spelt; and told me that she did not know if it was two names (perhaps Marie and Bonny, Marie being often pronounced Marry in her part of the world), or if it was maybe Latin (*Merit a Bene?*) or some corruption from the Napoleonic wars (Married to Boney!)'

As it turned out, these were all very shrewd observations – not least the Yorkshire connection. John S. Glover's version of the query came from Rawdon, Leeds: 'My friend Arnold and I are both from Yorkshire and occasionally I use the expression "Bonny to Marry" meaning when two people are alike in some way, i.e. both extremely dull or unpleasant or nasty or suited together by a characteristic not considered to be virtuous. My friend Arnold insists that the expression is "Marry to Bonny".'

To provide a *possible* (and to my mind intriguing) solution to all this, Marian Bock enrolled her nephews, Sam (8) and Ben (6) Erickson, who are leading authorities (in their age group) on pirates of history and fiction – 'and daring buccaneers in their own right'. It appears that two of history's most famous female pirates were Anne Bonny and Mary Read. Some of the ships they attacked were Yorkshire ships and the man who captured them, Captain Jonathan Barnett, was from a Yorkshire family. The ladies were tried at Spanishtown, Jamaica, in 1720, and sentenced to hang but got away with it. A book about them and a website run by a descendant of Captain Barnett may be found on the internet.

And there I was, thinking that 'marry to bonny' was in some way connected to the pledge made by wives in the Middle Ages 'to be bonny and buxom in bed and at board'. This was interestingly quoted by Archbishop Runcie when he discussed the pre-marital advice he had given to Prince Charles and Lady Diana before marrying them in 1981.

Chapter 18

... AND WAVED HER WOODEN LEG

Nonsense plays a big part in the coining of domestic phraseology, rhymes and so on. Nowhere is it so apparent as in the category of mangled words. This is a trait common to many families, namely, the deliberate mispronunciation of words, usually following accidental garbling. Denis Norden admitted on Quote ... Unquote *(21 May 1996) that in his family they adopted children's sayings, such as* **'horse rubbish'** *for 'horse radish'. Then there are other quite common usages such as* **'semi-skilled milk'** *and* **'Nealopitan ice-cream'**. *On* Quote ... Unquote *(23 October 2006), Nick Higham, the BBC News correspondent, confessed that his family, too, very much went in for inversions, e.g.* **'par-carks'** *for 'car parks',* **'wish-dosher'** *for 'dishwasher'; and* **'marker-supit'** *for 'supermarket'.*

I am able to date very precisely when one such inversion entered my family's language. In 1981, while jet-lagged, I was watching an episode of Whatever Happened to the Likely Lads *on TV in a hotel in Hong Kong. One of the lads had a Scandinavian girlfriend who talked about a* **'screw-cork'** *for opening bottles. From that day on, it has been what my wife and I have invariably called it. More nonsense follows. See also* **'too late, too late ...'** *(page 367–70).*

all balls and bang me arse! Sheer nonsense. An intensifier of the basic **all balls!** British use, probably since the 1910s.

The *OED2* finds a letter written in 1781 by one 'S. Crispe' stating, 'Physic, to old, crazy Frames like ours, is **all my eye and Betty Martin** – (a sea phrase that Admiral Jemm frequently makes use of).' Grose's *Dictionary of the Vulgar Tongue* (1785) has: 'That's my eye betty martin, an answer to any one that attempts to impose or humbug.' The phrase is used in *Punch* (11 December 1841). *Apperson* has 'Only your eye and Miss Elizabeth Martin' in 1851. The shorter expressions 'all my eye' or 'my eye' predate this.

As to how it originated, *Brewer's Dictionary of Phrase & Fable* (1894) has the suggestion (from Joe Miller, 1739) that it was a British sailor's garbled version of words heard in an Italian church: '*O, mihi, beate Martine* [Oh, grant me, blessed St Martin]', but this sounds too ingenious and, besides, no prayer is known along those lines. Probably there *was* a Betty Martin of renown in the 18th century – *Partridge/ Catch Phrases* finds mention of an actress with the name whose favourite expression is supposed to have been 'My eye!' – and her name was co-opted for popular use. Some people use a 'Peggy Martin' version.

always pull the strings on a banana – they give you stomach ache A superstitious piece of nonsense that I certainly remember from my own childhood. Quoted in *More Momilies: As My Mother Used to Say*, ed. Michele Slung (1986).

asparagus veins Mangled words for 'varicose veins'. Mrs Olga Sweeney, Devon (1995), listed this among those used in her family: 'leg-ends' for legends; 'joe-beacon' for Jacobean; 'copper knickers' for Copernicus; 'super flewus' for superfluous. 'And we all use the term "hyperdeemic nerdle" (as heard on [the television programme devoted to humorous "out-takes"] *It'll Be Alright On the Night*).'

Jean Parker wrote (2002), 'I seem to be the only person who has ever heard of the following rhyme, which seems utter nonsense':

> **The blind man saw a hare**
> The dumb man said, 'Where?'
> The deaf man said, 'There.'
> The man without legs ran after it
> The man without arms caught it
> And the naked man put it in his pocket.

Now, after having done a bit of digging, I offer the view that this is yet another version of established nonsense verse ideas that can be traced back to the one-line proverbial expression, 'A blind man may catch a hare' – which appears in Chaucer's *The House of Fame*, about 1383, 'As a blind man stert a hare'. By about 1620, J. Taylor, *A Kicksey Winsey*, has it in a rhyme:

> By wondrous accident perchance one may
> Grope out a needle in a load of hay;
> And though a white crow be exceeding rare,
> A blind man may, by fortune, catch a hare.

Iona and Peter Opie, in *I Saw Esau* (1947), discuss the then currently known lines –

> One fine day in the middle of the night
> Two dead men got up to fight.

> A blind man came to see fair play,
> A dumb man came to shout hurray.

In *The Lore and Language of Schoolchildren* (1959), the Opies find yet another attempt at the theme, from an edition of *Ditties for the Nursery*, printed about 1830:

> Two dead horses ran a race,
> Two blind [men] to see all fair,
> Two dead horses ran so fast
> The blind began to stare.

'Once when we visited my mother in hospital, she whispered confidentially, "That woman in the next bed – her husband, he can't read or write, you know. Not a word!" Then, after a pause, "**But they had the children**." This became chorused after any subsequent glaring non-sequitur, for which she was famous' – Paul Cloutman, London SW11 (1995).

'I'm writing to ask if anyone knows the meaning of (and I don't mean to be rude here), "**Cock your leg up and shout 'butter'!**" My grandmother used to say the phrase jokingly when we were young children to make us laugh. She doesn't know where it comes from; it was just something that her own mother used to say when she was young. If it helps, my grandmother was born and raised in Jarrow' – Judith Saunders (2006). Well, does anyone else know this?

**'Disappeario crescendo', as the monkey said when the marble clock
fell over the precipice** 'I only ever heard my father say this. It could
be said in consternation, when something suddenly fell; indignantly, if
something suddenly went missing; quietly and resignedly, if something
looked as though it had gone for good. And so on' – Mrs Frances
George, Overton, Hampshire (1995). An incomprehensible Wellerism,
indeed. Compare AS THE MONKEY SAID (page 320).

'My grandmother used to say, "He'll **end up in Dickie's meadow**"
to mean "in bad trouble"' – Mrs Monica van Miert, Tyne and Wear
(1996). The allusion is probably to Bosworth Field, where King
Richard III was defeated and killed in 1485. However, a simpler
explanation has also been offered. Grose's *Dictionary of the Vulgar
Tongue* (1811) defined 'dickie' as a 'donkey', so if you were in dickie's
meadow you were in the mire. See also AS QUEER AS DICK'S HATBAND
(page 238–40).

fat sorrow's better than lean Donald Rimes of Ashford, Middlesex,
wrote (1993), 'A Londoner myself, I was intrigued by this phrase used
by my wife's Yorkshire grandmother.' As well he might be. Presumably
it means, 'It's better to be miserable in comfort.'

David Williams recalled his mother, the Welsh poet Myfanwy Haycock,
reading him this poem when he was a small boy in the 1950s:

> **Fire! Fire! Mrs Briar!**
> Where? Where? Mrs Blair
> Down town, Mrs Brown.

Any damage, Mrs Gamage?
None at all, Mrs Ball.

The Opies appear to overlook this rhyme but it is in *The Annotated Mother Goose* (1962) as:

> 'Fire, fire!' cried the town crier;
> 'Where? Where?' said Goody Blair;
> 'Down the town,' said Goody Brown;
> 'I'll go see't,' said Goody Fleet;
> 'So will I,' said Goody Fry.

The annotation to this is that 'in Puritan Boston, you were called "Mister" only if you had the franchise ... A person without such property, and therefore without the right to vote, was called "Goodman" and his wife "Goodwife" or "Goody".' Perhaps this suggests an American origin for the rhyme? Whatever the case, I rather like the name 'Goody Blair' for the former occupant of 10 Downing Street, though I'm not so sure about 'Goody Brown' for his then neighbour, the Chancellor of the Exchequer, at No. 11.

Fred Fenackerpan (or **Fannackapam** or **Fenackerpan** and so on)
Partridge/Catch Phrases suggests that this was a one-word catchphrase used to convey 'Nonsense!' or 'I don't believe that!' Partridge found no citations before the 1960s, but one of these, a novel set in the First World War, derives it from a ditty or ballad of that time with the title 'Fred Fenackerpan, or the Hero Who Made Victoria Cross'.

In 1932, however, the name was popularized in the form 'Fred Fannakapan' as the title of a comic song written and composed by Reg Low and sung by Gracie Fields. It tells of a family waiting to inspect a daughter's suitor. They have an elaborate tea laid on but when he eventually turns up, he has been at the dentist and can't eat anything.

I think this song was merely written around a name that already existed.

'What I have always imagined to be a family saying turns out to be a Scots expression. "(Go/get) **away to Froochie**," we used to say when I was a kid, meaning, "Stop talking nonsense/we don't believe you." There actually is a place called Freuchie in Fife, to which liars and leg-pullers could be sent. One of the Scottish papers not many years ago suggested it had some antiquity. My impression is that at one time Freuchie was well known, and had much the reputation in Scotland that Gotham had in England' – W.P. Brown, Aberdeen (1994).

how long is a piece of string? An answer to an unanswerable (or poorly posed) question. Date of origin unknown but probably by the 1920s. Suggested answers include, however, 'Twice the length from the end to the middle' or 'Equidistant from the centre'. Used as the title of a book of scientific puzzles by Rob Eastaway and Jeremy Wyndham (2002). 'BBC staff sign own expenses . . . Asked how many claims for under £100 an employee could make, a spokesman for the corporation said, "How long is a piece of string?"' – *Metro* (London) (15 August 2002). Similar questions (akin to meaningless riddles) are: **'How many legs does a shark have?' 'How high is up?'** and **'How high is the moon?'** – hence the song 'How High the Moon' by Lewis/Hamilton (1940).

how many beans make five? A joke riddle, but also a catchphrase uttered as an answer to an impossible question (along the lines of HOW LONG IS A PIECE OF STRING? above, etc.). A Miss Alice Lloyd was singing a music-hall song in November 1898 which contained these lines:

You say you've never heard
How many beans make five?
It's time you knew a thing or two –
You don't know you're alive!

Miss M.L. King, London sw3, told me (1993) that a/the correct answer is 'Two in each hand and one in the mouth'. On the other hand: 'Two in each hand, and one up your — ' – *Wickenden*. Other answers include: 'Two beans, a bean, a bean and a half, and half a bean' – Veronica M. Brown, Wigston, Leicestershire (2002); 'One bean, two beans, a bean-and-a-half and half a bean'; 'One and a half, and a half of one, one and three quarters, one quarter and one'; 'Half a bean, bean, bean and a half, two half beans and a bean'; 'A bean, a bean, a bean and a half, half a bean, and a bean'; 'One and another and two and a t'other'; 'A bean and a half, a bean and a half, half a bean, and a bean and half'; 'A bean and a half and half a bean, a bean and a quarter and a quarter of a bean, half a bean and a bean'.

'I see,' said the blind man (when he couldn't see at all) There are many variations of this piece of nonsense. '"I see," said the blind man. "You're a liar," said the dumb' – mother of Stella Richardson, Essex (1998). 'My family had a particular saying from a previous generation for when, after an explanation, "the penny dropped": "I see," said the blind man. And do you know what he did? He took up a cup and saucer' – Martin Tunnicliffe, West Midlands (2000). 'If my mother could not give an answer to a question, she would say, "I see, said the blind man to his dumb and deaf daughter who was blowing steam off cold cabbage"' – Mrs J. Wood, Nottinghamshire (2000).

Partridge/Catch Phrases has this from America by the late 19th century, as also, '"I see," said the blind man, as he picked up his hammer and saw.'

'Growing up in the Thirties and Forties in Dundee, I found that my mother, who had Irish antecedents, seemed to have a saying to cover every situation, so you knew the state of play immediately. A particular favourite was used in situations where she was looking for an explanation for some misdeed or other and, if she did not believe the facts being offered up, she would say, rather drily, "'I see,' said the blind man and waved his wooden leg'" – Tom Stewart, Orpington, Kent (2002). Compare TOO LATE, TOO LATE (page 367–70).

I stood on the bridge at midnight ... From a delicious nonsense rhyme that used to be recited by the grandfather of Stella Richardson, Essex (1998):

> I stood on the bridge at midnight
> And a thought came into my head.
> What a fool I was to be standing there,
> When I might have been in bed.

I wish I were a little rock ... In the 12th and 13th editions of *Bartlett's Familiar Quotations* (1948 and 1955) (but no later), there is a little poem, 'The Weary Wisher', ascribed to a certain Frederick Palmer Latimer (1875–1940):

> I wish I were a little rock,
> A-sitting on a hill,
> A-doing nothing, all day long,
> But just a-sitting still;
> I wouldn't eat, I wouldn't sleep,
> I wouldn't even wash –
> I'd sit and sit a thousand years,
> And rest myself, b'Gosh!

Could this rhyme have any connection with TO SIT LIKE PIFF(E)Y? (page 43).

in days of old when knights were bold and monkeys chewed tobacco
'A promising start to a story which does not, however, materialize' –
used by the mother of Marjorie Wild, Crediton, Devon (2000).

I seem to recall from my youth a somewhat frisky rhyme beginning,
'In days of old when knights were bold ...' – but can't remember what
happened after that. Tony Malin, Blandford Forum (2003) provided
this full example:

> In days of old when knights were bold
> And women weren't invented
> You stuck your prick in a telegraph pole
> And had to be contented.

And Veronica M. Brown, Wigston, Leicestershire (2002):

> In days of old when knights were bold
> And paper was not invented
> They wiped their arse on a piece of grass
> And walked away contented.

not last night but the night before ... 'I first learnt this chant, a little
naughty, in 1924/5' – Gordon Shilleto, Goring, Berkshire (2001):

> Not last night but the night before
> Two tom cats came knocking at the door.
> I went downstairs to let them in
> And they knocked me down with a rolling pin.

The rolling pin was made of brass
And I fell down on my ... ask
Me no more questions, tell me no more lies
I saw a Chinaman doing up his ... flies
Are a nuisance, bugs are worse,
This is the end of my little verse.

Compare ASK (ME) NO (page 321).

well, now then, sir, Miss Bankhead! In 1993, Carol Williamson of Huntly, Scotland, recalled that her mother (raised on American radio in the 1930s) used to say this regularly. 'Obviously the Miss Bankhead was the original Tallulah, but whose catchphrase was it? I think it might have been Meredith Willson, who wrote the play *The Music Man*.'

Indeed. Thomas Millstead of Chicago came up with the information: 'The phrase was used by the composer and orchestra leader Meredith Willson on actress Tallulah Bankhead's radio program *The Big Show* (mid to late 1940s). It was called "big" because it was a one and one-half hour variety show, very long for radio in those days. Mr Willson (who later wrote the famous Broadway show *The Music Man*) led the orchestra and also had many speaking opportunities. Miss Bankhead, of course, had an exceptionally deep voice. Thus Mr Willson's frequently addressing her as "sir". On *The Big Show*, he also employed a choral group that interacted with him by speaking conversationally instead of singing. He called this act "Meredith Willson and His Talking People".'

'When we were young our parents often took us on Sunday afternoons out to somewhere nice in the countryside to have a cream tea or a picnic, but always on our return home as soon as Father had switched off the engine he would say, **"Olive oil and Tinkerty Tonk!"'** – Mrs Ann Matthews, Ludwell, Dorset (1995).

Partridge/Slang has 'tinkety-tonk' as a farewell remark (like 'toodle-pip').

More mangled words. 'My father, a proficient reader and speller, purposely mispronounced "picturesque" as **"picture-skew"** and "marmalade" as **"mar-mal-a-dee"** – Mrs K.A. King, Gloucestershire (1995).

'When we see cakes in a baker's window, we say, **"Struck through the heart like a penny treacle tart**." Friends, I am sure, think we are mad, but it's like a private joke to us and it's good to think that my grandparents are still alive in word if not in person' – Gail Cromack, Carmarthenshire (1998).

there were two ghostsisisis ... I was sent this curious rhyme for analysis, not having come across it before:

> There were two ghostsisisis
> Sitting on postsisisis
> Fighting with the fistsisisis
> 'Til blood ran down their facesesesis.

Compare this version from *I Saw Esau* (1947) by Iona and Peter Opie:

> There were three ghostesses
> Sitting on postesses

Eating buttered toastesses
And greasing their fistesses
Right up to their wristesses.
Weren't they beastesses
To make such feastesses.

The Opies comment: 'This rhyme may originally have been intended to poke fun at the speech of country bumpkins. In some dialects, words ending in "st" kept the ancient plural – as "nestes" and "frostes". Often this was extended to yet another syllable, and a farm labourer might be heard saying, "They there postesses are all rotten."'

thirty days hath September ... 'Our father died when we were small children. When our mother taught us a ditty about how many days there were to each month, she told us our father had always said this' – Larryu Martinels and Donnamarie Leemarde, Coffrane, Switzerland (1995):

Thirty days hath September,
April, June and no wonder.
All the rest have peanut butter
Except Pasadena
Which has the Rose Bowl.

Molly Gibson of Eastleigh then came forward with the version:

Thirty days hath Sept*ober*
April, June, and no wonder,
All the rest have peanut butter,
Except my second cousin Henry,
Who married a chiffonier,
Which is a tall thing with drawers.

This was sent in by Muriel Smith of Maidenhead and was quoted in *The Quote ... Unquote Newsletter* (July 1997):

> Dirty days hath September,
> April, June and November.
> All the rest are dirty too
> Except February –
> and that's positively filthy.

The next came from Sheila and Ron Pidgley. Something like it has been ascribed to the poet Thomas Hood (1799–1845):

> Dirty days hath September,
> April, June and November.
> February's days are quite all right.
> It only rains from morn to night.
> All the rest have thirty-one
> Without a blessed gleam of sun.
> And if any of them had two and thirty
> They'd be just as wet and just as dirty.

This came from Margaret Procter (1997):

> Thirty days hath September,
> April, June and no wonder,
> All the rest have porridge for breakfast,
> Except my grandma
> And she rides a bike.

A bizarre disc with the title 'I'm in Love with my Little Red Tricycle' was recorded by one Napoleon XIV in 1966 and would seem to be based on this last version:

> Thirty days hath Septober,
> April, June and no wonder,
> All the rest have peanut butter,
> All except my dear grandmother.
> She had a little red tricycle.
> I stole it. Ha ha ha!

And one more for good measure:

> Thirty days hath September,
> All the rest I can't remember.
> The calendar hangs on the wall;
> Why bother me with this at all?

The original rhyme for remembering the number of days in the month was first recorded in the late 16th century.

three towels to use and one to stand on ... Long, long ago, in a galaxy far, far away, someone asked where this slightly sick rhyme about towels came from:

> Said Papa with gay abandon
> Two to use and one to stand on.

Apparently, it is not, as one might have suspected, one of Harry Graham's 'Ruthless Rhymes' or even a 'Cautionary Tale' by Hilaire Belloc. Joe Kralich found this lurking on the internet. I think we may safely ascribe it to Anon:

> Father took his children three
> Bathing. They were drowned, but he

Drying cried in wild abandon,
'Three towels to use and one to stand on.'

to the woods! 'Can anyone tell me where the following piece of dialogue comes from?' – Ludwig Witt (2001):

> To the woods, to the woods.
> But I'm only 13.
> I'm not superstitious.
> I'll call the vicar.
> I am the vicar.
> To the woods, to the woods.
> Anything but the woods.
> Anything?
> To the woods.

Partridge/Catch Phrases describes this as 'the well-known children's dialogue game' and a 'simple, and basically innocent [exchange with which] young Servicemen seek to divert the boredom of life in the barracks, mid C20', when discussing the catchphrases '**I *am* the vicar!**' and 'To the woods!' Obviously, these dialogues took many forms.

I can remember my father telling me this rhyme, probably in the late 1940s. Anonymous, of course, and written probably before 1900, I'd say, as is evidenced by its inclusion in Carolyn Wells, *A Whimsey Anthology* (1906):

> **A tutor who tooted the flute**
> Tried to tutor two tooters to toot.
> Said the two to the tutor

'Is it harder to toot or
To tutor two tutors to toot?'

In fact, the American anthologist includes this in a section of limericks 'by Carolyn Wells', so who am I to deny her the credit, at this distance?

In 2000, Brian Holser's mum wanted to pin down an old song that included the line, **'With her one eye in the pot, and the t'other up the chimney'**. Sydney Treadgold happily responded, 'Since I never throw anything away, I was able to dust off an ancient copy of *The Scout Song Book* where "The Drummer and the Cook" is described simply as a "Capstan shanty".' It begins:

Oh there was a little drummer and he loved a one-eyed cook
And he loved her, O he loved her though she had a cock-eyed
look.

The refrain is:

With her one eye in the pot, and the t'other up the chimney
With a bow-wow-wow, fallal the dow-a-diddy bow-wow-
wow ...

This is an anonymous domestic rhyme, source and date unknown:

Quick! Quick! The cat's been sick.
Where? Where? Under the chair.
Hasten! Hasten! Fetch the basin.
Alack! Alack! It is too late,
The carpet's in an awful state.

No! No! It's all in vain,
For she has licked it up again.

'My father, being a great one for the "bon mot" and the mixed metaphor, would say, "**You can lead a horse to water but a pencil must be lead**"' – Mrs Mary Froom, Devon (1995).

'I had a great aunt who lived in the Yorkshire Dales. She never seemed to get anything right. One of her pet sayings was this: **'Them cuckoos are singing like larks this morning ...'** – Mrs Betty Watts, Bletchley, Milton Keynes (1996).

Chapter 19

TIME FLIES, THE MONKEY SAID

'A saying from my maternal grandfather who died in the early 1960s was: **"Time flies, the monkey said, as he chucked the clock over the wall"'** *– Ann Bamford, Cumbria (2006). This is another Wellerism and also known (by 1974) in the form '*... **as the monkey said when it threw the clock at the missionary***'. And yet again:* '**Time presses, the monkey said, as the grandfather clock fell on him.**' *More sayings on time:*

I'm all behind like the cow's tail What people, like my wife, say when they are behind with their tasks. The expression 'all behind like *a* cow's tail' has also been used to describe a person who is always last or is of a day-dreaming disposition. 'C.H. Rolph' wrote in *London Particulars* (1980), 'Grandma Hewitt [his grandmother] was a walking repository, rather than a dictionary, of clichés and catchphrases; and I have often wished she could have been known to Mr Eric Partridge during the compilation of his delectable dictionaries. Both she and I ... could predate many of [his] attributions. Here are four examples ... all of which were common currency in my Edwardian childhood: "Just what the doctor ordered", "Are you kidding?", "Cheats never prosper", and "All behind like a cow's tail".'

There is also, of course, the expression 'All behind like Barney's bull' – see I'M LIKE BARNEY'S (page 138).

'In our house, when we are running late and all the clocks strike, the cry goes up, "**And all's yet unachieved!**" "Where's that from?" I asked my husband recently. He confidently plumped for *The Lady's Not For Burning* [play by Christopher Fry]. But I said, no, *The Love of Four Colonels* [play by Peter Ustinov]. Turned out I was right' – Thelma Pearce, London SW17 (1992).

beating about the bush What bush are we talking about? Why beat it, anyway? Is there any subtle meaning we are missing here? This probably derives from bird hunting where beaters drive them out of bushes so they can be shot. The basic expression would seem to be 'Don't beat the bush while another takes the bird' (i.e. don't allow someone else to profit from your exertions). Now more commonly, 'Don't prevaricate – get to the point.' So one is saying, 'Don't waste time on preliminaries.'

the early bird catches the worm ... The proverb has been known since the 17th century. Tim Northwood of Trowbridge, Wiltshire (2005), has known this development of it for over 50 years:

> 'The early bird catches the worm'
> Is a proverb often taught.
> But the sage who wrote it forgot to say:
> 'It's the early worm that's caught.'

As *ODP* points out, the corrollary '**... It's the second mouse gets the cheese**' has been attributed to the US comedian Steven Wright.

haven't I been telling you for the past half hour, I'm coming in a minute? 'My mother used to say this' – E. Jean Crossland, Nottinghamshire (1994).

heavens, eleven o'clock and not a whore in the house dressed! This is a thing people say simply to register that 'time is getting on' and they are behindhand. When Derrick Carter of Southwold, Suffolk, wrote to the radio show in 1991 to tell us about an unusual saying of his mother's, he cannot have foreseen the wave of nostalgia he would precipitate. Whenever her domestic programme was falling behind badly, Mr Carter remembered, his mother would say, regardless of the time, 'Heavens, eleven o'clock and not a whore in the house dressed!'

But where had she got this expression from? Mr Carter remarked that both his parents were keen theatre-goers in the 1920s and 30s, and he wondered if his mother might have been quoting a line from a play – though whether one can imagine such a sentiment getting past the blue pencil of the Lord Chamberlain's Office in the days of stage censorship is a different matter.

What is interesting about this expression is that, whereas many 'family sayings' are incomprehensible to outsiders, this one was known to other *Quote...Unquote* listeners. Mona Howard of Hampstead said she believed the full version was, rather: 'Heavens, eleven o'clock and not a whore in the house dressed, not a po emptied and the streets full of Spanish sailors...' Jo Smithies, Isle of Wight, recalled the maternal 'Heavens! four o'clock and not a whore washed and the street full of sailors'. Christopher J. Anderson, Surrey, came up with *his* mother's subtly different 'Heavens! Ten o'clock! Not a bed made, not a po emptied, not a whore in the house dressed and the Spanish soldiers in the courtyard!'

Maude Gifford, Suffolk, said her mother used to say, 'Goodness gracious me, not a girl washed and the street full of Spanish soldiers!' Miss M.L. Fountain of Wembley passed on to us that her brother recalled it, not as a mother's saying, but as something he heard in his days in the navy, in the form: 'Ten o'clock already – no pos emptied, no beds made and a street full of matelots.'

F.H. Loxley, Bristol, dated from 1944 his first hearing of this cry (in the *army*): 'Eight o'clock, and not a whore in the house washed and a troopship in the bay.' Vernon Joyner, Surrey, on the other hand, settled for 'Eleven o'clock, not a whore washed, not a bed made, and the *Japanese fleet* in town!'

Seeking enlightenment, as we do, from the works of Eric Partridge, we find that he only once turned his linguistic attention to the comparatively simple phrase 'eleven o'clock and no pos emptied' – though 'no potatoes peeled' and 'no babies scraped' are mentioned as variants.

In Paul Beale's revision of *Partridge/Catch Phrases*, there is a 1984 reference to a version used by Terry Wogan on his breakfast radio show (after giving a time-check) – '[It's eight twenty-five] ... and not a child in the house washed.' Indeed, the saying has a pronounced Irish air to it. John Millington wrote (1998), 'My wife's mother was from Dublin and spoke of going to the Gate and Abbey theatres before the 1914–18 war. I have seen and heard plays by various Brendans, Seamuses etc., but have never come across this. It was, and still is, said when an unexpected, but known, visitor arrives: "The gas man! Come in, Sir, excuse the cut of the place, Sir. Not a child in the house washed yet, himself coming in any minute and no-one to go for the soap."'

The 'whores/pos/sailors' version is possibly a colourful elaboration of this basic expression. But how do so many people know it? Perhaps, after all, it might just have escaped the stage censor's blue pencil. One could certainly imagine a pantomime dame attempting something similar. In the 1980s, the comedian Les Dawson is reliably reported to have uttered the 'no pos emptied' line in drag. Rupert Hart-Davis in *The Lyttelton Hart-Davis Letters* (Vol. 3, 1981) writes in a letter dated 9 June 1958, 'In the words of the harassed theatrical landlady, "Half-past four, and not a po emptied".'

Whether all or part of the expression is a quotation from a play, or not, one does keep on being drawn back to a possible theatrical origin. The earliest printed reference found to date is in *The Spectator* (24 April 1959), in which Patrick Campbell recorded that 'ten-thirty, and not a strumpet in the house *painted*!' was a favourite saying, apparently in the late 1930s, of Robert Smyllie, editor of the *Irish Times*.

Ravey Sillars of the Isle of Arran told me (2000) that her father, who had fought in the First World War and died in 1940, used to say, 'Look at the time – and not a whore in the house painted!' David D. Higgins, West Yorkshire (2001) relayed a yet further variation: 'Good heavens, the house full of Chinamen and not a pot washed'. An even more substantial variant was reported by M. Stratford, Isle of Wight (1998): 'My mother, busy with five children, suddenly realizing the time was getting late, would look at the clock and exclaim, "Good grief, six o'clock and no sausages pricked!"'

Jillian Oxenham, Pembrokeshire (1994) wrote, 'Although my Cornish husband categorically denies that his mother ever said this, in the seafaring communities of Cornwall, on inquiring, and being told, what time it was, a gasp was often followed by this memorable phrase: "Not a whore in the house washed and Jack coming up the road!"' E.N. Rouse, Worcestershire (2000), wrote, 'Father, when asked the time would say,

'— o'clock, and Lizzie not here yet.' Could this be related in some way?

Compare: 'Look at the time and the bairn's dress is only half made!' and 'Look at the time – and not a dish washed' – from Maurice Dougan, Edinburgh (2003).

Ian Forsyth asked (2005), 'Why do crossword compilers habitually use "the enemy" as a clue for "Time"? My two or three books of quotations do not throw any light on it.' Well, the short answer is: 'Because of the saying **"how goes the enemy?"** for "what's the time?"' The slightly longer answer examines where this originated. It occurs, for example, in Dickens – *Nicholas Nickleby*, Chap. 19 (1839) – but the real origin is a play by Frederick Reynolds called *The Dramatist*, Act 1, Sc. 1 (1789).

A character called 'Ennui the Timekiller' 'whose business it is to murder the hour' (I'm quoting Partridge's *Catch Phrases* here) has this: '(*takes out his watch*) How goes the enemy – only one o'clock! I thought it had been that an hour ago.' When he finds that it is, in fact, past two o'clock, Lord Scratch asks, "And you're delighted because it's an hour', and he replies, 'To be sure I am – my dear friend to be sure I am, the enemy has lost a limb.' *Brewer's Dictionary of Phrase & Fable* had it (until it was accidentally left out of the 2005 edition), with the explanation: 'Time is the enemy of man, especially of those who are behindhand.' The *Oxford Dictionary of Quotations* had the quotation until it was dropped by the editor of the 4th edition.

how long have you got? Response to a simple question that is apparently going to take a long time to answer because it is so complicated and detailed. From the 1990s onwards, especially.

'My mother was born in Gosport in 1893. If she were in a hurry, she would say, **"Oh dear, I'm getting married tomorrow and I've the man to find and the money to borrow'** – H.M. Harpam, Stratford-upon-Avon (2002).

just in time; or, born in the vestry! Said about a late arrival. The writer Antony Jay on *Quote ... Unquote* (29 March 1994) recalled that this is what his mother would say when arriving late. *Partridge/Catch Phrases* noted, 'Obviously, applied [and referring] to a wedding held only just in time to prevent the coming child from being adjudged illegitimate.' Paul Beale added, 'Perhaps modelled on typical Victorian novel-titles.'

'My mother, who was born on Tyneside, would say when her children were "playing for time", **"Less of your hunker sliding."** Apparently North East miners call their haunches "hunkers"' – Mrs S.F. Cooper, Co. Durham (1995).

not in a month of Sundays Not for a very long time, if ever. 'About a task that would never be accomplished' – Stella Richardson, Essex (1998). *OED2* has the phrase 'month of Sundays' = 'long time' in a Captain Marryat novel *Newton Forster* (1832).

In our household, when someone asks, **'What's the time?'** and the answer happens to be (as it does, frequently, for some reason), **'Half-past nine'**, the original inquirer chimes in with, **'Knickers on the line.'** One of a number of ritual additions, this was imported by my wife from her

Buckinghamshire childhood of the 1950s. In a section called 'Crooked Answers' in *The Lore and Language of Schoolchildren* (1959), Iona and Peter Opie print two versions of a rhyme from Alton, Hampshire:

> What's the time?
> Half past nine
> Put the napkins on the line.
> When they're dry
> Bring them in
> And don't forget the safety pin.

And:

> What's the time?
> Half past nine
> Hang your breeches on the line.
> When the copper
> Comes along
> Pull them off and put them on.

In her book *Daddy, We Hardly Knew You* (1989), Germaine Greer described how she had researched her father's true history to find out the answers to questions about him that had always tantalized her. Along the way, she recorded Reg Greer's way of putting down children's questions. For 20 years, if asked, '**What's the time?**', he would invariably reply, '**Must be. Look how dark it is.**'

Chapter 20

ALL THE SHOUTING IN THE WORLD . . .

All the shouting in the world won't make it right – *'This is what a person says when railing at cruel fate'* – Wickenden. *Here are some more reflections on the workings of fate – some comic, some philosophical, some plain sad:*

all good things must come to an end A proverbial expression meaning 'enjoyment/pleasure cannot go on for ever'. Said on the completion of absolutely any activity that has been good fun and usually spoken with a touch of piety. *ODP* points out that the addition of the word 'good' to this proverb is a recent development. 'To all things must be an end' can be traced back to the 15th century. There is a version from 1440 and, as 'everything has an end', the idea appears in Chaucer's *Troilus and Criseyde* (1385). The Book of Common Prayer version of Psalm 119:96 is 'I see that all things come to an end.'

it's all in a lifetime (or **all in one's lifetime**) 'That's life, it's all part of life's rich pageant' – reflective, philosophical phrase, implying resignation to whatever happens or has happened. Since 1849. Mostly American use? P.G. Wodehouse concludes a letter (23 July 1923) in which he describes how he was knocked down by a car: 'But, my gosh! doesn't it just show that we are here today and gone tomorrow! ... Oh, well, it's all in a lifetime!' Hence the title of Walter Allen's novel *All in a Lifetime* (1959).

all such things are sent to try us A common expression used when things go wrong or against us. Quoted in Richard Hoggart, *The Uses of Literacy* (1957): 'Here, as in some others, the connexion with religion is evident.'

'One quote from *Much Binding in the Marsh* [BBC radio show, 1947–53] has become a family catchphrase ever since childhood. Sam Costa, feeling hard done by, would go into an inaudible muttering session, finishing with, "**And I always get the tip-up seat.**" This is used by anyone who thinks they're being put upon' – Jenny Searle, Welwyn Garden City, Hertfordshire (1981).

another page turned in the book of life! A conversational reflection on a death. One of the numerous clichés of bereavement, designed to keep the awfulness of death at bay by means of comfortingly trite remarks. I heard it in about 1960, spoken after the first funeral I attended.

The notion of life as a book whose pages turn can be invoked on other occasions as well. On 1 September 1872, the Revd Francis Kilvert wrote in his diary, 'Left Clyro for ever. A chapter of life closed and a leaf in the Book of Life turned over.'

In its original biblical sense, the said book is a record of those who will inherit eternal life (as in Philippians 4:3 and Revelation 20:12).

'My mother always used the expression "**as sure as God made little apples**" when she believed something would come to pass' – Anon (2003). I am not sure what the origin of this saying is, though I guess it is American. It makes a little more sense if the full version is used, namely, 'as sure as little green apples grow on little green trees'.

'For years I have been trying to find the source of a phrase my father *always* quoted as he started the car at the beginning of a journey: '**And away we go, with the best of luck, and a tin of Tickler's Jam ...**' – Rob Gower (2001). *Partridge/ Catch Phrases* has 'Tickler's Jam' meaning 'army rations'. One might also note the echo of the line from a First World War song, 'Over the top with the best of luck/Parley-voo'.

In 2004, David Critchlow set me the task of finding out where this near-platitude or bromide came from: '**I was told to cheer up, things could be worse. So I cheered up and, lo, things did get worse.**' David says he first heard it in 1947 but is sure that it is much older. Maybe. I've no idea. Meanwhile, Jonathan Scott sent me this version on a wall plaque, made in Canada in the early 1970s:

> One day as I sat musing,
> Sad and lonely,
> And without a friend,
> A voice came to me from out
> Of the gloom saying,
> 'Cheer up, things could be worse!'
> So I cheered up – and sure enough,
> Things got worse.

everything comes to he who waits – only some of us wait a bloody sight longer than others – *Wickenden.* The basic proverb, 'All things come to those who wait', dates back to the 16th century, though with different wording.

hope for the best, expect the worst and take what comes An anonymous motto, quoted by Arthur Marshall on *Quote . . . Unquote* (1 August 1987), who said that he was told it by a no-nonsense President of a Women's Institute. Apparently, it originated with Queen Alexandra (1844–1925), who used to write it in people's birthday books.

if they fell down a sewer they'd come up smelling of roses 'On someone always having good luck' – *Wickenden*. The *OED2* does not find 'to come out of something smelling of roses', meaning 'to emerge with an unblemished record', before 1968.

it could have been worse – it might have been raining Mock consolation in the form of a fairly well-established rueful comment. In 2004, T.A. Dyer pointed me in the direction of what just might be the original utterance. Field Marshal The Viscount Slim in his volume of memoirs *Defeat Into Victory* (1956) is describing the low point of the retreat of forces under his command in Burma (1942): 'The situation was grave ... when even the most confident staff officer and the toughest soldier want holding up, and they turn where they *should* turn for support – to their commander. And sometimes he does not know what to say ... "Well, gentlemen," I said, putting on what I hoped was a confident, cheerful expression, "it might be worse!" One of the group, in a sepulchral voice, replied with a single word: "How?" I could cheerfully have murdered him, but instead I had to keep my temper. "Oh," I said, grinning, "it might be raining!" Two hours later, it was – hard ...'

Viewing again the Mel Brooks film *Young Frankenstein* (us 1974), I let out a little cheer when Dr F. (Gene Wilder) and Igor (Marty Feldman) are disinterring a body in a graveyard. Says Dr F., 'What a filthy job.' Replies Igor, 'Could be worse.' 'How?' 'Could be raining.' And then it starts to pour down.

it isn't always dark at six 'At the lowest is the acceptance of life as hard, with nothing to be done about it: put up with it and don't aggravate the situation' – a comment on this traditional saying by Richard Hoggart in *The Uses of Literacy* (1957). He also includes: '**Life is no bed of roses**',

'Tomorrow will take care of itself', 'Ah well, we live in hopes' and 'We're short of nowt we've got'.

'The senior English tutor at my school (Dunstable School, Beds.) was Mr C.L. Harris, brother of Christopher Fry, incidentally, and he was frequently heard to mutter, in a sneering tone:

> **There's nothing new,**
> **And there's nothing true,**
> **And it don't signify!**

'The frustration at being unable to identify the source has been eating me away ever since!' – John A. Plowman, Yeovil, Somerset (1998).

Well, 'it don't signify', on its own, goes back through Dickens and Swift to about 1729. As for the rest, Sylvia Dowling pointed out that *Benham's Book of Quotations* has 'Nothing's new and nothing's true and nothing matters', attributed to Lady Morgan, the popular novelist (1776–1859).

Joe Kralich discovered an article, 'David Copperfield and Arthur Pendennis', in *The Times* (11 June 1851). It was unsigned but apparently was the work of Samuel Phillips. He tantalizingly wrote, 'The *morale* might almost be summed up into the American's creed, "There's nothing new, there's nothing true, and it don't signify".' So who was this American?

Marian Bock found Sir Richard Burton, the explorer and translator, up to the same trick. In his notes to *The Kasidah of Haji Abdu El-Yezdi* (1880), he wrote, 'But our Haji [one who has made the pilgrimage to Mecca] is not Nihilistic in the "no-nothing" sense of Hood's poem, or, as the American phrases it, "There is nothing new, nothing true, and it don't signify".' Marian reported that two Burton experts both considered that 'the American' here means Americans in general. But, as she noted, Burton regularly assumes that everyone will know his sources. In the same passage, he quotes four lines of poetry by 'the light Frenchman'.

Then Mark English turned up the best 'earliest use' so far. In *Representative Men* (1850), R.W. Emerson (who was, of course, an American) wrote in an essay on Montaigne: 'Why should we fret and drudge? Our meat will taste to-morrow as it did yesterday, and we may at last have had enough of it. "Ah," said my languid gentleman at Oxford, "there's nothing new or true, – and no matter".'

As, presumably, this is Oxford, England, we may have evidence here that the phrase is not actually American in origin. Mark also found another non-American use in an issue of *Notes & Queries* dating from 1887: 'The Cornish version of this proverb has been known to me for many years: "There's nothing new, and there's nothing true, and it don't sinnify" (signify); and I supposed it to be peculiar to that country.'

we only live once (or **you only . . .**) A common proverb but little recorded in the books. The earliest citation to hand is from the *Los Angeles Times* (10 June 1923).

In 2005, Marie Crawford of Liverpool wrote, 'In the May Blitz of 1941, my mother lost her mother, her father, her brother, her sister, her nephew and an unborn child. There was no funeral but my mother placed an obituary notice in the *Liverpool Echo* which included the quotation':

'Who picked this rose?' said the gardener.
'I,' said the Master – And the gardener answered him not.

'The newspaper cutting was kept in a little drawer in my parents' bedroom and from an early age I would read it and remember feeling very sad. I was never able to ask my mother about it as she could not bear to talk about that terrible time. I seem to remember that the *Echo*'s offices had books of verses to choose from but I would love to know the source.'

The short answer is that we have not been able to find out where this familiar quotation originated. I presume the gardener is asking, 'Why did this person die?' and the Master is God or perhaps Jesus. Indeed, there would seem to be some sort of allusion to John 20:14–17, in which Mary Magdalene encounters Jesus at the sepulchre after the crucifixion and 'supposing him to be the gardener, saith unto him, Sir, if thou have borne him hence, tell me where thou hast laid him ... Jesus saith unto her, Mary. She turned herself, and saith unto him, Rabboni; which is to say, Master.'

The curious thing about the quotation is that, although the wording sometimes differs ('... and the garden/gardener fell silent/was silent', for example) there is never any more of it.

I have found it used countless times in In Memoriam notices, in Britain and especially the US. A tombstone inscription said to date from 1879 is reported to go: '"Who plucked that flower?" cried the gardener, as he walked through the garden. His fellow servant answered, "The Master". And the gardener held his peace.'

In the 1851–8 segment of George L. Prentiss, *The Life and Letters of Elizabeth Prentiss* (1882) – she was an American authoress – there is this, included in her description of the death of a child: '"Oh," said the gardener, as he passed down the garden-walk, "who plucked that plant?" His fellow-servants answered, "The MASTER!" And the gardener held his peace.'

I can well believe that it was a standard text in American funeral homes and newspapers, but why so obscurely allusive? John Julius Norwich reminded me that he included this (obviously close) parallel in his 1988 *Christmas Cracker*. It is from the ending to 'The Gardener', a short story in Rudyard Kipling's *Debits and Credits* (1926):

A man knelt behind a line of headstones – evidently a gardener, for he was firming a young plant in the soft earth. She went towards him, her paper in her hand. He rose at her approach and without prelude or salutation asked: 'Who are you looking for?'

'Lieutenant Michael Turrell – my nephew,' said Helen slowly and word for word, as she had many thousands of times in her life.

The man lifted his eyes and looked at her with infinite compassion before he turned from the fresh-sown grass toward the naked black crosses.

'Come with me,' he said, 'and I will show you where your son lies.'

When Helen left the cemetery she turned for a last look. In the distance she saw the man bending over his young plants; and she went away, supposing him to be the gardener.

John Julius notes that 'the all-important reference is to John 20:15', as I have pointed out above. Also it is poignant to know that Kipling lost his own son in the First World War and was instrumental in composing the official wording for memorials to the fallen.

Dr Trevor Griffiths contributed (2006) a telling reminiscence: 'I encountered the quotation in a book entitled *C.T. Studd, Cricketer and Pioneer* by Norman P. Grubb (1933). The situation was that Studd and his wife had lost a child at birth and someone sent them this message.

'I remember the quote very clearly because shortly after I had read it, my then Bible Class leader and his wife had a stillborn boy, and I copied it out on to a card I sent them. It was:

"Who plucked this flower?" cried the master. "I", said the Gardener, and the master held his peace.

'This particular use of the quote places it over one hundred years, in Victorian times, because the use of the word "master" refers not to Jesus but to the owner of the garden and the Gardener, written with a capital "G" refers to God.'

Chapter 21

A SURE SIGN OF FINE WEATHER

'My father (late schoolteacher of Nottingham) had a saying which he used to trot out when the weather looked a bit doubtful: **"If it looks like rain and doesn't rain, it's a sure sign of fine weather!"** *– George Hill, Bromley (2000). Weather words and phrases are often mighty strange and weather lore exceedingly unhelpful ...*

'The uncle and aunt who raised me in the 1920s taught me about thunder: "Don't be afraid – **it's only the angels moving their beds**"' – Ken Marshall, Basingstoke (1993).

Casson/Grenfell has the nannyism: '**Thunder is clouds knocking together**' and *Widdowson* has, from South Yorkshire: 'When thunder is heard, the child's fears are allayed by references such as "**T'od lad's rollin' barrels upstairs**" or in Lincolnshire, "**Elephants are dancing**".'

cold enough for a walking stick 'An uncle's favourite expression' – Margaret Thompson, Liverpool (1999). This was also said by the father of Lewis Conquer (2002), in addition to '**cold enough for two pairs of bootlaces**'. And there is '**cold enough for two hairnets**' – 'my father-in-law attributes this to a Northern comedian whose name momentarily escapes me' – Francesca Nelson (2002).

enough blue to make a pair of sailor's trousers This saying is listed in *Casson/Grenfell* as an example of 'nanny philosophy': 'If there's enough blue sky to make a pair of sailor's trousers then you can go out.' *Brewer's Dictionary of Phrase & Fable* (1989) glossed it as 'two patches of blue appearing in a stormy sky giving the promise of better weather' and notes the alternative 'Dutchman's breeches' for 'sailor's trousers'. Indeed, 'Dutchman's breeches' would seem to be the original version, as stated in William H. Smyth, *The Sailor's Wordbook* (1867): '*Dutchman's breeches*, the patch of blue sky often seen when a gale is breaking, is said to be, however small, "enough to make a pair of breeches for a Dutchman".'

heaven help the sailors on a night like this! 'My grandmother on the North East coast would exclaim this when the wind howled around the house' – Ian Forsyth, Co. Durham (2000).

Compare these sayings from *Partridge/Catch Phrases*: 'Pity the poor sailor on a night like this!'; 'God help sailors on a night like this'; and 'God help the poor sailors ...'

it's a monkey's wedding This is, apparently, a 20th-century African catchphrase, 'applied to weather characterized by a drizzling rain accompanied by a shining sun' – *Partridge/Catch Phrases*, and known by 1968. Sometimes this has been reported as '**it's a monkey's birthday**'.

For the same eventuality, there is also '**a fox's wedding and a monkey's dance**' – used when it starts to rain but the sun continues to shine and 'first heard in a military boarding school at Sanawar, India', by Grace Constable (2000). Interestingly, *Partridge/Slang* has 'monkey's wedding' as a naval term for an unpleasant smell. Given that foxes are also noted for their smell, could there be something to do with the smell of sun on damp ground going on here?

Compare: '**The Devil is beating his wife.**' *Apperson* dates from 1666 the proverbial expression, 'When it rains and the sun shines at the same time the devil is beating his wife.' Or '... is beating his grandmother ... he is laughing and she is crying.'

Widdowson notes: 'When rain falls while the sun is shining, a common saying is, "**It's only a sunshower; it won't wet you.**"'

'When a day dawns wet and stormy, or inclement in any way, as a reaction to people who call such days "nasty", my family's saying is: "**It's always a good day, but sometimes it's more difficult to tell**"' – Wendy-Ann Street, Ipswich (2002).

it's dark over Bill's mother's way An extremely well-known comment on the weather when rain threatens, sometimes with '**black**' in place of 'dark' and '**Will's**' instead of 'Bill's'. Paul Beale in his revision of Partridge/*Catch Phrases* mentions the expression 'It's a bit black over Bill's mother's' and gives an East Midlands source. H.S. Middleton, Shropshire, formerly of Leicestershire, whose brother was called Bill, wrote in 1993 to say how, in the early 1920s, a certain Len Moss had looked through the sitting-room window in the direction of Mr Middleton's home and said, 'It looks black over Bill's mother's.' Was this the origin of the phrase?

All I was able to tell Mr Middleton was that in 1930, the erudite journal *Notes & Queries* carried a query about this phrase in the form 'it looks pretty black over Will's Mother's'. Here it was described as an 'old Sussex' saying ... and there was no response to the query.

Barry Day, a Brit in New York, recalled that 'It's a bit black over Bill's mother's' used to be said a great deal by *his* mother when he was growing up in Derbyshire (1940s/50s). 'It was always said ironically,' he added. 'So I can confirm its Midlands usage.'

I first heard about it on a London radio phone-in (June 1990), in the form, 'It looks like rain ... over Will's mother's way.' In the language journal *Verbatim* (Autumn 1993), Alan Major discussed a number of 'Kentish sayings' and included 'out Will's mother's way', meaning 'somewhere else, in the distance, on the horizon'. Major added, 'Who Will's mother was is unknown, but there are several similar expressions, with word variations, used in other English counties. In Gloucestershire, the expression is "It's dark over our Bill's Mum's mind".'

The Revd P.W. Gallup, Hampshire, wrote in 1994 that he had traced the saying in eleven counties and commented on its age: 'I have friends in their late eighties who as children knew it well from their parents and say that it was then widely known and used. This suggests that the saying has been used at least by several generations.'

Since 1993, I have received a goodly number of claims from correspondents that they were personally acquainted with the original Bill and his mother.

lovely weather for ducks! What you say, philosophically, when it is raining. Although it must be ancient, I have not found a citation in this precise form before 1985. *Partridge/Catch Phrases* finds 'nice weather for ducks' in Philip Oakes, *Experiment at Proto* (1973). *Apperson* has 'Weather meete to sette paddockes [frogs] abroode in' from Heywood's *Proverbs* (1546) and 'another fine week for the ducks' in Charles Dickens, *The Old Curiosity Shop*, Chap. 2 (1840). He also suggests that the predominant form is 'fine weather for ducks'. 'Nice weather for young ducks and mud up to y'r knees when you goes round to the well' – Flora Thompson, *Lark Rise to Candleford*, Chap. 28 (1945).

a mackerel sky is very wet – or very dry The actress Siân Phillips chose this to illustrate the unhelpfulness of weather proverbs on *Quote ... Unquote* (13 April 1993). Mrs Barbara Williams, Plymouth, Devon, wrote (1993) that the version she grew up with was, 'Mackerel sky, mackerel sky/Neither wet, neither dry.' *Apperson* finds any number of explanations as to what a mackerel sky foretells and none of them is very helpful. For example from West Somerset (1886): 'Mackerel-sky! not much wet, not much dry.'

raining cats and dogs Meaning 'raining extremely heavily'. It was well-known by 1738 – according to Swift's *Polite Conversation* – though there is a 1652 citation: 'Raining dogs and polecats'. The poet Shelley wrote of 'raining cats and dogs' in a letter to a friend (1819).

There is no very convincing explanation for the phrase. According to the *Morris Dictionary of Word and Phrase Origins* (1977), it comes from the days when street drainage was so poor that a heavy rain storm could easily drown cats and dogs. After the storm people would see the number of dead cats and dogs and think it looked as if they had fallen out of the sky.

Brewer's Dictionary of Phrase & Fable (1989 edn) suggests, on the other hand, that in northern mythology cats were supposed to have great influence on the weather and that dogs were a signal of wind, 'thus cat may be taken as a symbol of the downpouring rain, and the dog of the strong gusts of wind accompanying a rain-storm'.

rain in June keeps all in tune In *Love from Nancy: The Letters of Nancy Mitford* (1993), reference is made to a letter to her from her sister Diana Mosley (dated 10 June 1946): 'About the time of the [V-Day] procession I saw Baker [the gamekeeper at Diana's home, Crowood] & said terribly wet. Yes he replied, his mind on farming, but they do say Rain in June keeps all in tune.' They do, indeed. An earlier form of the proverb (recorded in 1846) is: 'A good leak in June/Sets all in tune.'

Chapter 22

OLDER THAN MY TEETH

*When asked their age by inquisitive young persons, nannies and other such older persons are traditionally supposed to reply, '**A little older than my teeth and as old as my tongue**.' This is how the saying appears in* Casson/Grenfell, *but long before that Jonathan Swift had reversed matters in his* Polite Conversation *(1738) as, 'Why, I am as old as my Tongue, and a little older than my teeth.' 'When a child asks, "How old are you, Mummy?" the stock response is, "As old as my tongue and a bit older than my teeth"' – Widdowson. More evasions on the subject of age:*

'My mother would never tell me how old she was. When I asked her she would answer, "Twenty – **and the rest**." She never would say how many years the "rest" was' – Andrew G. Forsyth, Hertfordshire (1996).

'My Yiddische Mama, towards the end of her life, had everything under the sun wrong with her. When anyone asked, "How are you?", she would say, "**Apart from my health, I'm all right**." Now I'm nearly 80, I use the same answer' – Anne Lubin, Swindon (2002).

'It was 1929. I was just coming into my father's sitting room with afternoon tea when I heard a prim little 80-year-old just saying, 'Indeed, Mr Steen, I don't in the least mind dying – **but I have a great distaste for the preliminaries**.' I was 20 at the time but I've never forgotten and often quoted it! – Mrs S.L. Brunyate, Bangor, Northern Ireland (1996).

I was delighted when Mary Jaquet drew my attention to some verses entitled 'I Can't Remember' that she had seen printed in the church magazine of a Somerset village. They were found among the papers of Henry Adams (1907–2000) of Milverton and were ostensibly original, although they included four lines that have been the subject of one of our searches since 1998:

> I got used to my arthritis,
> To my dentures I'm resigned,
> I can manage my bifocals,
> **But Lord I miss my mind.**

In fact, I am now inclined to think that Mr Adams had merely copied out a poem variously entitled 'Join the Club!', 'An Ode to Forgetfulness' and 'A Little Mixed Up', which sometimes includes the above four lines and sometimes does not.

Findlay Dunachie meanwhile spotted the four-line version being ascribed to John Sparrow in Noel Annan, *The Dons* (1999), where it is given the title 'Growing Old':

> I'm accustomed to my deafness,
> To my dentures, I'm resigned,
> I can cope with my bifocals,
> But – oh dear! – I miss my mind.

Annan comments that this was frequently quoted and misquoted but seldom ascribed correctly. Sparrow, Warden of All Souls, Oxford, from 1952 to 1977, was no mean poet. Towards the end of his life, when I met him, he was, alas, well into his own 'missed mind' period, but I am not convinced that he originated this. He died in 1992. According to two sources, the above was also the version quoted (without attribution) by the former Liberal leader, Jo (Lord) Grimond (who died in 1993).

However, I think I may have discovered what prompted Annan to make the attribution. In Sparrow's *Grave Epigrams and other verses* (1981) there occurs this little piece entitled (with a nod, of course, to Galileo) *'Eppur si muove'*:

> To age and imbecility resigned,
> I watch the struggles of my failing mind:
> Lumbering along the all-too-well-worn grooves
> The poor old thing moves slowly – but it moves!

I was born in nineteen hundred and frozen to death A slightly facetious way of not revealing one's age. Veteran TV announcer

Macdonald Hobley said it on BBC Radio 2 *Where Were You in '62?* in 1982. Another version is '**. . . in nineteen hundred and mind your own business**'.

in Johnny Gough's garden Meaning 'in the cemetery' = 'dead'. Told to me on an LBC radio phone-in, London, in June 1990, but otherwise untraced and unexplained.

it'd be a blessing if the Lord called him/her 'Of a hypochondriac old person' – Stella Richardson, Essex (1998).

I. Moore of Manchester wrote (1994): 'My father was the youngest of a large family and when his older sisters read the deaths in the paper, they used to say, "**I'll just see who's given up smoking.**" For years, he used to think that if you gave up smoking, your name went in the newspaper.'

just because there's snow on the roof, it doesn't mean the boiler's gone out An older man's avowal that he is not finished yet – quoted by the actor Peter Jones (1920–2000) on *Quote . . . Unquote* (13 April 1993). A modern proverbial expression, I should think, and possibly American in origin.

many years ago . . . An introductory phrase from the writer and broadcaster Denis Norden's 'list of old person's phrases' – which he referred to on *Quote ... Unquote* (21 May 1996). He also mentioned **'when I was your age ...'** and **'... which was a lot of money in those days'**.

there's life in the old dog yet This expression of wonder may be uttered at the unexpected possession of some power by someone or something thought to be 'past it' (especially when referring to the person's love life). It was used as the title of a painting (1838) – precisely, 'The Life's in the Old Dog Yet' – by Sir Edwin Landseer, that shows a Scottish ghillie rescuing a deerhound which, unlike a stag and two other hunting dogs, has not just plunged to its death over a precipice.

three score years and ten What has come to be considered as a person's allotted span in biblical times, after Psalm 90:10: 'The days of our years are three score years and ten.' But in truth the Bible is simply suggesting that it is a good age to live to.

wear out the oldest first What an old person undertaking an onerous chore might say. This occurs in Jonathan Swift, *Polite Conversation* (1738) – which shows it must have had whiskers on even then:

Neverout: Miss, come be kind for once, and order me a dish of coffee.
Miss: Pray, go yourself; let us wear out the oldest first.

Chapter 23

IT'S CALLED MIND YOUR OWN BUSINESS

*This chapter is devoted to what I call 'fobbing-off phrases' – those
many expressions used by parents and nannies to deal with the endless
questions posed by children. Professor J.D.A. Widdowson, of the
former Centre for English Cultural Tradition and Language at the
University of Sheffield made these comments to me on this category
(2006): 'Folklorists commonly refer to these as put-offs, i.e. expressions
used to deflect questions, especially when the questions are addressed to
adults by children. In my experience, put-offs are typically used when
adults do not wish to divulge the true answer to a given question,
for whatever reason.'*

*'This asking of questions [by children]teased their mother and made
them unpopular with the neighbours ... One old woman once handed
the little girl a leaf from a pot-plant on her window-sill. "What's it
called?" was the inevitable question. "'Tis called mind your own
business," was the reply' – Flora Thompson,* Lark Rise, *Chap. 1
(1939). The concept of 'minding one's own business' occurs in Francis
Bacon's* Essays *(1625) but the dismissive injunction, 'Mind your own
business' does not seem to have been recorded before the 1880s.*

'My Cumbrian grandmother when asked a question would reply, "**The answer's a lemon.**" "Why?" we asked. "**Suck it and see**," was her response' – Janet C. Egan, Middlesex (2000).

This exchange brings together two well-known expressions, much used separately. 'The answer is a lemon', being a non-answer to a question or a refusal to do something requested of one, is probably of American origin and seems to have been in use by 1910. A lemon is acidic and sour, and there are several other American phrases in which a lemon denotes that something is unsatisfactory or not working properly. The lemon is also the least valuable object on a fruit machine.

'Suck it and see', meaning 'try it out', presumably derives from what you would say about a sweet – 'suck it and see whether you like the taste of it'. It was used as a catchphrase by Charlie Naughton of the Crazy Gang in the 1940s/50s, though it is probably of earlier music-hall origin – at least according to W. Buchanan-Taylor, *One More Shake* (1944). *Partridge/Slang* dates it from the 1890s. A correspondent, H.E. Johnson, suggested (1999) that it started with a *Punch* cartoon at the turn of the 19th/20th century, with the caption: '*First urchin:* "I don't know if this here's a plum or a beetle." *Second urchin:* "Suck it and see."'

as the monkey said ... Introductory phrase to a form of fobbing-off Wellerism. For example, if a child says it can't wait for something, the parent says, 'Well, as the monkey said when the train ran over its tail, "It won't be long now."' The singer/songwriter Dillie Keane, speaking in 1990, revealed that her Irish father would always repeat this, 'if, as a child, you said you couldn't wait for something'. According to *Partridge/Slang*, there is any number of 'as the monkey said' remarks in which there is always a simple pun at stake: e.g. '"They're off!" shrieked the monkey, as he slid down the razor blade' or '... when he sat on the circular saw'.

'This rhyme was oft-quoted at home during my childhood':

Ask no questions, hear no lies.
Ever seen a donkey doing up his flies
Are a nuisance, bees are a pest,
Rowntrees chocolate I like best.

– Bryn Strudwick, Basingstoke (2006).
Compare NOT LAST NIGHT (page 280).

because I say so! The most common parental statement? 'This was one of my mother's favourite retorts in my childhood – often illustrating her inability to give a reasonable response/answer after being asked 'Why?', as a consequence of a seemingly unreasonable and/or illogical order/request/statement! The incessant frustration led to a quest for perfection and my becoming a Work Study Engineer in later life where Critical Analysis was a key technique and one of the key areas in that technique was the 'Why, what, where, who and how?' research. After umpteen investigations, it emerged that one of the most common reasons for holding back progress and change, frustrating efficiency, or a manager "guarding" his territory was "We've always done it that way"!' – Bryan Taylor, Liskeard (2001).

From Jennifer Forsyth of Grange-over-Sands (1994): 'A family expression, now being used by the fourth generation, often startles the uninitiated. My mother's eldest sister, born in 1897, had been asked out to tea by a neighbour and she was to go there unescorted. This caused her some anxiety and she asked her mother, "What shall I say when I get there?" The reply didn't allay her fears and she kept on repeating, 'But what shall I say...?' Her youngest sister was quite exasperated by all this

shilly-shallying and crossly retorted, "Oh, say, '**Botty with drawers on**'"
– the rudest thing she could dream up in 1905. Since then, if there is
nothing to be said, it is "B.W.D.O.", which might be received on a
postcard from foreign climes, or as a response to routine family enquiries
on health or the state of the nation.'

bread and pullet [or **pullit** or **smell it**] A well-known riposte from a
parent when asked, for example, usually by a small person, 'What's for
tea?' Although it has been suggested that 'pullet' refers to the leftovers
that have to be pulled from the leg of a fowl, I think the following
explanations are more convincing:

 'My Victorian grandmother also used the phrase "Bread and pull it".
As she explained, you put a slice of bread into your mouth and pull it'
– Robin Steers, East Sussex (1995). 'I was reminded of my grandmother's
stock response. In childhood, I heard it as "Bread and tillet", and took it
as some kind of spread. Now I realize that she said "till it" (to it), being
of Scots descent' – Margaret Mitchell, Merseyside (1995). 'When as a
small child I asked my mother what was for dinner, I got "bread and
pullit" or "What do you fancy, a parrot or a monkey?" or "Legs of chairs
and pump handles"' – Enid Grattan-Guinness, Hertfordshire (1995).

 'As many may think it has nothing to do with chicken (pullet), I
believe it refers to the days when families were very large and there was
not much money to feed them. The idea was that they would have a
piece of bread and pull it as far as it would go, to make a small amount
of food feed several people' – Sheila J. Wilberforce, Argyll and Bute
(1996). 'My mother used to say "Bread and Pullett', supposedly a
reference to a poor family who had to take the bread and pull it to make
it go round' – Sylvia Dowling, Lancashire (1998). 'I recently came across
a Victorian recipe for "Pulled Bread". The white crumb was peeled from
the middle of a freshly baked, still warm loaf. This was then put in the
oven until golden brown' – John Smart, Essex (2000). 'Being brought
up in "straitened" circumstances in Sheffield just after the war, I was

frequently told by my mother that we would have to live on "bread and pullet" for the rest of the week. The invariable answer to the question "Why pullet?" was very simple: "To make it go further!"' – Peter Ellis, Market Bosworth (2002).

'I am reminded of my grandmother with whom I often stayed as a child. Me: "Grannie, what's for lunch today?" Grannie: "**Dried bread and scratch it.**" A Jamaican colleague says she has "dried bread and scratch it" from her family as well' – David Mills (2003).

So, the basic expression would seem to refer to bread without any addition of butter or jam, just plain fare.

Many other fobbing-off phrases exist in answer to the question, 'What's for lunch/tea/dinner?' *Widdowson* has: '**few broth**', '**fresh air and snowballs**', '**steam pasty**' or '**toughened dumplings out o' t'pan**' and adds that 'a much more direct reply is, "**What you get, and like it too.**"' *Casson/Grenfell* contributes the nannyism '**a rasher of wind and a fried snowball**'.

'My grandmother had a hard life, widowed in 1926 with six children and one on the way. This perhaps gave her a philosophical, albeit rather vulgar, outlook on life. If her hungry children clamoured to know what was for tea, she would reply, "**Cow's arse and cabbage**"' – Isabel Worcester, Surrey (2002). 'My mum (born 1904) when asked, "What's for dinner?" would say, "**Cow's cock and cauliflower**" – and she was a lady mostly' – Marian E. Rowe, Dunkirk, Kent (2004).

'My Cumbrian grandmother, when asked what was for lunch, would reply, "**Fried framlings and buttered haycocks**"' – Janet C. Egan, Middlesex (2000). A haycock is a heap of hay in a field, but what a framling is, I know not (except that Framling is the name of a place in Hertfordshire).

According to Ms J. Harrison of Powys, 1994, **knobs and chairs and pump-handles** 'was my mother's reply to our daily demands of "What's for dinner, Mum?" The vision of this has always fascinated me. Mum said her father always used to say it.'

Margaret Rowden, Somerset (1995) offered **liver with lace holes in,** while Janet C. Egan, Middlesex (2000) wrote that her Cumbrian grandmother would say, '"**Potatoes and point**" when asked what was for lunch …' –

'My mother, Winnie Barratt, who still lives in the Black Country, whenever asked what's for tea but doesn't know or else doesn't want to say, replies, "**Tripe and trolleybobs!**"' – Rob Barratt, Lostwithiel, Cornwall (2003).

Mrs Tickner of West Byfleet, Surrey, wrote (1994) to say that when asked, 'What have we for pudding?', her mother would reply, '**Wait-and-see pudding**', and this was also contributed by Marjorie Wild of Crediton, Devon (2000).

Compare: 'Patience pudding with wait-a-while sauce' – a nannyism in *Casson/Grenfell* – and THREE JUMPS AT THE CUPBOARD DOOR AND A BITE AT THE LATCH (page 335).

'What do you have there, Mum?' – '**Cat fur to make kitten britches**.' Source: David V. Barrett (2003). Compare LAROVERS FOR MEDDLERS (page 327).

the cat's eaten it In *Lore and Language* (July 1980), J.B. Smith noted that this 'evasive answer purporting to explain the disappearance of food, is an allusion to the tale-type exemplified by the Grimms' "Clever Gretel", a story which deals with the ingenious excuse devised by a greedy cook who eats the meal she is supposed to have prepared for a guest.'

In her book *Daddy, We Hardly Knew You* (1989), Germaine Greer recalls this expression of her father's: 'At the dinner-table where we children were forbidden to speak, he occasionally held forth … [but] if I pounced on some statement that seemed to me to reflect however dimly upon the real world [he would say], **"I've forgotten more than you're ever likely to know."** This fatuous hyperbole dismayed me ... but perhaps after all it was literally true. Daddy's whole life was an exercise in forgetting.'

This would appear to be a venerable put-down. Something like it has been found in 1685. The proverb 'We have all forgot more than we remember' was known by 1732.

'My Grandma, who was born in 1878 (big generation gap in our family), always used a saying that I have never heard anyone else say: **"Grease your bottom and slide down a rainbow."** This she would say if you were particularly pleased with yourself and singing your own praises' – Stella Ellis, Crowthorne, Berkshire (2002).

half past kissing time – time to kiss again 'In answer to the question, "What time is it?"' – *Widdowson*.

'Here is something my Mum used to say to us children all them years ago. When we complained, "Mum, these crusts are so hard", she would say, **"Harder when there are none, my dear"**' – Mrs Tickner, West Byfleet, Surrey (who was 84 when she wrote in 1994).

hay: horses eat it, cows chew it and it grows this high in China 'In response to use of "Heh?"' – John Alexander, Stockport, Cheshire (2000).

'When I was a child and my mother was talking to somebody and I said, as children do, "What did you say?", if she didn't want to tell me, she would always state, "**He's gone round the corner with a brick under his arm**." When I asked her what she meant, she said, "I've no idea. It's what my mother always said to me." I said it to my daughter and now my daughter says it to my granddaughter, with the same reply' – Frances Haskins, Wootton Bassett, Wiltshire (2001).

I hear you 'I hear what you say but am not going to do anything about it' – a Scots expression meaning that a remark is not worth considering or is untrue and is certainly not going to be responded to.

Notably used by Lord Reith to fob off suggestions by Malcolm Muggeridge in the BBC TV programme *Lord Reith Looks Back* (1967) – 'Presented with an argument that he intended to ignore, Lord Reith would say in a matter-of-fact way: "I hear you." It was an admirably plonking rhetorical device' – *The Listener* (5 May 1977).

Margaret Martin of New Malden, Surrey, wrote (1993), 'My mother communicated in epigrams. If I complained that I could not find something, I was told, "**I saw the dog eating something**." Needless to say, no dog!'

'If, as a child, you said, "I want something", they [my parents] would say, "**I want doesn't get**"' – Sarah Hall, Eye, Suffolk (2005).

I think this is a universal nannyism, though *Casson/Grenfell* has it as, 'I want gets nothing'. Compare: **I want never gets**. 'If one said, "I want …", we would be told, "Want never gets" or "Want will be your master"' – Miss O.E. Burns, Stourbridge, Gloucestershire (1995).

'My Liverpool Nan had a wealth of sayings. If anyone said, "I've got an idea!", she would retort, "Well, **sew a button on it!**"' – Paul Thompson, Scone (2004).

'Whenever I made an extravagant or boastful utterance, my grandmother would say, '**I've heard geese fart before in windy weather.**' – George Goldsmith-Carter, Kent (1989). Date of origin unknown. Another correspondent recalls this as, 'I've heard ducks fart before.'

'We have a saying in our family. It is, "**If I knew the answer to that, I'd know the answer to everything.**" This is usually said when there is no answer' – A. Weston-Webb, London SE24 (2004).

'"Where are you, Mummy?" is responded to with, "**I'm in my skin**"' – *Widdowson*.

'When asked where somebody was, my mother would reply, "He's in his skin. When he jumps out, you jump in" – in other words, "Look for yourself!"' – Gwen Croally, Sheerness, Kent (2003). 'In his skin' is also in *Partridge/Catch Phrases* as an answer to 'Where's so-and-so?'

larovers for meddlers and crutches for lame ducks (sometimes **lareovers** or **layoes** or indeed any spelling you care to choose) If someone asks, 'What have you got there?' this is the reply. Possibly a Northern dialect expression originally, but now quite widespread. Could 'meddlers' be 'medlars', i.e. the fruit (also a term for the female genitals, as it happens)?

Philip N. Wicks, Northamptonshire, recalled (1994), 'When as a small child I asked my mother [who hailed from Norfolk], "What's in there?", regarding the contents of any unreadable packet or blank blue grocer's bag, she would reply secretively, "Leerooks for meddlers and beans for gooses eyes." I've wondered for forty years what she meant.'

'My mother used to quote this to us as kids and I have always wondered as to its origins – "Leos for meddlars and crutches for lame ducks … there's a mop in our backyard, go and suck it!"' – Peter Reeve, Nantwich, Cheshire (2006).

Partridge/Catch Phrases finds a version already in use by 1668. *Apperson* explains 'larovers' as 'lay-overs' – things laid over, covered up, to protect them from meddlers – and concludes: 'Almost every county has its variation probably of this phrase. The most common form in which it survives, however, is "Layers for meddler".'

A surprising occurrence is in Chap. 32 of Margaret Mitchell's *Gone With the Wind* (1936). Scarlett O'Hara, when asked who in Atlanta is going to lend her the money that she needs to pay the taxes on Tara, avoids answering the question by saying, 'archly', 'Layovers catch meddlers.'

The *Morris Dictionary of Word and Phrase Origins* (1977) confirms American usage: '*layover to catch meddlers* is a dialect variant of a very common answer used by adults to evade a direct answer to children's questions. Instead of saying to the child, "It's none of your business," he would be told, "It's *layover to catch meddlers*." So what's a *layover?* you ask. A *layover* is a trap for bears or other unwary animals, made of a pit covered with boughs. And a *meddler*, of course, is a person who interferes in other people's business. The phrase was recorded in Eastern and Southern states as long ago as 1890. It also appears as *larovers for meddlers, layos to catch meddlers* and even as a single word, *larofamedlers*.'

Another explanation is that 'lay-holes for medlars' are what you put the fruit in to ripen. *Partridge* also gives the variant '**crutches for meddlers and legs for lame ducks**'.

No easy solution to this one. Compare CAT FUR TO (page 324); IT'S A WHIMWHAM (page 338).

'My mother and her mother used an expression that I've never heard used by anybody else. If we children (I'm 65 now) ever asked for something that was totally out of the question or unreasonable they would say, **"Go and have a roll with your leg up."** As a youngster, I thought they were referring to the bread-type roll and couldn't see what that had to do with my request. Nor why raising one leg was important. Years later, I realized they meant to physically roll over – which you couldn't do, could you, not with your leg up?' – Allan Williams, London SE20 (2001).

'My mother-in-law, Elsa Buckley, always referred to someone in a bit of a flap as "having a fit with her leg up". Was it simply a Buckley family saying?' – Linda Buckley (2004). Well, obviously this was not restricted to the Buckleys, but we still do not know how it arose.

'My mother, an inspired cook, if asked the source of a particular recipe, would invariably reply, **"I made it up out of my own head and there are plenty of ingredients left"**' – Kenneth F. Buckingham, Surrey (1995).

'In the mid-1950s, all my little brother wanted for Christmas was a toy bus exactly like the one he'd had the previous year but which had been lost or broken. My parents scoured almost every toy shop in the city, to no avail.

'In order to explain Father Christmas's inability to supply the right bus, my parents told him that, unfortunately, **"the naughty fairies have burnt the factory down!"** (Well, we did live in Liverpool!)

'Now, in our family, if anyone asks for something which is completely out of the question (new car, diamond ring), someone always tells them, with great regret, "Oh, I'm sorry, the naughty fairies have burnt the factory down"!' – Laraine Mundell (2006).

In 2003, Michael Abbott of Northampton recalled that many years before, when he was in the Royal Navy, 'If a mate wanted something, say a light for a cigarette, and you couldn't oblige, the reply was, "Sorry – **but I've a photo of General Buller ...**" He added, 'In spite of a chest-full of medals, Buller seems to have been a spectacularly disastrous general in the Boer War. But I wonder just how that phrase about having a photo of him arose – and whether anybody else knows it?' Whatever the case, Michael said he now did actually have a photograph of General Buller ... in his bathroom.

This opened the floodgates of memory and these are just some of the other, similar push-off remarks in response to a request for a match or indeed anything, that I was told about:

'No, but I have a photo of Lloyd-George in my pocket' (Richard Till); 'No, but I've got a picture of Lord Roberts' (Eve Tyndall); 'No, but I have a very interesting photo of Lord Roberts with one shoe on' (Norman Mude); 'No, but I've got a picture of a dead horse' (Mike MacSween); 'No, but I've a sharp piece of string'/'No, but I've an Auntie in the Royal Marines' (Iain Coker); 'No, but I've got a brother who's a monk on the back of a custard packet' (Geoff Grandy); 'No, but I've got a sister in the WAACS' (Geoffrey Wilson); 'No, but I've got a sister who's a Girl Guide, and a wheelbarrow with a wooden leg' (Christine Miller).

David Jones quoted these unhelpful responses from J.P.W. Mallalieu's novel *Very Ordinary Seaman* (1944): 'No, but I've a bag that had cakes in it!', 'No, but I've got a sister in the Wrens!' and 'No, but I've got an aunt in Australia!' Peter Higginbotham also recalled the nudging 'Have you got a match?' 'No, not since Errol Flynn died' – which I will let you work out for yourself – and, in response to the same question, '**Yes, my arse and your face.**'

'The correct reply to "Have you got a match?" when I was a youth was always, "Your face, my arse." This was further adapted by my friends to the query "king-kong?" when anybody wanted a light. This from the playground insult, "What are you going to do for a face when King Kong wants his arse back?"' – Alana Hunter, Plymouth (2004).

'When I did my National Service, many years ago, a common reply to the question, "Got a match?" was, "Yes. Your face and the east side of a cow going west!" A bit vulgar, but quite funny – at least we thought so' – John Nicholls (2004).

oh arr ... (or **oh ah**) A non-committal response to something said when it is considered unlikely or preposterous or dubious. It sounds like an imitation of a country yokel determinedly unimpressed by what he has been told. These examples are all from P.G. Wodehouse: '"Ronald has just announced his intention of marrying a chorus-girl." "Oh, ah?" said Lord Emsworth' – *Summer Lightning*, Chap. 18 (1929).

'The first time I met him, we had barely finished the initial pip-pippings when he said, apropos of nothing, "My father was a professional cricketer." If there's a good answer to that, you tell me. I thought of saying, "Mine had a white moustache," but finally settled for, "Oh, ah," and we went on to speak of other things' – in a letter (24 August 1932). '"Oh, Mr Wooster," he said, meeting me on the stairs ... "You were good enough to express an interest in this little prize for Good Conduct which I am offering." "Oh, ah?"' – *Very Good, Jeeves*, 'The Love That Purifies' (1930).

Queen Anne's dead A phrase used to put down someone who has just told you something that you know already. H.L. Mencken's *Dictionary of Quotations* (1942) glosses it slightly differently: 'Reply to an inquiry for news, signifying that there is none not stale.' He also supplied the alternative 'Queen Elizabeth is dead' and said that both forms appear to date from about 1720.

In George Colman the Younger's play *The Heir-at-Law* (1797), there occurred the line 'Tell 'em Queen Anne's dead'. She actually died in 1714. *Apperson* dates 'Queen Anne is dead' to 1722, in a ballad: 'He's as dead as Queen Anne the day after she dy'd' (which doesn't seem to convey the modern meaning of the expression); and 'Queen Elizabeth is dead' to 1738 in Swift's *Polite Conversation*:

> What news, Mr Neverout?
> Why, Madam, Queen Elizabeth's dead

Partridge/Slang also dates 'My Lord Baldwin is dead' to 1670–1710.

An American equivalent is, 'Bryan has carried Texas' – presumably referring to William Jennings Bryan (1860–1925), who ran three times unsuccessfully for the US presidency.

'When I revealed some world-shattering piece of news, my mother (born in the 1890s) would look at me, shake her head and say, "Yes, dear, and Queen Anne's dead and her bottom is cold"' – Alan Huth, Alassio, Italy (2005).

right after I eat this orange 'My wife (who is American) introduced me to this saying. It is used in answer to a question along the lines of, "When are you going to get around to doing the washing up, the ironing? etc" and means "In my own good time"' – Simon Rickman (2004).

she's run away with a dead soldier to France 'When we were children and asked our father where our mother was, he would always say this' – Anonymous correspondent (2003).

shut your mouth, here comes a bus What you say to a child who has his/her mouth open. 'When I was a child my grandmother, if I had my mouth open in a typically idiotic gape, would say this' – Peter Toye

(2000). 'Close your mouth, there's a bus coming' – in script of ITV's *Inspector Morse*, 'The Remorseful Day' (15 November 2000).

sit down, your bottom is making buttons Carol Smith, the producer of *Quote . . . Unquote* for many years, told me her mother used this very frequently. But what is meant by it?

'When we were very excited, my maternal grandma would say, "Your backside's making buttons"' – Pat Stimpson (2003). 'Another oft-repeated phrase of my grandmother's used to be directed at any person who could not settle and whose behaviour verged on what nowadays we would call "hyper-active" – "Boy, your arse makes buttons!"' – Graham Sparrow, Bunwell, Norfolk (2004).

To 'make buttons' was known by the 1830s as the nervous fingering of button-holes by someone under pressure or interrogation. Perhaps the phrase just refers to the fidgetty movements made when *sewing on* buttons?

'When I was a child I remember that whenever one of us said, "Where shall I sit?" or "There's no seat for me", my parents used to reply, "**Sit on your thumb but mind the nail**"' – Wynne Kelly, West Midlands (1998). Wynne went on to say, 'Recently I heard a relative of French Canadian origin say something in French when her children asked her what there was to eat. She said, "*Mange ta main, et garde l'autre pour demain* [eat your hand and save the other for tomorrow]." So it's not only British parents who irritate their children!'

sky-blue pink with a finny haddy border 'This was my mother's invariable answer to any question when we were children' – Julie Hickson (2000).

Compare 'sky-blue tail', 'bottom pink' and 'little thin flowery border' under NEAT BUT NOT GAUDY. Marjorie Wild, Crediton, Devon (2000) recalled 'sky-blue-pink' and 'sandy-grey-russet' as nonsense descriptions. 'As a small child, when I asked an aunt what was the colour of something, she would teasingly reply, "Sky-blue scarlet, the colour of a mouse's fart" – to the annoyance of other adults. I have never heard this from anyone else, and have no idea whether or not it was my aunt's original' – Mrs J. Jones, Shrewsbury, Shropshire (1993).

Well, *Partridge/Slang* has 'sky-blue pink' for 'colour unknown or indeterminate', since about 1885. *Casson/Grenfell* has, in answer to the question, 'What shall I wear?' – 'Sky blue pink.'

'A few weeks ago, whilst in Oldham town centre, I overheard the following said by an older lady (grandmother?) to a little boy getting tearful and a bit stroppy: "**You'll have something to cry about if somebody kidnaps you**"' – Duncan Loft, Manchester (2003). A nannyism in the making?

that'll stop you farting in church 'This was the family saying that was invariably used by my father when he was obliged to act in order to prevent us youngsters from meddling with anything dangerous or from straying beyond control. He would place something beyond our reach or lock it away. He would say it to his ducks and chickens, too – and to himself when he considered that he had put right someone who had chanced their arm with him' – Jim Diston, Minehead, Somerset (1994).

Partridge/Catch Phrases suggests that a politer form of this remark is 'that will stop him laughing in church' and that the original 'that will teach him to fart in chapel/stop their farting in chapel' (i.e. 'that'll stop them from taking liberties') is possibly an English public school expression of the 1930s.

that's for me to know, and you to wonder – *Wickenden*. Or, 'That's for me to know, and you to find out.' Fobbing-off phrase recalled by Jenni Murray on *Quote . . . Unquote* (3 April 2000).

'When the children keep asking, "Where are you going?", the mother replies, **"There and back to see how far it is"**' – *Widdowson*. Also between children and not just between an adult and a child. Included by John Titford in his column for *Family Tree Magazine* (December 1994).

Partridge/Catch Phrases has the expression specifically as a *child*'s response to 'Where are you going?'

Widdowson also gives '**off to Timbuctoo**' and '**to see my Aunt Fanny**' in answer to the same question.

there's more knows Tom Fool than Tom Fool knows As 'more know Tom Fool than Tom Fool knows', this is quoted as 'the old English proverb' in Daniel Defoe, *Colonel Jack*, Chap. 17 (1723). 'When my children were small and wondered how we knew some of the things that they did, the conversation would go: "How do you know?" – "There's a lot of people know Joe what Joe don't know"' – Mrs K. Polond, London SE23 (1995).

three jumps at the cupboard door and a bite at the latch In reply to the child's question, 'What's for dinner?' The number of jumps may vary. 'A jump at the cellar door, and a bite at the latch' – *Widdowson* from Sheffield, in answer to the question, 'What's for tea?'

'Whenever I asked my maternal grandmother, a hardworking Lancashire woman, what was for dinner, she would always reply, "Three jumps 't cupboard door and a bite 't latch"' – Martin Taylor, Surrey

(2003). 'More common in Cheshire was the phrase, "Three kicks at the pantry door, and a bite at the latch"' – Michael Haighton (2003). 'If a child asks what is for dinner, the reply may be, "A run round t'table and a kick at t'cellar door"' – *Widdowson*.

David Mills's grandmother's version (2003) was: '"Three jumps at the cupboard door." I called her bluff more than once and would go to the cupboard door, jump three times and say, "I'm still hungry."'

'What's for dinner? Three jumps at the pantry door and four if you're hungry' – included by John Titford in his column for *Family Tree Magazine* (December 1994).

Then there is also **two jumps at the pantry door and a bite off the latch.** Fobbing-off phrase 'in response to someone asking what the next meal is' – Stella Richardson, Essex (1998). Also in *Widdowson*, who has 'two jumps at the cupboard door and a bite at the knob' from Swinton, Lancashire.

From the theatre director Sir Peter Hall's memoir *Making an Exhibition of Myself* (1993): 'When I asked why I didn't have any brothers or sisters, my mother, with a slight sniff, would produce one of her aphorisms: **"We couldn't do for two what we can do for one."'**

what do you think that is – Scotch Mist? 'This is a term of incredulity, quite common in my family, used usually by a slightly irritated utterer when confronted by someone who fails without good reason to recognize the obvious' – William McKee, Kingswood, Surrey (2004).

'what?'s dead long ago and 'pardon?' took its place Said to a person who asks 'What?' An archetypal nannyism. Used in the script of ITV's *Inspector Morse*, 'The Remorseful Day' (15 November 2000).

what's that got to do with the ——— ? Meaning 'What you have just said is irrelevant.' Just a few variations …

Brewer's Dictionary of Phrase & Fable (1894 edn) finds in classical literature: 'What has that to do with Bacchus?'

'T.S. Eliot at one point said he doubted that Mr Coward had ever spent one hour in the study of ethics; "What has that got to do with the price of eggs?" Noel wanted to know' – Cole Lesley, *The Life of Noel Coward*, Chap. 15 (1976).

Sir Joh Bjelke-Peterson, Premier of Queensland, was reported in *The Australian* (1 May 1985) as saying of something he thought was irrelevant, 'That's got nothing to do with the price of butter.'

'What's that got to do with the price of carrots?' was the example I gave in my book *The Gift of the Gab* (1985).

'What's that got to do with the Prince of Wales?' – told to me on an LBC radio phone-in, London (1990), but otherwise untraced and unconfirmed. And which Prince of Wales was being talked about, unless this is a simple price/prince play on words?

Partridge/Catch Phrases has 'What's that got to do with the price of eggs?' as being of American origin. Indeed, it is uttered in the film *While You Were Sleeping* (US 1998).

'When my children were young and far from clean and tidy, I would say, "The state of you and the price of fish!"' – Patricia Harrison, Hertfordshire (1999). 'What's that got to do with the price of fish?' – Jane Bird, North Yorkshire (2000), quoting a friend.

'When I was a child in Canada, the expression commonly used was, "What's that got to do with the price of tea in China?"' – Reg Norman, Somerset (2000). 'What's that got to do with the price of bacon?' – Tony Malin, Blandford Forum, Dorset (2003).

'My father (and therefore now all his children/grandchildren) always used to say about anything that was not relevant to the subject/argument, "What's that got to do with the underground railway?"' – Graham Feldman, Jerusalem, Israel (2005).

what's that when it's at home? 'A question asked about an unusual name' – *Wickenden*.

I think this is more widely used about anything the speaker is unsure of. *Partridge/Catch Phrases* has it as a tag 'implying either derision or incredulity', with a citation from 1914.

'In my childhood there was one particular saying my mother used, which I have never heard anywhere else. If she was making something and I became too inquisitive and asked what it was, it was always the same answer: "**It's a whimwham for a duck's bridle.**" In other words, mind your own business' – Mrs E. James, Somerset (1995). Variations on this theme include the spelling 'wimwam' and the concluding phrases '... for a goose's bridle' '... for ducks to perch on' '... for a treacle mill' '... to wind the sun up'.

'When we came home from school and asked hungrily, "What's for lunch?" our mother replied curtly, "Whimwams for ducks to peak on"' – Owen Wainwright, Guernsey (1996). Graham Aldred said (1998) that his mother would always use this same phrase when she couldn't be bothered to give a full explanation in answer to the question 'Mum, what's that?' or 'What's it for?'

'When I asked what something was, my mother would say, "They are wim-wams for goose's bridles to run through"' – Mike Killen (1998). 'My mum always said (and said that her mum always said), "Wigwams, for ducks to pee upon" when asked, "What's for tea?", or "What are you doing?", or anything she couldn't be bothered to answer' – Steve

McGuigan (2000). 'My mother used to say, "A wig-wam to wind the sun up" or "Layalls for meddlers"' – John Alexander, Cheshire (2000). Indeed, compare LAROVERS FOR MEDDLERS ...

Apperson has 'A whim-wam from Yocketon. A whim-wham to wind the sun up. [Answers by old folk to inquisitive young people who interrupt them]' – from *Cheshire Proverbs* (1917).

'My grandparents said, "A wigwam to wind the moon up with"' – Veronica M. Brown, Wigston, Leicestershire (2002).

Compare: 'A wingwam for a goose's bridle', 'A whimwham from mustard town', 'A whimwham to wind mustard mills up with' – all from *Widdowson*.

who ate all the pies? An insinuation about a fat person – in any context, but especially in football, where the saying originated. Indeed, it is a question posed by English football fans of any overweight player and possibly derives from the tradition of eating meat pies at half time. It is sometimes sung to the tune of 'Knees Up Mother Brown'. Impossible to say who it was first aimed at but, in the 1990s, Mick Quinn of Newcastle United and Portsmouth was very much associated with the cry.

In 2005, Terence James emailed to say he had heard of a crowd shouting at a similarly portly player at Carrow Road, the ground belonging to Norwich City, of which club Delia Smith, the cookery writer, was famously a director. The cry from the terrace there was rumoured to be, 'Who ate all the Boeuf Bourguignon?'

'My husband's grandmother (who comes from Liverpool) is fond of saying, **"Who's kicked your donkey over?"** when someone is being petulant – or in place of another favourite of mine, **"He's thrown his teddy out of the pram"**' – Zoe Chamberlain, Shropshire (2002).

Partridge/Catch Phrases has this as 'What's knocked your donkey over?',
meaning, 'What has upset you?' 'Why are you so disgruntled?' and dates
it from before 1950.

'My mother had a dislike of the pronoun "she". As a child, if ever I
referred to her as "she" in the course of conversation, she would
immediately interject, "**Who's she, the cat's aunt?**" – Barry Gayton,
Norfolk (1996).

From Stella Gibbons, *Cold Comfort Farm*, Chap. 6 (1932): '"She comes
from up at the farm" … "Who's 'she'? The cat's mother?" snapped the
shawl. "Speak properly to the young lady."' I think 'cat's mother' may be
the more popular version.

the wind will change and you'll be stuck like it 'If I looked sulky' –
Alison Adcock, Oxford (2004). 'If you pulled a face, my mother would
say, "One day the wind will change and your face will stay like that"'
– Gervase Phinn, former schools inspector turned best-selling storyteller
(2006).

Y's a crooked letter Fobbing-off response to children who ask 'Why?'
questions – Valerie Grosvenor Myer, Haddenham, Cambridgeshire
(1996). 'Because Y is a crooked letter and can't be straightened' – Stella
Richardson, Essex (1998).

Another way of dealing with 'Why?' is to reply '**Z**' – said Christopher
Matthew on *Quote … Unquote* (13 October 1998). This may be related
to the response, 'Because Y's a crooked letter and Z's no better', reported
by J.B. Smith in *Lore and Language* (July 1980).

you don't give donkeys strawberries A phrase for 'when children wished to partake of special grown-ups' food' – Mrs Robin Pearson, Burgh by Sands (2000).

Compare: my own mother-in-law – or so I am reliably informed by someone better placed to know – used to say this when describing someone who was extremely enthusiastic about something (and not just food). She came from Buckinghamshire and it may be a local expression.

'My wife's family use a phrase which seems to be applied to foods that are liked and disappear with speed, "Like strawberries to donkeys"' – Alan Bailey (2005).

'There is definitely something we need to know about donkeys and strawberries. As we were picking fruit in a friend's garden recently, I had a sudden flashback. When the world was young, if pet or a child was wolfing down titbits without proper appreciation and demanding more, my late mother would say, "It's like feeding a donkey on strawberries"' – Ian Forsyth, Durham (2006).

See also DONKEY'S BEEN ON (page 18).

you give my bum the toothache 'Old family saying from my mother when she was really fed up with us' – Mary Coulter, Middlesex (2000).

you have made your bed and now you must eat it A nannyism and a play upon the proverb 'As you make your bed, so you must lie on it', which was known by the 16th century, according to the *ODP*.

'I prefer "You've buttered your bread and now you must lie in it". The German equivalent (as used by the Kaiser to Bethmann Hollweg in 1914) appears to be, "You've cooked the broth, now you must eat it"' – Veronica M. Brown, Wigston, Leicestershire (2002).

**you know what thought did – killed the cat and only thought he did
it** An expression open to many variations. 'When children fail to check
facts and say they *thought* something was the case when it was not so,
the usual retort is, "You know what Thought did? He only thought he
did"' – *Widdowson*.

'When as children we said we "thought something", my Yorkshire
Grandma would say, "You know what thought did – killed the cat and
only thought he did it." My Edinburgh husband knows the expression
as, "... planted a chicken thinking it would grow a hen"' – Margaret
Barrow, Buckinghamshire (1995).

Compare: 'Do you know what thought did? It followed a donkey-cart
and thought it was at a funeral' – said by the paternal grandmother of
Kathleen B. Crossen, Belfast (1997). Or '... he followed a muck cart and
thought it was a wedding' – Stella Richardson, Essex (1998).

'If I was trying to explain myself (for something that I shouldn't have
done) by saying, "I thought it was all right", my mother (who was from
Yorkshire) had an intriguing response. Me: "Mum, I thought it was all
right for me to use the dining table as a cutting board." Mum: "Aye,
well, you know what Thought did. (Pause.) He did it in his pants"'
– Bob Herbert, London SE23 (2002).

Partridge/Slang also lists these continuations: '... ran away with
another man's wife', '... lay in bed and beshit himself, and thought he
was up', and '... No, 'e never! 'E only thought 'e did!'

Hence, presumably: 'My Dad has an unusual quote that he heard
from his father: "Thought thought his bottom was falling out of bed,
so he got out and put it back in again"' – Steven Mithen (2004).

you'd be late for your own funeral A nannyish admonition to someone
who is chronically unpunctual. Origin and date unknown.

you're a blether-cum-skite and the ducks will get you 'As a child, I think I must have been quite a chatterbox. One of my grandmothers had a way of stopping the flow. If I were going on a bit or exaggerating, she would laugh and clap her hands and say this to me' – Eva Bates, Carrickfergus (2002).

NB A 'blatherskite' is 'one who blathers' and the *OED2* gives it of American origin by the mid-19th century.

'When I was sent on an errand (as a girl), I always got waylaid or diverted and was greeted on arrival at home by the expression: **"You're a fine one to send for sorrow"**' – Mary J. Price (2001).

Chapter 24

NOW WASH YOUR HANDS

The simple fact about letting it be known that you are going to the lavatory is that no one ever says the direct, 'I am going to the lavatory.' Instead, they employ longer, more colourful and above all inventively euphemistic expressions. Frank Deakin of Wilmslow coined the word 'loophemism' for this phenomenon in 1995. What follows merely scratches the surface of this topic. In my earlier book A Man About a Dog: Euphemisms & Other Examples of Verbal Squeamishness *(published by Collins Reference, 2006), there are over a hundred of them ... But 'bathrooms' are not just 'lavatories', so while we in there, we'll look at other related phrases, too.*

The phrase **answer the call of nature** has been known since 1761, when Laurence Sterne's *Tristram Shandy* had that a character 'hearkened to the call of nature'. 'The calls of nature are permitted and Clerical Staff may use the garden below the second gate' – *Tailor & Cutter* (1852). '"What were you up to in Causey Spinney last Monday?" ... "Call o' Nature, please, sir"' – Flora Thompson, *Lark Rise*, Chap. 3 (1939). 'When I was aft obeying a call of nature ... a huge tunny had delivered a sideways smack at my nakedness with his 160 lbs. or so of cold fish' – Thor Heyerdahl, *The Kon-Tiki Expedition*, Chap. 6 (1950). 'Call of nature "sent [the publisher Robert] Maxwell overboard" ... He would frequently get up in the middle of the night and found it more convenient, as a lot of men do on a boat, to relieve themselves over the side as it was moving' – headline and text, *The Independent* (21 October 1995).

Hence, jokes along the lines of 'Have you had the call?' – as in the BBC radio show *Round the Horne* (28 March 1965). There is also the variant, **to answer a certain requirement of nature.** The **call of the great outdoors** may also be used in the same way, although the phrase 'great outdoors' was originally used simply to describe 'great open space' (by 1932).

By about 1900, **to do a number one** or **two** had become in nursery talk, 'to go the lavatory' – 'one', to urinate, 'two', to defecate. 'This little ginger [kitten] is going to do a number one if we're not careful' – Angus Wilson, *No Laughing Matter*, Chap. 2 (1967); 'When I had done Number two, you always washed them out yourself before sending them to the diaper service' – Mary McCarthy, *Birds of America* (1971).

> Red, white, and blue,
> Dirty kangaroo,
> Sitting on the dustbin
> Doing his 'Number Two'.

– rhyme quoted in Iona & Peter Opie, *The Lore and Language of Schoolchildren* (1977).

'"**Doing a Sophia**" was said in my wife's family when someone disappeared to the loo just as everyone was about to sit down to a meal. This was a habit much practised by Great Aunt Sophia' – Tony Morrison (2006).

to go and change the water in the fish bowl 'My son used to say this' – L. Middleton (2001).

'My father used to say, "**I'm going to look at Africa**", despite the fact that we were living in India!' – Mrs R. Collins, Norfolk (1998).

to go and see a man about a dog A loophemism – but not always. The expression can mean: (1) To undertake any illicit or unmentionable job or task while providing this excuse for leaving the scene. (2) To go and have a drink, while withholding the fact that this is the purpose of your exit. (3) To go to the lavatory. Since the mid-19th century. A caption to a Ghilchik cartoon in *Punch* (22 January 1930) is: 'The Age Old Excuse. Cave-dweller: 'I won't be long, dear. I've just got to see a man about a brontosaurus.' But to which of the meanings does this refer?

    Partridge/Catch Phrases seems to suggest that the phrase originally indicated that the man was about to 'visit a woman – sexually', then that he was 'going out for a drink', and then that he gave it 'in answer to an inconvenient question'. Only fourthly, does it list 'go to the water-closet, usually to "the gents", merely to urinate'. At one time, *Brewer* also preferred the 'concealing one's destination' purpose of this phrase, suggesting that it was a late 19th-century American expression, and gave an example of its use during Prohibition as disguising the fact that the speaker was going to buy illegal alcohol from a bootlegger. A later edition suggested that the phrase meant that the speaker was pretending that he would see a man about placing a bet on a dog race (but this strikes me as too literal).

Sticking to what I take to be the now primary meaning: it has been suggested that 'dog' is some sort of rhyming slang for 'bog', a well-known term for a lavatory, but this is not true rhyming slang and does not convince.

To unravel all this a little: the earliest citation for the phrase, in any meaning, is Dion Boucicault's play, *The Flying Scud, or a Four-legged Fortune*, Act 1 (1866), where a character says, 'Excuse me Mr Quail, I can't stop; I've got to see a man about a dog.' Here the meaning would appear to be that he is providing a limp excuse for absenting himself. This does not support an American origin for the phrase, for Boucicault was Irish and working mostly in London. However, there does seem to have been a US origin for the drinking/Prohibition meaning. In Barrère & Leland's *Dictionary of Slang* (1890) is this definition: '*To see a man* (American), to go and have a drink at the bar.' Later, *American Speech*, Vol. 3 (1927) has: '*See a man about a dog*, to go out and buy liquor.' Early citations for the 'go and take a leak' application are lacking, in any country.

There is also a further way in which this phrase is commonly used. Professor J.D.A. Widdowson, of the former Centre for English Cultural Tradition and Language at the University of Sheffield, made these observations to me (2006): 'I have spent quite a lot of time investigating the language used in social control of children and among these have recorded numerous instances of "to see a man about a dog" used as a put-off to deflect children's insistent or persistent questions to an adult. The recorded examples with this particular function greatly outweigh those used purely euphemistically. My own mother frequently used the saying in this way.

'My friend and colleague Jean Alexander confirms that the same expression was commonly used in her family in her childhood in Stockton-on-Tees. She adds, very pertinently, that children in our days (some 60 years ago!) would be regarded as being very impertinent if they were to address such questions as "Where are you going?" etc. to their parents or other adults.'

to go and splash one's clogs as one's back teeth are all awash – John Hill, Dorset (1996). Compare BACK TEETH SUBMERGED (page 64).

to go and turn one's bike round Widely used. 'I have heard that one being used here in Suffolk and was given this explanation. Back in the days when policemen used cycles on the beat, the Suffolk and Norfolk bobbies would meet on the county boundary. They had a chat, attended to the wants of nature, then "turned their bikes round", hence the old saying!' – Marie Laflin, Suffolk (1995).

'At a recent tennis tournament at our small village club one of our ladies (middle-aged like myself) left the court saying, "I'm just going to turn the *vicar's* bike round" ' – Mrs H. Ball, Flackwell Heath, Buckinghamshire (1996).

'My usual saying, **"I've got to go and wring out my socks"**' – Ted Farley, Kent (1996).

'When I was a pupil at Bolton School (I started the year after Ian McKellen left, so he will confirm what I say, depending on his memory), we were instructed that if ever we wished to go to the toilet, we should ask "**to go down**". Why, I haven't a clue, other than that the toilets were on the lowest floor of the building' – Brian Robinson (2001).

'My grandmother, when escorting us out and about as children, was apt to ask whether we needed to "**pay a visit to the House of Commons**"' – Chris Gamble, Norfolk (2003). She was not alone in using this expression.

'Our juniors have an interest in the Old English word for faeces. They use it a lot – the ones from polite homes do, I mean homes that talk of No. 2 and "going to the House of Commons"' – A.S. Neill, *That Dreadful School*, Chap. 7 (1937).

'And Willy Nilly, rumbling, jockeys out again to the three-seated shack called the House of Commons in the back' – Dylan Thomas, *Under Milk* Wood (1954).

Compare: 'When I was in France in 1968, the usual phrase for this situation was *"Je vais chez Louis Quatorze"*' – Mrs J. Barton, London N1 (2003).

to go to the loo A euphemism for going to the lavatory that was well-established in well-to-do British society by the early 20th century and in general middle-class use after the Second World War. Of the several theories for its origin, perhaps the most well known is that it comes from the French *gardez l'eau* [mind the water], dating from the days when chamber pots or dirty water were emptied out of the window into the street and recorded by Laurence Sterne as *garde d'eau* in *A Sentimental Journey* (1768). This cry was also rendered 'gardyloo' in old Edinburgh and recorded by Tobias Smollett in *Humphrey Clinker* (1771).

However, Professor A.S.C. Ross, who examined the various options in a 1974 issue of *Blackwood's Magazine,* favoured a derivation, 'in some way which could not be determined', from 'Waterloo'. At one time people probably said, 'I must go to the water-closet' and, wishing not to be explicit, substituted 'Water–loo' as a weak little joke. The name 'Waterloo' was there, waiting to be used, from 1815 onwards.

Even in flats or bungalows, a host is liable to ask, '**Would you like to go upstairs?**' Since the early 20th century?

'I was working in an office and a female Latvian sat next to me. When a male member of staff had left the office and was wanted on the phone etc., our Latvian friend would say, "**He has gone where Kings go alone**". Similarly when a female was missing, she had always gone "where the Queen goes alone"' – Miss Rosemary C. Black, Sutton Coldfield, West Midlands (1995).

The Revd John Hagreen, Kent (1996), added, 'I heard the euphemism "*Où le roi va seul*" in southern France in the late 1920s.'

Prof. Robin Jacoby, Oxfordshire (1999), mentioned the Russian euphemisms '**I'm going where even the Tsar goes on foot**' and '**I'm going where even the Tsar removes his gloves**.' Compare: 'A place where even the King goes on foot – *enfin,* the toilet chamber' – Aldous Huxley, *Time Must Have a Stop* (1946).

to have a whistle 'One of the many euphemisms for male urination – particularly among the boating fraternity' – John Phillips, Looe (*sic*), Cornwall (1996).

to look at the garden Meaning 'to go to the lavatory out of doors'. Compare 'I will but look upon the hedge' – which is what Autolycus says, when he means this, in Shakespeare, *The Winter's Tale*, IV.iv.827 (1611).

Robert Clayton, Cardiff, wrote (1995), 'My father loved reading, particularly non-fiction, and when I was a schoolboy in Beaumaris, Anglesey, in the 1950s, he read a book about a primitive tribe living in the jungles of South America. They would gather round the camp fire and, when one of them wished to visit the toilet, he would stand up and announce his intention to the whole assembly, which would then chorus, **"May you do so mightily!"** On his or her return from the jungle, they would announce, "I have done so mightily!"

'This became the norm in our family for many years – you can imagine the effect on friends who came to visit ...'

A cautionary rhyme exhorting bathroom users to behave themselves is remembered by many, but it has not proved possible to trace its source. It was often to be found on a plaque in bathrooms, probably by the 1920s/30s. One such version was illustrated and signed by the artist Mabel Lucie Attwell (1879–1964). The text would appear to be as follows:

> **Please remember – don't forget**
> **Never leave the bathroom wet.**
> Nor leave the soap still in the water –
> That's a thing we never oughter.
> Nor leave the towels about the floor
> Nor keep the bath an hour or more

When other folks are wanting one,
Please don't forget – it isn't done.
And if you'd really do the thing,
There's not the slightest need to sing.

to powder one's nose A loophemism – for females only. It was in use by the 1920s, in the UK and US, but in the latter less so because of possible confusion with a side-effect of cocaine-sniffing. *OED2* doesn't find it before 1921, when Somerset Maugham daringly put it in his play *The Circle*. Cole Porter also included it in a song for *The New Yorkers, 1930* – though there is some doubt as to whether the song was actually used in the show.

A little later than this: 'We are invited to wash our hands, or, if we wear dresses, to powder our noses' – Isaac Goldberg, *The Wonder of Words*, Chap. 6 (1938). Then from Edward Albee, *Who's Afraid of Virginia Woolf?*, Act 1 (1962):

> *Honey*: 'I wonder if you could show me where the ... I want to ... put some powder on my nose.'
> *George*: 'Martha, won't you show her where we keep the ... euphemism?'

to be shown the geography of the house i.e. to be shown where the lavatory is. Hence, '**the geography**' can also be taken to refer to the whereabouts of the lavatory. Probably by the mid-19th century.

'For a man to show a woman the way to the lavatory ... an evasive phrase had to be used ... "Have you been shown the geography of the house?"' – Robert Graves, *Lars Porsena, or the Future of Swearing and Improper Language* (1920); 'It is all very baffling for the uninitiated foreigner, who when his host offers to "show him the geography of the house" finds that his tour begins and ends with the smallest room' – A. Lyall, *It Isn't Done* (1930). '**The smallest room**' is, of course, another loophemism.

'A friend of mine asked the Bobby on the beat, "**Where can I spend a penny without paying anything?**" The Bobby showed us the way' – Mrs Dorothy B. Alexander, Shropshire (1996).

As for the basic phrase, 'to spend a penny', the first public convenience to charge one penny opened in London in 1855. So I am curious about this from Chap. 6 of Charles Dickens, *Dombey and Son* (1846–8): 'The young Toodles, victims of a pious fraud, were deluded into repairing in a body to a chandler's shop in the neighbourhood, for the ostensible purpose of spending a penny.' What was going on here? (*OED2* does not have a citation for the phrase before 1945.)

the usual offices The lavatory and also straightforward washing facilities in a house: 'You will find the usual offices at the end of the corridor.' In use by the 1930s, though the term 'office of ease' had been used for 'privy' since the early 18th century. 'The bathroom's to the right and the usual offices next to it' – John Braine, *Room at the Top*, Chap. 1 (1957).

Chapter 25

EXCLAMATION MARKS!

Here you will encounter cries, curses, expletives, oaths – in fact, anything that is likely to have an exclamation mark put after it about the home . . .

bad cess to them! 'My Irish grandmother used to say this when she wished someone ill – a way of saying "Bad luck to them!" I only recently noticed it in Trollope's *The Macdermots of Ballycloran* (1847) – his first novel, set in Ireland. The word "cess" refers to a tax or assessment levied in that country' – Elizabeth Seager, Oxfordshire (2000).

of all the blood and stomach pills! A euphemistic oath, of not very clear origin. 'The exclamation, "Of all the blood and stomach pills", was used by my grandfather in utter exasperation when he had come to the end of his tether with something' – Stephen Marsden (2006).

bloody Sunday! I was hesitating whether to include this, as I was not certain how much of a domestic saying it was. Then I did a little research into how the title of the film *Sunday Bloody Sunday* (UK 1971) was arrived at and concluded that it was. Aware as I was of the infamous 'Bloody Sundays' in British, Russian and Irish history (1887, 1905 and 1920, respectively), I could not quite see the relevance of them to the film's story of a man-loves-boy-loves-girl relationship, even though that is told on a daily basis, starting on a Friday and climaxing a week later on a Sunday, when it finally runs into the sand.

Then I read Penelope Gilliatt's introductory essay to her published screenplay. It transpires that she had always wanted to call the film simply *Bloody Sunday* for a good reason: 'Sunday nearly always being bloody in the minds of English children: the day of stasis; of grown-ups going to sleep after too heavy a lunch ...'

Then 'some young eager beaver' working for the film company threw a spanner in the works by pointing out the historical 'Bloody Sundays'. Gilliatt persisted with her domestic theme: 'The total bloodiness of Sundays from childhood to death is due, I think, to the enslaving legend we have made for ourselves, with the help of the enslaving Old

Testament, that time off is fun and work is at the behest of others.' She did allow that, 'Sundays are bloody indeed. Wars break out on Sundays.'

But the word *bloody* continued to worry the American front-office people. Other titles were floated, including *Apex* and *Triangle* and *Every Day of the Week.* Finally, the matter was resolved by, I think, the producer Joseph Janni (though Gilliatt does not name him directly), who said, 'I've got it. *Sunday Bloody Sunday.*' No comma.

I should think the film probably popularized the basic phrase again just in time for it to be applied to the 'Bloody Sunday' that occurred in Northern Ireland early the following year and which, as it happens, was itself depicted in a film with the title *Bloody Sunday* (Ireland/UK 2001). In 1973, the UK/US group Black Sabbath released an album with the title *Sabbath Bloody Sabbath,* which was kind of neat.

Bob's your uncle! is an almost meaningless expression of the type that takes hold from time to time, here meaning 'and there you are/there you have it!/all will be well/it's as simple as that'. It was current by the 1880s but doesn't appear to be of any hard and fast origin. It is basically a British expression – and somewhat baffling to Americans. There is the story of one such [the director and playwright Burt Shevelove] – according to the actor Kenneth Williams on *Quote ... Unquote* (24 July 1980) – who went into a London shop, had it said to him, and exclaimed, 'But how on earth do you know – I do have an Uncle Bob!?'

In 1886, Arthur Balfour was appointed Chief Secretary for Ireland by his uncle, Robert Arthur Talbot Gascoyne-Cecil, 3rd Marquis of Salisbury, the Prime Minister. Is that where the phrase came from, as some people fervently believe?

Miss M.L. King, London SW3 (1993), wrote, 'Whenever anyone says it, I reply, "**And Fanny's your aunt**" – I don't know why.' Peter Davies, Hertfordshire (1999), had, rather: 'Bob's your uncle, Fanny's your aunt, and the baby's name is dripping.'

go and boil your head! i.e. 'Go away, don't be silly!' Probably by 1900, especially in Scots use. 'A strange phrase used in my family: when annoyed with younger members of the family, older ones would say, crossly, "Oh, go and boil your head!" Most mysterious! And almost impossible to do …' – Carol Irving, London sw6 (2006).

The writer and jazz singer George Melly described on *Quote … Unquote* (27 May 1997) how his paternal grandmother exclaimed on being offered some (then rare) Danish Blue cheese in the late 1940s, '**Dash me wig**, where did you get that?' This turned into a Melly family saying. When cheese was fancied, you said, 'I'll have a bit of dash-me-wig.' George had earlier recounted all this in his memoir, *Rum, Bum and Concertina*, Chap. 12 (1977).

OED2 has 'dash my wig' as a 'mild imprecation' by 1797. As 'dash my vig' it appears in R.S. Surtees, *Handley Cross*, Chap. 50 (1843). From *Punch* (20 February 1864): 'New Danish oath – "Dash my Schles-wig!"' *Brewer* (1894) finds in addition 'Dash my buttons!' and explains: '*Dash* is a euphemism for a common oath; and *wig*, buttons, etc., are relics of a common fashion at one time adopted in comedies and by "mashers" of swearing without using profane language.'

I'll go to Putney on a pig! An expression of surprise or astonishment, in use by the mid-19th century. *Partridge/Slang*, however, has that 'go to Putney (on a pig)!' was the equivalent of saying 'go to Hell!' In whichever way it was used, the lure of alliteration seems the predominant reason for the phrase. 'When my grandfather had a bad hand in family card games and didn't know what to play, or in any circumstances when he was similarly "stuck", he would say, "Well, I go to Putney." After a long pause, playing for time whilst working

out his strategy, he would add, " ... on a shutter'" – Sue Wright (2003).
A shutter is an improvised litter or stretcher.

'My father-in-law had a number of pet sayings, mainly from the First
World War, I think – like the expletive, "**Good Gordon Highlanders!**"
Whenever life became a bit difficult he would say, "**Everything's in
favour against us!**"

Another, not actually used by him as a "saying" but which instantly
became a part of the family's language, and still is: fuming over his
cleaning lady's latest saga of breakages, he spat out, "She does not know
it yet – but **that lady is due for non-retention!**" – which is now the
standard description in our household for anything that has to be
emptied out!' – P. Skilling, London w2 (1996).

good heavens, Mrs Evans, the child has a bald head! 'I have always
been intrigued by this saying, used by my late grandfather (whose
mother's maiden name happened to be Evans) to express surprise'
– Ann Peterson, Thornaby (2001).

hard cheese! Tough luck! Known since the late 19th century and
possibly linked to the meaning of 'cheese' as 'the best thing'. Hard
cheese is not the best.

'Always quoted when a fly was killed or, later on, whenever anybody got
killed in a radio or TV programme: "*He* **won't be called Clarence any**

more ..." I think it came from a melodrama my parents saw in their courting days in the very early 30s, possibly at the New Cross Empire' – Enid Grattan Guinness, Hertfordshire (1993).

Betty Burke, Wiltshire, came up with a possible source. She remembered from her schooldays an example in an English grammar book ('probably illustrating the accusative case') – 'They used to call him Clarence, but they call him nowt now, for I murdered him last Monday.'

Poor Clarence, whichever one he was! He had an interesting death, of course, and not with a fly-swat, in Shakespeare's *Richard III* (1592–3). Indeed, it was suggested (2000) that 'He won't be called Clarence any more' was an overheard playgoer's reaction to the character's murder.

Partridge/Slang remarks of the name: 'Like, though less than, *Cuthbert*, apt to be used as a jocular colloquialism.' Paul Beale told me, 'A Punch cartoon of 2 February 1916 may be relevant; it shows an officer and a sergeant discussing a distant sentry: '*Officer.* "Why do you think he wouldn't make a good corporal?" *Sergeant (indicating sentry).* "'Im a corporal! Lor Lumme! Why, 'is name's Clarence!"'

Music-hall historians Max Tyler and Michael Kilgarriff both thought they had resolved the matter by finding the lyric of a song entitled 'Murders', written and composed by Dick Henty, sung by George Grossmith Jnr (among others) and interpolated in *Tonight's the Night* at the Gaiety Theatre, London, in 1916. It tells of the way the singer has rid himself of various people who annoy him – his laundress, a street-organ player, his mother-in-law and his landlady's son. Of the last:

> I rented some apartments in a very quiet street,
> The cooking was delicious, and the landlady was sweet,
> But she had a horrid little boy with curls upon his brow,
> She used to call him Clarence – but she calls him *nothing* now.
>
> I murdered him one evening, I thought his time was up,
> And afterwards I took his charming mother out to sup,
> She little thought while eating the most expensive fruit,
> That I'd murdered little Willie, in his little velvet suit.

The change of the boy's name from Clarence to Willie in the last line is confusing and some performers have used 'Clarence' in both places. It is possible that 'little Willie' is just a way of referring to one's offspring (whatever his name) – as in the Donald McGill postcard joke 'Can't see my little Willy' – but it is unsatisfactory here.

However, Enid Grattan Guinness, when told of all this, referred the matter back to her (by now) 92-year-old mother, who said, no, she did not think it came from a song but from a monologue heard at an Oddfellows' Smoking Evening. Ah well … the search continues.

Hell's bells and buckets of blood! 'An expression of annoyance, remembered from the 1930s' – Mrs M.B. Bedwell, West Sussex (1996). *Partridge/Slang* has this as a 'mock ferocious' extension of the basic 'Hell's bells!' = hell! Compare: 'Instead of swearing, my mum (born 1904) would say, "Court plaster, bladder of lard, dandelions, old buckets, go to Helston with you" – said at a rate of knots and sounding quite atrocious' – Marian E. Rowe, Dunkirk, Kent (2004). Partridge explains 'Bladder of lard' = bald-headed.

here we go! Let's begin (any activity). *Partridge/Catch Phrases* suggests this dates from the mid-19th century but provides no proof. *OED2* finds the similar 'Here goes' by 1829. I include it here in the light-hearted sense reflected in the cry, 'Earwigo! – as the earwig said as he fell off the wall.' As used by Tony Hancock in BBC TV, *Hancock's Half Hour* (The Reunion Party) (25 March 1960).

Mrs D.R. Richard, Bumbles Green, Essex (1995), sent me first of all what she took to be a toast: '**May your rabbits never die!**' which her father used often, and which she assumed he had made up for himself. But, then, while reading her father-in-law's diary of the Empire Cruise of 1923–4, she found that, as a naval officer, he had had to attend a very long and dull party at a big house in Canada. 'It was not possible to get away until 3 a.m.,' Mrs Richard reported, 'by which time he said of his hosts, "I hope all their rabbits die."' Next thing, her husband was reading Dorothy L. Sayers, *Have His Carcase*, Chap. 7 (1932), in which Lord Peter Wimsey phones Harriet Vane and during the conversation says, 'All right, and **I hope your rabbit dies**.' So that was it. 'This expression was in current use in my schooldays in the early 1920s and always ended any acrimonious argument or dispute' – Anonymous octogenarian (1996).

Many other people responded that they knew the curse in extended versions. 'I first heard it from my husband and his mother, who were brought up in the Dewsbury area of Yorkshire. In full, and sounding particularly vindictive, it ran, "Well, all I hope is that his rabbit dies – and he can't sell the hutch' – Ruth Daughtry, Ashbourne, Derbyshire (1996). This same version was heard 'from a Yorkshireman who grew up in Leeds in the 1930s' – Miss Mary Lanning, Bristol (1996). Also sent by Miss D.B. North, West Yorkshire (1996). 'The parting shot after a quarrel was frequently, "I hope yer rabbit dies" but with even more withering scorn went on into "an' yer can't sell t' skin"' – Anne Gledhill, Mirfield, West Yorkshire (1996). 'My mother used to say, "I hope your rabbits die and your rhubarb won't grow" in the 1930s' – Stella Richardson, Grays, Essex (1996). 'When I was young (before the war of 1939–45) we used to say, "May your rabbits die and your toenails grow inward for evermore!" This was in Birmingham' – Mrs H.E. Beech, Staffordshire (1997). 'As I am Yorkshire born, I often use the curse even now, but my version is again a different one. I say, "I hope your rabbits die and your white mice turn black"' – Mrs Sylvia Armstrong, Kent (1997).

Stella Gibbons, *Cold Comfort Farm*, Chap. 16 (1932) has her doughty heroine apparently adapt the phrase: '"Then you're a crashing bounder," said Flora, vigorously, "and I hope your water-voles die."'

After much of this had been exposed (and note the strong Yorkshire involvement), Mrs Richard commented (1996), 'It is strange that all the sayings are in the form of curses. My sister and I are again wondering if our father did in fact make up the toast version.' Well, perhaps not: *Partridge/Catch Phrases* has 'May your rabbits flourish!' as a popular farewell (from Australia) since about 1930.

I should cocoa! 'I should think not!' – a slightly dated British English exclamation, current by 1936. Longman's *Dictionary of English Idioms* (1979) adds a word of caution: 'This phrase is not recommended for use by the foreign student.'

But why 'cocoa'? As always when in difficulty over a phrase origin, turn to rhyming slang. 'Cocoa' is from 'coffee and cocoa', almost rhyming slang for 'I should hope so!' Often used ironically. However, Tony Percy wrote (2005), 'I have always been rather sceptical of the frequent explanation that it is a form of rhyming slang for "I should say so!" I remember being very surprised when John Cleese used it in *Fawlty Towers*, in 'The Wedding Party' episode, when the enchanting Mrs Peignoir challenges Basil with the following words: (coquettishly) "I'm not having you knocking on my door in the middle of the night!", and Basil replies: (falsetto) "Ha ha ha ha ha … I should coco! [*sic*]" (I quote from the text.)

'I hadn't heard this expression used since the 1950s and cannot place where I heard it (probably radio). However, the meaning here appears to be more "I should think not!" rather than "I should hope so" (and the meaning you attribute to it is also negative). I wonder how Cleese recalled it, and why did he spell it without the 'a'? Is the rhyming slang more subtle? Could it possibly be an indirect rhyme (like "titfer") – perhaps "cocoa drink" = "think"? And has anybody else used it in public media or print since the 1950s?!' We are still looking.

I'll be jiggered! A sort of oath. The *OED2* has the verb 'to jigger' as a 'vague substitution for a profane oath or imprecation – origin disputed'. Known by 1837. Possibly it has something to do with a slang expression meaning 'to shut up, imprison'.

I'll go to the foot of our stairs! Many people are puzzled by this old Northern English expression of surprise or amazement and can't understand why it is used. It means, presumably, that the short walk to the place mentioned would allow the speaker to recover equanimity. Or perhaps it meant it was time to give up and go to bed? Professor Ron Leigh commented helpfully (2002), 'The saying was very common in Sheffield when I grew up there. As you probably know, Sheffield is very conscious of its proud tradition of being underwhelmed by startling news. So, on being told some amazing story, a typical Sheffielder will dryly respond, "I'll go to the foot of our stairs", indicating, "How very unimpressed I am".'

It was reportedly used by Tommy Handley on the BBC radio show *ITMA* (1940s) and elsewhere. It is also said to have been used by the entertainer George Formby (1904–61) as 'Eeh, I'll go to the foot of our stairs', as also, 'Eeh, I'll go to our 'ouse [pronounced 'our rouse']' – Robina Hinton, Suffolk (1999).

Chris Littlefair gave this variation from the North-East (2000): 'I'll go to the bottom of our garden.' Compare: 'In this area (Chipping Campden, Gloucestershire), I have often heard and used, "Well, I'll gutta [go to] Sezincote"' – Andy Doran (2002). Indeed, there are similar expressions of amazement incorporating journeys to France, Hanover, Jericho and Putney: 'I have tried in vain to trace the origin of the expression, "Well, I'll go to France!" This was used to express amazement and incredulity. I associate the use with the North of England where I heard it many times in the 1950s/60s' – Robert Atkinson, Winchester (2002). 'My mother, who died recently, aged 96, was prone in her younger days when surprised by anything to remark,

"Well, I'll go to Hanover!"' – Joan Wintle, London NW9 (2003). *Partridge/Slang* has it that 'go to Hanover = go to Hell', but I fail to see a connection here. See also I'LL GO TO PUTNEY (page 358).

A last word on the subject: an anonymous correspondent (2002) referred to a Lancashire usage in about 1950: 'The full expression is: "I'll go to the foot of our stairs and pump thunder!" It means, "I am so surprised (by what you have just told me, say) that I have a great disturbance in my bowel and must remove myself from the parlour and go to a private place while I expel internal gases."'

it's enough to make a parson swear 'I recall members of my family saying this after some aggravation' – Colleen Spittles, Kent (1993). Indeed, it is a well-known expression and quite old. Edward Ward used it in *Hudibras Redivivus* (1706): 'Your Folly makes me stare;/Such talk would make a Parson swear', and it appears in Swift's *Polite Conversation* (1738). 'My father, who never used strong language, in spite of having been in the navy, used to say such things as "Damn and set fire to it" and "It's enough to make a parson swear and burn his books"' – Janet C. Egan, Middlesex (2000).

my stars and green garters! 'My late mother had this saying when something surprising occurred' – Anne Rowlinson, Stockport (2003). *Partridge/Slang* finds 'my star and garter!' and 'my stars and garters!' as elaborations of 'my stars!', by 1850, and probably adopted as though in response to the brightness of breast-worn decorations. Whatever the form, it is an expression of astonishment. The Star and Garter is a name given to several British pubs, especially those at Windsor and Putney. It alludes to the Most Noble Order of the Garter, the highest order of knighthood (founded by Edward III in about 1348), and to the star that is an important feature of the insignia. The Royal Star and Garter

Homes at Richmond, Surrey, were originally established for wounded war veterans. *Stars and Garters* was the name of an ITV series (1963–6) which presented variety acts in a (fake) pub setting.

no peace for the wicked (or **no rest ...**)! Light-hearted exclamation by someone who is being harried by demands from other people or is snowed under with work. By the 19th century, possibly in imitation of certain biblical passages, e.g. Isaiah 48:22: 'There is no peace, saith the Lord, unto the wicked' and 57:21: 'There is no peace, saith my God, to the wicked.' Another version: '**no rest for the weary!**'

O, ye of little faith! A generalized admonition to doubters, based on the biblical use. It occurs several times in Matthew and Luke in the New Testament. It is usually Jesus upbraiding his disciples or others for their doubts.

rabbits! What you say on waking on the first day of the month. I still do it myself, though usually after I have said something else, which I'm sure spoils the effect ... The idea is to bring yourself luck and no doubt it springs from the general association of hares and rabbits with good luck (rabbit's feet, and so on).

In *A Dictionary of Superstitions*, edited by Iona Opie & Moira Tatem (1989), the earliest record of this custom dates only from 1919. However, the particular routine recorded at that date involved saying 'Rabbits' three times just before going to sleep on the last day of the month and then 'Hares' three times on waking next morning. There are many variations – one, for example, has the cry as 'White rabbits!' Another involves the paying of a forfeit to a person who gets in first with the cry.

and the same to you with [brass] knobs on! A pretend rude response. 'With knobs on' simply means 'generously embellished'. *Partridge/Slang* suggests it was known by 1910. In 1987, Margaret Walsh of Auckland, New Zealand, told me of her baroque version: 'Same to you with brass fittings and a self-starter.'

well, stagger my belly and tits, if it ain't Sir Jasper! 'My father (late schoolteacher of Nottingham) when considerably surprised'– George Hill, Bromley, Kent (2000).

Presumably, this is a relative of the man referred to in the expression 'Oh, Sir Jasper, do not touch me!', a cry from a ribald rugby song (current mid-20th century) about a most 'immoral lady/as she lay between the sheets/with nothing on at all'. And, presumably, this alludes to a vile seducer called Sir Jasper in some actual melodrama. There is a Sir Jasper Fidget in William Wycherley's play *The Country Wife* (1675), but he is quite the reverse of a vile seducer.

the things you meet when you haven't got a gun! 'What you say after meeting someone strange' – Rosie Cullen, with a saying of her grandmother's (2001). 'I offer you a versatile saying used regularly by my (Irish) father, Bill Coulter – often associated with driving past a pretty girl: "The things you see when you haven't got your gun"' – Jeremy Coulter, Maidenhead (2003). '"The sights you see when you haven't got a gun" – referring to people wearing outrageous attire' – Robert Swaffer, Peterborough (2003).

'too late, too late!' shall be the cry ... This seems to be the basis of a series of fairly nonsensical expressions, uttered when some opportunity has been missed. 'Too late, too late, shall be the cry,/Arnold the ice-cream man's gone by' is to be found in the Peter Nichols play *The Freeway*, Act 1, Scene 3 (1974). 'My father, who is from the West of Ireland, says, "Too late, too late, will be the cry,/When the man with the oranges has passed by"' – from an anonymous correspondent (1995). Alison Klenar (2000) recalled from her childhood, '"Too late, too late," the maiden cried,/"I'd rather have my haddock fried!"'

Compare what *Partridge/Catch Phrases* calls originally a military catchphrase – 'Too late! too late!' spoken in a high falsetto, after the story of 'that luckless fellow who lost his manhood in a shark-infested sea very soon after he had summoned help'.

Another possible origin: John Gray of Sutton wanted to know (1993) the source and correct form of a couplet that his father used to quote at him when he was a boy:

> Too late, too late, shall be the cry
> When you see — passing by.

Sir David Hunt, the diplomat and *Mastermind* champion, suggested that this was probably a corruption of a hymn to be found in the 19th-century Sankey and Moody hymnal. Indeed, the final couplet of the concluding verse of 'Jesus of Nazareth passeth by' by Miss Etta Campbell and T.E. Perkins is:

> 'Too late! too late!' will be the cry –
> 'Jesus of Nazareth *has passed by.*'

This came as a revelation to Stuart Holm of Norwich, who recalled living in Morecambe when he was a student at Lancaster University in the late 1960s. 'A regular Sunday ritual was a stroll along the promenade with a few fellow students. Among the delights on offer, a street trader was usually to be found selling a variety of wares to the accompaniment of the inevitable sales patter. He adapted "Too late, too late" as part of his sales pitch, leading on one memorable occasion to the unforgettable phrase, "Too late, too late will be the cry, when the man with the gents fully automatic umbrella passes you by." Umbrella was pronounced "umbarella" and the overall effect so amused my friend Ross Reynolds and me that it became a catchphrase for the rest of our time at university.'

Llywela V. Harris, St Davids, Dyfed (1994), remembered from her childhood the pithier 'Too late, too late, the pawnshop's shut!' Jaap Engelsman, Amsterdam, noted (1996), 'A well-known Dutch catchphrase is *Te laat, te laat, sprak Winnetou, het zaad is al naar binnen toe* (or *Helaas, helaas, sprak* ...), meaning '"Too late, too late (Alas, alas)' spoke Winnetou, the sperm's gone in already." The Red Indian Winnetou appeared from 1893 onwards in a series of popular novels by the German author Karl May (1842–1912).'

'too late, too late!' the — cried and waved his/her wooden leg
Obviously related to the previous phrase. T.A. Dyer, London SW12, noted (1993) that his father used to say (in the 1940s), '"It's come too late!" the lady cried, as she waved her wooden leg – and passed out.'

In about 1984, an American professor queried the saying, '"Aha!" cried she, as she waved her wooden leg, and died' – which is clearly linked.

'"Too late, too late," the maiden cried/Lifted her wooden leg, and died' – Mrs K.W. Kent, Lancaster (1994).

Donald Hickling, Northamptonshire, recalled a nonsense poem that his father brought back from the First World War which included the phrase, 'Waving her wooden leg in dire despair.' He added that his family would exclaim it whenever a disaster-prone neighbour hammered on the party wall.

P.S. Falla, the translator, wrote (1996), 'There is, "Ha, ha" she cried in Portuguese/And waved her wooden leg." I have heard the first line of this in French also!'

'This saying I have only heard via my mother, and she is 86: '"Oh good,' she said, as she swung her wooden leg, 'only one boot to clean"'' – from Margaret Addicott, Hertfordshire (1996).

Remembered by Rip Bulkeley, Oxfordshire (1998), from an American source: 'Ha ha! she cried, waving her wooden leg. Only one shoe to clean.' But also from his Yorkshire Granny 50 years ago: '"Help! Help!" she cried, and waved her wooden leg.'

'"Aha! cried the Duchess, as she waved her wooden leg", also the variant, "Oho! she cried, as the cock flew at her" were both used as jokey exclamations by our Nanny (born 1897), and we were so used to hearing them as children in the 1950s that we never questioned her about where they came from' – Nick Bicat, Oxfordshire (2000).

'Too late! Too late! the Captain cried, and shook his wooden leg' – Tom Doyle, Madrid, Spain. Adam Wilkins, St Albans, Hertfordshire (2000), remembered from his grandfather, '"Too late, too late," she cried as she waved her wooden leg three times in the air.'

'"Too late, too late," the maiden cried, as she waved her timber limber' – remembered by the mother of Marjorie Wild, Crediton, Devon (2000).

'"'Oh, thank you, sir,' she said, as with a smile she waved her wooden leg" – heard from my father and only once heard from another man at work' – Derek Armstrong (2000).

Clearly, the cry is not 'too late, too late' in all versions, but the emphasis remains upon the wooden leg, as in these citations from the US: '"Aha!" she cried, as she waved her wooden leg and died' – Anonymous, 'Some Wellerisms from Idaho' in *Western Folklore* 25 (1966); '"Hurrah!" as the old maid shouted waving her wooden leg' – Herbert Halpert, 'Some Wellerisms from Kentucky and Tennessee' in *Journal of American Folklore*, No. 69 (1956).

'twas ever thus! An exclamation of mild despair at some example of inefficiency or incompetence and meaning almost the same as the modern 'So what's new?' It does not occur in Shakespeare or the Bible. In fact, the only examples I have turned up (and without the fatalistic edge) are: as the first line of 'Disaster' by C.S. Calverley (died 1884):

''Twas ever thus from childhood's hour!' – this is a parody of lines from Thomas Moore's 'The Fire Worshippers' in *Lalla Rookh* (1817): 'Oh! ever thus from childhood's hour!'); and, as the title, ''Twas Ever Thus', given to a parody of the same poem by Henry S. Leigh (1837–83). His version actually begins, 'I never rear'd a young gazelle.'

Ollie exclaims it in *The Laurel and Hardy Murder Case* (US 1930).

Compare: 'What would you, ladies? It was ever thus./Men are unwise and curiously planned' – James Elroy Flecker, *Hassan* (1922).

Va-va-va-voom! Essentially a showbiz catchphrase and outside the scope of this book – but it has taken on a life of its own and ought to be considered here. The phrase underwent a revival in the UK during 2004 through its use (with one 'Va' deleted) in TV commercials for Renault cars featuring the footballer Thierry Henry.

It has even been included in an edition of the *Concise Oxford English Dictionary*, where it is defined as an expression of the quality of being exciting, vigorous or sexually attractive.

Originally, it was the catchphrase of an American TV comedian of the 1950s, Art Carney. He used the phrase in the character of Newton the Waiter on *The Morey Amsterdam Show* and of Ed Norton, the sanitation engineer, in *The Honeymooners*. He also recorded a jolly song with the title in 1954.

'One day, on a picnic, after some exciting horseplay, I shouted, "**Whoa, Emma!**", which resulted in a horrified silence and glare from Grandma, whose name it was. Well, I didn't know where this expression came from anyway' – Margaret Smith, Barnstable, Devon (2001).

'When I was young in the 1950s, elderly gentlemen often used the phrase "Whoa, Emma" if one was in a hurry. I suspect it could be a music-hall catchphrase – did Gus Elen say it to his (off-stage) horse in his dustman act?' – Keith Thomas, Crosby, Lancashire (2002).

Indeed. *Partridge/Catch Phrases* has this as 'a warning to a person of either sex to be careful' and dates it to 1900–40. Previously, 1880–1900, it had been 'directed at a woman of marked appearance or behaviour in the streets' and before this, in 1878, there had been a Henry Daykins song, *Whoa, Emma!* whose opening words were, 'A saying has come up' – suggesting that it was perhaps a catchphrase newly in vogue at that time.

Benham's Book of Quotations (1948 edn) has the 'London street saying' as 'Wo, Emma! Mind the paint! *c.* 1878–1890' and adds, 'Herbert Daykin [sic] is said to have composed a song about this saying, *c.* 1878. A song "Mind the Paint," by N.G. Thomas, does not seem to have been published till 1887.'

The only actual song with the title 'Whoa! Emma!' I have been able to locate is certainly from 1878, but written and composed by John Read. It does not contain the words 'Mind the paint', so Benham may have conflated two songs. A comedy short with the title *Whoa, Emma!* was released in the US in 1926 and another song with the title was written by Dorothy Fields and Harry Warren for the film *Texas Carnival* (US 1951).

winter drawers on! A jocular exclamation when the weather turns cold, punning on 'winter draws on' but referring to 'drawers' as warm knickers or underpants. *OED2* has the phrase 'winter draws on', in a straightforward sense, by 1910. Compare SPRING IN THE AIR (page 44).

ye gods and little fishes! A mock-heroic exclamation of contempt or indignation, possibly derived from some 19th-century drama. 'But out of school, – Ye gods and little fishes! how Tommy did carouse!' – Louisa M. Alcott, *Little Men*, Chap. 2 (1871).

Chapter 26

AFTER BURPS AND BOTTY-BURPS

And now we turn to phrases surrounding the usually unmentionable occurrences of belching and farting ...

the back door's open again 'A phrase for passing wind' – L. Middleton (2001).

better out than in What you say having belched. Quoted in Mary Killen, *Best Behaviour* (1990). Or when farting, according to *Partridge/Catch Phrases*, where Paul Beale dates it to the 1950s.

'Like all youngsters, I was taught to say "excuse me" when breaking wind. My mother would always then say, **"That's OK, an empty house is better than a bad tenant"'** – Dryden Henderson, Cropston, Leicestershire (2001).

'My grandfather observing a silent fart: **"That one had its carpet slippers on"'** – Betty Roe, London W10 (1995). The writer Andrew Davies was quite open in referring to his mother-in-law's expression after a fart: 'Oh, it's just a little wee one in its stockinged feet' – on *Quote . . . Unquote* (10 May 1994). Compare SILENT BUT DEADLY (page 379).

Dorothea Jamieson of Devizes, Wiltshire (1992): 'We have two expressions which have been adopted by the family. Just after the First World War when 'flu and consumption were rife – neighbours of my mother were afflicted and a girl from the country came to Southsea to help their household. My grandmother was rather sorry for this Winnie and asked her to tea. As she ate, she belched and said, **"Manners! – I always sez that when I does that."'**

more tea, Vicar? A correspondent who, understandably, wished to remain anonymous, advanced this family phrase 'for after a fart, or to cover any kind of embarrassment'. Well, yes, it is associated with genteel, suburban manners, but originally (perhaps 1920s/30s), it was one of those things you said to distract attention from a burp or a belch or what the broadcaster Carol Vorderman has been known to refer to as a 'botty-burp'. The Revd Phil Goodey of Bideford wrote to *Quote . . . Unquote* (2002) to ask for this information because, as he says, 'Whenever I visit a parishioner, someone always manages to arrange it so that my host says, "More tea, Vicar?" and everyone laughs . . .'

Paul Beale collected various forms for a revision of *Partridge/Catch Phrases*, including: 'Good evening, vicar!'; 'No swearing, please, vicar' (said facetiously to introduce a note of the mock-highbrow into a conversation full of expletives); 'Another cucumber sandwich, vicar?' (after an involuntary belch); 'Speak up, Padre!/Brown/Ginger (you're through)' (as a response to a fart).

In *Politics, Prayer and Parliament* (2000), David Rogers declares, 'The phrase, "More tea, Vicar?" has entered the language as shorthand for comfortable suburbia.' Hence these stories: '"More tea, Vicar?" asked Lady Lavinia as she poured the tea with her other hand' and 'One day the young Vicar was visiting two elderly ladies. Whilst he was sitting on the shiny sofa, he passed wind mightily and noisily. As the echoes died away, one of the ladies filled the embarrassing silence by asking, "More tea, Vicar?" "Oh no!" he replied. "It makes me fart!"'

pardon, Mrs Arden, there's a pig in your garden! What you exclaim after belching or burping, or audibly farting, in order to deflect attention from yourself.

In 1997, the *Sunday Telegraph* Magazine started a picture puzzle series under the title 'Pardon, Mrs Arden' and I was asked where the phrase came from. I had never heard it, but these citations were soon summoned up: 'It was blissful to lie in my adjoining single bed, watching her undress down to her vest and pink satin bloomers, averting my gaze while she used what she called the "Edgar Allan", then listening to the crunch of biscuits, the slurp of gin and tonic and the occasional gentle belch, followed by an apologetic murmur of "Oops! Pardon Mrs Arden!"' – *Daily Mail* (19 March 1994); 'Every time you said "pardon" to old Charlie, who worked on the farm, he would answer: "Pardon, Mrs Arden, there's a pig in your garden"' – *The Daily Telegraph* (29 January 1994).

At this point, my wife woke up and added (from her Buckinghamshire childhood) the variant '… there's a pig in your *back* garden', plus the rejoinder, 'That bain't no pig, that be my son, John.' Curiouser and curiouser.

Latterly, it has been suggested to me by two independent sources that there was a novelty song with the title 'Pardon, Mrs Arden', sung in pantomimes of the 1930s/40s. One source recalls that it went on:

> Oh, his fur is as soft as silk,
> All he wants is a saucerful of milk.
> There's a kitten in your garden
> Saying miaow, miaow, miaow, miaow
> Isn't it a pity that it's such a pretty kitty
> Saying miaow, etc.

I have been unable to trace the sheet music for this.

Obviously, this is the same song as was reported having been sung in a show at the Theatre Royal, Manchester, in 1937/8, with the words:

> Pardon, Mrs Arden,
> There's a kitty in your garden
> And it goes miaow, miaow, miaow, miaow.
> All it wants is a saucer full of milk,
> Feel her coat, for it's just like silk,
> So!! Pardon, Mrs Arden,

> There's a kitty in your garden,
> And it goes miaow, miaow, miaow, miaow.

However, it does seem to be the case that there was an 1870s music-hall song that is quoted in Vyvyan Holland's book *Son of Oscar Wilde* (1954) as:

> Parding Mrs Harding,
> Is our kitting in your garding,
> Eating of a mutting-bone?
> No, he's gone to Londing.
> How many miles to Londing?
> Eleving? I thought it was only seving.
> Heavings! *What* a long way from home!

This couplet may also have been included:

> I'm sorry, Missus Dewsberry
> I haven't seen her since last Tuesberry.

H. Montgomery Hyde's *Oscar Wilde* (1976) has the first two lines as, rather:

> Beg your parding, Mrs Harding,
> Is my kitting in your garding?

Kathleen Strange remembered the first three lines (in 1997, when she was 92), as:

> I beg your parding, Mrs 'Arding
> Is my kitting in your garding
> Eating of a herring-bone?

Geoffrey Grigson's anthology *The Cherry Tree* (1959) has yet another version:

> Beg parding, Mrs Harding,
> Is my kitting in your garding?
> Is your kitting in my garding?
> Yes she is, and all alone,
> Chewing of a mutting bone.

Yet More Comic and Curious Verse (1959) has:

> ''Parding, Mrs Harding,
> Is my kitting in your kitching garding,
> Gnawing of a mutting-bone?'
> 'No, he's gone to Londing.'
> 'How many miles to Londing?'
> 'Eleving.'
> 'I thought it was only seving.
> Heavings! what a long way from home!'

'My version of the "burp" saying – what my mum used to say to me when I was young, is as follows' – Pam Ball, Suffolk (2001):

> Good heavens, Mrs 'Arding
> There's a chicking
> In your garding
> With a wooden leg
> Tied up with a piece of string.

A number of correspondents have even more recently recalled the use of this phrase in connection with farting. John Gage, Buckinghamshire (2001) wrote, 'If, as a child, I passed wind, my mother would chastise me with the admonition, "Pardon, Mrs Arden, your cat's in my garden."'

My old friend David Kennard, whose birth surname was Arden, wrote (2001), 'At my earliest school, a kindergarten in Belsize Park, and at my first Prep School in Croydon, I was often teased with the rhyme: "Ooh beg pardon, Mrs Arden,/For doing nasties/poopoo in your garden." This was almost invariably triggered by someone in the playground breaking wind. The connection between this teasing and my last name made it an easy decision for me to accept my stepfather's family name upon my adoption.'

All in all, it is not hard to see how the expression 'Pardon, Mrs Arden' has developed.

sure, and it's a poor arse that doesn't rejoice 'My Irish grandma, when somebody broke wind' – Pat Stimpson (2003).

silent but deadly Of a fart. By the early 1990s? From Helen Fielding, *Bridget Jones: The Edge of Reason*, Chap. 11 (1999): 'In aeroplane in sky. Having to pretend to be very busy wearing walkman and writing as ghastly man next to self in pale brown synthetic-type suit keeps trying to talk to me in between silent but deadly farting.' Compare HAD ITS CARPET (page 374). Curiously enough, there is a feature film with the title *Silent But Deadly* (US 2002), but I doubt if there is any connection ...

'When driving in the country pre-war, with its appropriate smells around farms, my father always used to say, "**What a smell of broken glass!**"' – Jocelyn Linter, Essex (1998).

Partridge/Slang has 'smell of broken glass – a strong body-odour, e.g. in a Rugby footballers' changing-room after a game ... earlier C20' and compares 'There's a smell of gunpowder – someone has broken wind, late C19.'

But how does glass come into it? Patrick Hughes suggested (2002) that 'broken glass' is Cockney rhyming slang for 'the smell of my dirty arse'. 'My mother (1905–86) and her sisters used to come out with "a smell of broken glass" as a jocular comment on a fart in company' – David Wilson (2006).

'As a child in Dublin in the 1930s, this was a euphemism in our household when anyone broke wind. Mother always said, **"That's the wind that shakes the barley"'** – Mrs F. Walden, Croydon, Surrey (2006). This memory was brought back when Ken Loach entitled a film about the Irish Civil War of the 1920s, *The Wind That Shakes the Barley* (UK 2006). It is from an Irish folksong, very relevant to that time, about a man lamenting the death of his loved one:

> And on my breast in blood she died
> While soft winds shook the barley.

Chapter 27

THANK YOU AND GOODNIGHT

By the mid 20th century, I should think, the phrase '**thank you and goodnight**' *had become a dismissive catchphrase – for example, it was used in this way on the BBC radio show* Beyond Our Ken *(13 May 1960). When the popular Controller of BBC Radio 4, Helen Boaden, was given a farewell party in December 2004, this phrase was inscribed on the invitations – presumably by someone too young to appreciate how entirely inappropriate it was ... Here now, finally, is a selection of domestic cries of a valedictory nature.*

don't do anything I wouldn't do! A nudging farewell remark, perhaps dating from about 1900. In BBC TV, *Hancock's Half Hour* (The Reunion Party) (25 March 1960), a barman says it twice to Hancock, who is about to go to a party. Some people add, 'Which should give you plenty of scope', adding nudge to nudge.

I'll show you the back of my hand i.e. 'I'll bid you goodbye' – in a mock dismissive gesture, as though about to slap or 'show the knuckles to' the other person. Chris Littlefair reported it from the North East (2000). The version 'Here's the back of my hand to you!' is in Swift's *Polite Conversation* (1738).

Compare the modern expression, 'Talk to the hand', in full, 'Talk to the hand, 'cos the face ain't listening' or ''Cos the ears aren't listening', or ''Coz the face don't give a damn' etc. – a rude, dismissive remark made with upraised hand, meaning, 'I won't listen to what you're saying and I won't even look at you.' This dates from the early 1990s, possibly with lip-synching drag queens, but most people came to know it from the *Jerry Springer Show*, where it was very popular with scrapping guests. Hence, its apotheosis, if that's the word, in the stage show *Jerry Springer the Opera* (2005).

if you can't be good, be careful! Nudging farewell remark, sometimes completed with 'and if you can't be careful, name it after me' – or 'buy a pram'. *H.L. Mencken's Dictionary of Quotations* (1942) calls it an American proverbial expression, though the *ODP*'s pedigree is mostly British, finding its first proper citation in 1903 – from A.M. Binstead, *Pitcher in Paradise*. In 1907, there was an American song called 'Be Good! If You Can't Be Good, Be Careful!' written by Harrington Tate. There is also the follow-on: '... and if you can't be careful, remember the date'.

I must love you and leave you Since the 19th century there has been this semi-proverbial, semi-jocular farewell. During the Vietnam War, one of the few memorable patriotic slogans, current from 1969, was 'America, Love It or Leave It'. This was perhaps inspired by the song 'Love Me or Leave Me' (1928, hit version 1955). *Love 'Em and Leave 'Em* was the title of a Louise Brooks film (US 1927).

'My late husband would always say when someone was leaving our house, "Well, goodbye and **thank your mother for the rabbit**" (or sometimes it would be "dripping")' – Mrs B. Penberthy, Cullompton, Devon (2002).

'One of our family quotations whenever anyone leaves the house is, "Ta-ra, duck [pronounced dook], thank your mother for the rabbit!"' – Rae Deane, Nottingham (2003).

'Thank you, mother, for the rabbit' is also a catchphrase attributed to the comedian Larry Grayson (1923–95) when he used to appear under his original stage name of Billy Breen, though *Partridge/Catch Phrases* has it reported by 1969, which might mean it was older.

KEYWORD INDEX

GENERAL INDEX

Cloutman, Paul 141, 274
clumsiness 15–16
Cobb, Irvin S. 161
Cockney rhyming slang 196
codes 179, 183, 185
coffee 65–6
Coghill, Mary 138
Cohen, J.M. 180
cold 112, 308, 372
Cole, John 150
Coles, David 248
Coles, Margaret 164
Colin, Sid 183
collectors 48–9
Collier, Jane 76
Collins, Mary 181
Collins, Michael 28
Collins, R. 347
Colman, George the Younger 331
compliments 62, 181
Conan Doyle, Arthur 151
confidentiality 15
confusion 235
Congreve, Lady 124
Connolly, Billy 227
Connolly, Cyril 134
Conquer, Lewis 146, 308
Constable, Ena 132
Constable, Grace 309
Conway, Jaquie 114
Cooke, Brian 202–3
Coombs, Pat 168
Cooper, Gary 42
Cooper, James Fenimore 43, 202
Cooper, Lorna 177
Cooper, Margaret 193
Cooper, S.F. 295
Cornelissen, Douglas 158

Cornford, Tim 19
Coronation Street (TV show) 244
correctness 58
Corrie, Joe 158
Costa, Sam 298
Cotterill, Ted 136
Cottle, Jacqueline 75
Cotton, Sir Bill 173
Cotton, Billy 173, 194
Cotton, Charles 118
coughing 190–1, 194–5
Coulter, Bill 367
Coulter, Jeremy 367
Coulter, Mary 341
country bumpkins 283
Country Life magazine 124
Coupe, R.W.D. 114
Courts, Kay 114
Coward, Mat 20–1
Coward, Noel 242–3, 337
Cowley, Violet 209
Cox, Jane Cannon 147–8
Craggs, R. 216
Craig, Robert 141
Craster, Jean 57
Craster, John 57
Craton, Andrew 251
Crawford, Joan 222–3
Crawford, Marie 303
Crawford, Michael 244
Criomhthain, Tomás Ó 135
Crispe, S. 272
Critchlow, David 154, 300
Croally, Gwen 327
Cromack, Gail 79, 282
Cromwell, Oliver 239
Cromwell, Richard 239
Crossen, Kathleen B. 342
Crossland, E. Jean 291

Crowe, William 195
crusts 83
Cryer, Barry 122
Cullen, Rosie 14, 91, 367
Culmer, Valentine 192
Cunningham, Kate 138

Daily Mail (newspaper) 376
Daily Telegraph, The (newspaper) 233, 376
Dalton, Ann 214
Daniel 50
Daniells, Chris 69
Dann, Paul 262
darts 20–1
Daughtry, Ruth 362
David 202
Davie, Donald 88
Davies, Andrew 44, 374
Davies, Carole-Anne 128
Davies, Peter 357
Davies, Stephen W. 41
Dawson, Les 293
Dawson, Peter 266
Day, Barry 310
Daykins, Henry 372
De La Mare, Walter 38
Deakin, Frank 345
Dean, Bob 69, 97
Deane, Rae 383
death 24–5, 189–90, 191, 193, 299, 303–5, 314, 316
Defoe, Daniel 335
Delaney, Shelagh 18
Delderfield, Eric R. 17
Dellino, Clive 258
Diamond, Anne 233
Diamond, Paul 169
Diana, Princess of Wales 269

patience 166–7
Pattison, Margaret 69
Paul, William Drummond 196
Paul–Jones, Richard 175
Pavlova, Anna 23–4
Payne, J. 256, 263
Payne, J.H. 199
Peacock, Thomas Love 77
Pearce, Thelma 290
Pearson, D.A.G. 55
Pearson, Hesketh 23
Pearson, Kenneth 208
Pearson, Robin 341
Peebles, M.S. 183
pen friends 210
Penberthy, B. 17, 73, 383
Pepys, Samuel 156
Percy, Tony 231, 363
Perkins, T.E. 368
Perry, Joan 129
personal characteristics 233–69
Peterson, Ann 48, 359
Pettifer, Isabel 221
Philip, Prince, Duke of Edinburgh 241
Philip, Margaret 29
Phillips, John 351
Phillips, Samuel 302
Phillips, Siân 311
Phinn, Gervase 95, 221, 340
physical characteristics 219–27
Picarda, Noel 258
Pidgley, Sheila and Ron 284
pigs 68, 70, 79
pitch-dark 14–15
Pitt, William 132

Plant, Michael 48–9
Platt, Ken 243
Plowman, John A. 302
Pocock, David 66
politics 40
Polond, K. 335
pomposity 49–50
Pool, Kate 39
Poole, Jim 88
Poole, John 257
Pope, Alexander 245
porridge 74
Porter, Cole 185, 353
portions 72
potatoes 68, 75
poverty 129, 132–3, 234
Pratchett, Terry 231
prayers 22
preaching 91–2
pregnancy 112, 170
Prentiss, George L. 304
prevarication 290
Price, Colin 18
Price, Mary J. 86, 267, 343
Price, Pamela Vandyke 124
Priddy, Robert 32, 194
prioritisation 47–8
Procter, Margaret 284
Prohibition 348
proverbs 63, 77–8, 83, 130–1, 141, 149, 150, 152, 154, 155, 158, 159, 166, 168, 175, 180, 199, 200, 210, 212, 291, 298, 300, 302–3, 309, 312, 316, 325, 341
Pulleyblank, Mary 167
Punch magazine 39, 69, 87, 125–6, 142, 143, 171, 181, 245, 246, 250, 272, 320, 347, 358, 360

Purvis, Roger D. 260
put downs 200, 260, 262
puzzles 14

Quayle, Sir Anthony 89
Quick, Diana 121
Quinn, Mick 339

Rabelais 29
Race, Steve 17
rain 309, 310–11, 311–12
Randegger, Alberto 200
Ransome, Arthur 58
rationing 73
Rattray, Revd Lorna 38
Rawicz, Marjorie M. 239
Rawles, E.Y. 217
Rawles, Margaret 200
Ray, John 210, 251
Raymond, W. 188
Rayner, D.F. 177
Read, John 372
Read, Mary 269
Read, Phil 238
Reader's Digest 162
recognition 24
red-heads 54
Redfern, Walter 215
Reece, Fred 246
Reed, George 130
Reed, Henry 150, 227
Rees, George 178, 249
Rees, Lilian Rose 130, 178, 249
Rees, Phil 128
Rees, Vivien 145
Reeve, Peter 328
Reith, Lord 326
religion 151, 298
Renault 371
repetition 29